Landscapes of the Soul

C. G. Jung and the Exploration of the Human Psyche in Switzerland

scapes

of

Land the Soul

C. G. Jung and the Exploration of the Human Psyche in Switzerland

SWISS NATIONAL MUSEUM
SCHEIDEGGER & SPIESS

6   *Foreword*
       Denise Tonella

8   *On the Exhibition: A Brief Psychogeography of Switzerland*
       Stefan Zweifel

13   **IN PICTURES I: LANDSCAPES OF THE SOUL**

30   *From Freud's Psychoanalysis to Jung's Analytical Psychology*
       Stefan Zweifel

38   "The Swiss Line in the European Spectrum," C. G. Jung

40   *A New Grammar of the Mind—in the Swiss Spirit*
       Alain de Botton

48   "The Navel of the Dream," Sigmund Freud

50   *Geneva: A Stage and "Gateway" for Psychoanalysis*
       From J. J. Rousseau to Sabina Spielrein and Beyond
       Michael Jakob

56   "Psychogeographic Reveries," J. J. Rousseau

59   **IN PICTURES II: SIGMUND FREUD**

74   *The Last Turn? Ethnopsychoanalysis in Zurich in the 1980s*
       An Eyewitness Account and Rather Daring Hypothesis Forged with Hindsight
       Peter Schneider

80   "A Brief Ethnopsychoanalysis for Children," Paul Parin

82   *Leading Women in Psychoanalysis—A Short Guide*
       Ita Grosz-Ganzoni

90   "In Freud's Practice," Anna Guggenbühl

95   **IN PICTURES III: C. G. JUNG**

112   *C. G. Jung as Thinker and Author*
Murray Stein

118   "Descent into Hell in the Future," C. G. Jung

120   *The Domestic Interior as the Scene of Work on the Unconscious*
The Desks of C. G. Jung and Sigmund Freud
Lothar Müller

126   "Estranged Intimacy," correspondance between Sigmund Freud and C. G. Jung

132   *Imagination, Creativity, and Archetypes*
Elizabeth Leuenberger & Verena Kast

138   "Geneviève and the King," Meret Oppenheim

140   *Emma Jung: A Pioneer in Swiss Depth Psychology*
Thomas Fischer

148   "The Anima as an Elemental Being," Emma Jung

151   **IN PICTURES IV: HOSPITALS AND ART**

168   *Psychiatry: Child of an Ambivalent Modernity*
On the History of Psychiatry in Nineteenth and Twentieth Century Switzerland
Urs Germann

174   "Pataphysics of Pathology," Blaise Cendrars

176   *Not Simply a Diminutive Adult. On the History of Child Psychiatry*
Ursina Klauser

182   "The Origin of the Child's Words Papa and Mama," Sabina Spielrein

184   *Heroic Epics and Their Shadows. C. G. Jung in Pop Culture*
Christine Lötscher & Gesa Schneider

190   "For Madmen Only," Hermann Hesse

192   *Art and Insanity: A Crack in the Wall*
Otto Gross and the Resistance to Psychiatry and Psychoanalysis
Stefan Zweifel

200   "The Clown of God," Vaslav Nijinsky

202   **APPENDIX**

Foreword

Switzerland is "home to mappers of the mind," its "psychogeographic space a psychoanalytic hub of worldwide renown."

That was what the author and curator Stefan Zweifel told us when he came to pitch his idea of an exhibition about what he called Switzerland's "landscapes of the mind." We needed no further persuasion. Mental health, which in recent years has become a major social issue, has deep historic roots in Switzerland. It was also clear to us that Carl Gustav Jung, as the founder of analytical psychology, would play the pivotal role in the Swiss National Museum's exhibition on the subject opening in Zurich in 2025.

With our ever-faster pace of life, pressure to perform, growing inequality, global crises, social media with its unrelenting comparisons, cyberbullying, information flood, and the oppressive burden of being constantly spoiled for choice, the human psyche is challenged as never before. The past few decades have seen psychological well-being elevated to a factor worthy of attention, so that "mental health issues" are less taboo and can be talked about more openly. Our mental-health awareness is changing.

The subject of our exhibition is mental health as reflected in the light of history. By adopting not just historical, but also social as well as artistic perspectives, the exhibition seeks to make sense of the many different approaches taken to managing the mind. What has emerged can be seen as a "psycho-geography" of Switzerland that visualizes very clearly for just how long and in how many different ways we have been trying to get to the bottom of the mysterious human psyche. Our journey takes us from the philosopher Jean-Jacques Rousseau to painters such as Henry Fuseli and pioneers of psychoanalysis such as Sigmund Freud and Lou Andreas-Salomé or Emma Jung-Rauschenbach. Another focus is Switzerland's psychiatric hospitals from Zurich to Geneva, where the methods developed for keeping the psyche in check included such dubious innovations as electroshock therapy.

Enthroned at the heart of the exhibition is C. G. Jung's *Red Book*, a work that enables us to venture beyond the purely medical and scientific aspects of the subject and to advance into the cultural, spiritual, and mythological dimensions of the mind. As Jung was the one who made Zurich a major center of psychotherapy, a critical look at him and his followers is just as much a part of the exhibition as are the psychoanalytic methods of today. Young people who have struggled with mental health issues will also be heard.

This anthology of essays was conceived as a tie-in with the exhibition. All twelve essays follow the common thread of the exhibition by describing Switzerland's many "landscapes of the mind." The role played by women in the development of psychoanalysis is also accorded the attention it deserves.

My first debt of thanks is to the curator Stefan Zweifel, who was the prime mover behind both the exhibition and this publication. This is not the first time that Stefan Zweifel has played a key part in an exhibition at the Swiss National Museum, and it goes without saying that he was the ideal choice for a project about psychoanalysis in Switzerland. Not only has he given us an exciting journey through the history of psychoanalysis and its role in art and culture, but he also invites us to join him on historical forays into the history of psychiatry, Switzerland's psychiatric hospitals, and some of the key concepts of psychoanalysis. Sincerest thanks are also due to Pascale Meyer, who brought her personal enthusiasm, organizational talents, and considerable experience to bear on the demanding task of project management. I would also like to thank Valérie Lüthi and Sophie Dänzer for contributing to the content as well as handling the necessary coordination work. As scenographer, Alex Harb proved skillful at according Zweifel's creativity the space and scope needed to maximize its impact.

Numerous works of art were included as a way of visualizing the theories and notions of the human psyche as no other medium could, as were a number of documents from the holdings of the Jung Family Archive and other memorial institutions, many of which have never before seen the light of day. In extending my heartfelt thanks to all our individual and institutional lenders, I would therefore like to give special mention to the Stiftung der Werke von C. G. Jung and the Stiftung C. G. Jung Küsnacht. Sincere thanks also go to all those foundations and private individuals who believed in our project and lent us financial support, most notably the Kulturstiftung UBS, the Stiftung der Werke von C. G. Jung, the Stiftung zur Förderung der Psychologie von C. G. Jung SFPJ, the Susan Bach Foundation, and Dr. Nancy Swift Furlotti. I am also deeply grateful to Mayo Bucher, Maya Hoffmann, Ursula Hauser, and John Neumeier for lending us particularly relevant works of art.

Working together with the authors of the texts, our publisher Scheidegger & Spiess and the book designer Martina Brassel was a great pleasure, and we are deeply grateful to them all. In closing, I would like to extend my warmest thanks to my colleagues and co-workers at the Swiss National Museum and to all the many other individuals who have had a hand in seeing this project through to completion.

Denise Tonella
Director of the Swiss National Museum

The Matterhorn now crowns the pile of unanswered letters on my desk. I gladly accept the small particle of Switzerland in the symbolic sense you suggest, as homage from the only country in which I feel a man of property.

Sigmund Freud to Oskar Pfister, thanking him for the gift of a silver Matterhorn paperweight, May 10, 1909

Our loveliest mountain, which dominates Switzerland far and wide, is called Jungfrau—the Virgin. The Virgin Mary is the female patron saint of the Swiss—a living reminder that the virgin mother is the earth.

C. G. Jung, "The Swiss Line in the European Spectrum," 1928

On the Exhibition:
A Brief Psychogeography of Switzerland

Switzerland has been home to soul-seekers such as J. J. Rousseau and C. G. Jung since time immemorial, and it both historically and currently boasts more centers of psychiatry, psychology, and psychoanalysis than almost any other country. Together they form a network covering almost every inch of the map, from Geneva to Zurich, from Kreuzlingen to Bern, from Basel to Monte Verità. Switzerland's importance as a psychogeographical space and psychoanalytical hub, moreover, extends far beyond the its own borders, the summit that outshines all the others being Sigmund Freud's momentous encounter with C. G. Jung at the Bürghölzli psychiatric hospital in 1908.

Switzerland was *Sigmund Freud's First Country*, to quote the title of Anton M. Fischer's book, which is to date the only major study of this phenomenon. And thanks to the election of Jung as first chairman of the International Psychoanalytic Society, Zurich, in 1910, it would soon become what Freud hailed as the "world capital of psychoanalysis"—an accolade that would be repeated during the unrest of 1968 and remain into the 1970s. Even today, Zurich has more psychoanalysts per square kilometer than any other city.

This is a story full of dramas and dramatic turns of event. At least initially, Jung vehemently defended Freud's theories of drives and dreams, and changed his mind only after the two men traveled to America together. Then, in his now legendary *Red Book* begun after his crisis of 1913, he started to record his own dreams and from them derived his first intimations of the archetypes underpinning the collective unconscious. There, the anima and animus as the two sides of every self, as well as figures such as "the eternal child" and the "great mother" gradually coalesced into psychic constellations, whose reach extended far beyond psychological practice and into the world of art and literature, even finding their way into Hollywood screenplays.

Psychogeography:
Switzerland as a Map of the Soul

The land of dark forests, serene lakes, and deep tunnels has long been the scene of excavations in search of the human soul. It was here that Rousseau penned his *Confessions* of 1765, and with it an unsparing auto-analysis of his own childhood and childhood "perversions." Rousseau, armed with a pack of "Jass cards" in his pocket, would later roam the forests of the Jura Mountains—his writing room—writing down directly on the cards what was on his mind. He then expanded these notes into his last work, the *Rêveries du promeneur solitaire* (*Reveries of a Solitary Walker*, 1782) with the famous account of his time on Ile St. Pierre in Lake Bienne: this "fifth reverie" shows how the landscape was affecting his train of thought and tinging his sentiments—as when he lay down in a little boat on the shore of the Ile St. Pierre and let the waves rock him to and fro, lulling him into memories of his childhood.

Among those to follow in this soul-seeker's footsteps were the various painters of erotic dreams and nightmares such as Henry Fuseli, who had ladies balance hairdos like giant phalli on their heads even as nightmares wrought mischief on their breasts; then there were the wandering ponderers who cast a long shadow of their own, as in the Engadine, where Friedrich Nietzsche became one of the first to suspect that the *Ich* (ego) was perhaps just an illusion, given that we were all riding "on the back of a tiger"—the tiger being the darkest urgings of our unconscious. The artist Thomas Hirschhorn's *Nietzsche-Map* is in itself a kind of inner map of his brain extending into the present. Meanwhile, at Monte Verità, the Austrian psychoanalyst Otto Gross was dreaming of orgies that might liberate him from all father figures and at the same time discovering the dark truth about all social utopias—as well as driving his lover to death by cocaine. Just as anxious to flee the spider of "reason," whose rational threads hold oppressive everyday life together, was Friedrich Glauser, who in his novel *Matto regiert* (1936) had Police Constable Studer analyze the "madhouse of Münsingen," though he himself had been allowed to marry his last lover only on condition that he first have himself sterilized. Similarly tragic is the tale of the Swiss writer Annemarie Schwarzenbach, whose androgynous appearance resisted the kind of black and white categories used for psychiatric assessments and whose lesbian lust was stigmatized as "abnormal"—until she left the Prangins hospital that had been treating her with electroshock therapy and not long afterwards died in Sils-Maria, her jaw broken and as misunderstood as ever.

Around mid-century, Switzerland's hospitals, with Freud and Jung at the helm, finally began treating the "mentally ill" with more than just straitjackets and cold baths. The country became the first place outside Italy to apply both electroshock therapy and insulin shock therapy, treating such famous patients as the dancer Vaslav Nijinsky at the Bellevue Sanatorium. Meanwhile, the pharmaceutical company Ciba Geigy, acting in complicity with Roland Kuhn as the head of the psychiatric hospital in Münsterlingen, tested thousands upon thousands of pills on oft-unsuspecting patients—at least until 1957, when the first antidepressant "Tofranil" was hailed as a "pharmaceutical turnaround," even though it did but half of what was promised. These days it is in psychoactive substances such as LSD that most hopes are placed, leaving open the question of how the necessary trials might look. Anticipating another therapeutic turnaround, an enthusiastic media has evoked the image of a hallucinogenic rainbow arcing back to the year 1949, when LSD was first tested at the Burghölzli.

It is hard to think of anywhere else where psychiatric medicine's brightest and darkest aspects have been so closely intertwined, or that can boast so many pioneering psychoanalysts who did work of truly global reach. Among them was Ludwig Binswanger, whose *Daseinsanalyse* helped heal both the art historian Aby Warburg and the artist Ernst Ludwig Kirchner in Kreuzlingen; Jean Piaget in Geneva who developed his child developmental psychology in dialog with his own analyst Sabina Spielrein, a pioneering child psychologist in her own right; Goldy Parin-Matthèy, Paul Parin, and Fritz Morgenthaler, are best known for their invention of ethnopsychoanalysis, which they put to the test in both Zurich and Africa, applying tools such as Hermann Rorschach's famous inkblot test; and such pioneers of Jung's analytical psychology as Jolanda Jacobi, Marie-Louise von Franz, and Verena Kast.

Jung's practice had long been a beacon shining out into the wider world, and this effect was further enhanced by the founding of the Psychoanalytical Seminar Zurich (PSZ) in 1968. From the mid-1970s onwards, therefore, Zurich really became a Mecca of psychoanalysis, and the PSZ the largest psychoanalytic society in the world, at least for a while. Before long, however, this same "Mecca" was spawning all manner of colorful psycho-sects, including some dedicated to the scientific study of psychoactive substances.

It was the psycho-boom of the 1980s, coupled with the problem of drug addiction undeniably on display in the Platzspitz Park behind Zurich's Swiss National Museum, that finally persuaded doctors and psychologists, psychiatrists and psychoanalysts to set aside their professional jealousies and make a concerted effort to remedy that wretched situation, while at the same time showing the woodcut-like division of psychoanalysis into Freudian or Jungian categories to be more of a still wet watercolor, its fluid, intermingling colors making it a fitting psychogram of the present.

Bibliography:

Ludwig Binswanger and Aby Warburg, *Die unendliche Heilung. Aby Warburgs Krankengeschichte*, edited by Chantal Marazia and Davide Stimilli, translation by Sabine Schulz, Zurich/Berlin 2007.

Gregor Busslinger, Emilio Modena and Claudio Raveane et al. (ed.), *30 Jahre Psychoanalytisches Seminar Zürich Stadt der Seelenkunde. Institutionalsierung/ De-Institutionalisierung*, PSZ: Zurich, vol. 48 (2007).

Anton M. Fischer, *Sigmund Freuds erstes Land – eine Kulturgeschichte der Psychotherapie in der Schweiz*, Giessen 2013.

Barbara Handwerker Küchenhoff and Doris Lier (ed.), *Psychoanalyse in Zürich*, Bern 2012.

Thomas Kurz and Anneke Lubkowitz (ed.), *Psychogeografie*, Berlin 2020.

Marietta Meier, Mario König, Magaly Tornay, *Testfall Münsterlingen: Klinische Versuche in der Psychiatrie, 1940–1980*, Zurich 2020.

Ursula Rütten (ed.), *Beziehungsgeflechte: Korrespondenzen von Goldy Parin-Matthèy, Fritz Morgenthaler und Paul Parin*, Vienna 2019.

Rita Signer (ed.), *Hermann Rorschach (1884–1922), Briefwechsel*, Bern 2004.

Dark nightmares and wild forests: Switzerland has always been a landscape of the mind. The first to explore the influence of the Swiss landscape on the psyche was the philosopher J. J. Rousseau, who famously went for walks in the woods ("my study") and in his *Confessions* undertook the first ever "auto-analysis," even inquiring into the role of sexuality in his early childhood. His follower in this respect was the philosopher Friedrich Nietzsche, who debunked the illusion of the self as a wholly conscious ego, arguing that it is the unconscious drives in the "cellar" that define us.

The Swiss artist Thomas Hirschhorn charted Nietzsche's thinking as a mental map, and in doing so drew on the work of the Parisian Situationists, who in 1957 charted the French capital's psycho-geographic hotspots and frontiers on a map of their own. Where are Switzerland's frontiers and hotspots? This question had been answered purely intuitively by the artist Annemarie von Matt in *Helvetisches Verkehrs-NETZ*—a year before the Situationists. Many escaped in their imagination the web of reason and the confines of normality by building their very own zeppelin, like the patients at the Waldau hospital.

HENRY FUSELI
The Nightmare, 1790–1791

ADOLF WÖLFLI
Zungsang = Skt. Adolf = Roosali, 1917

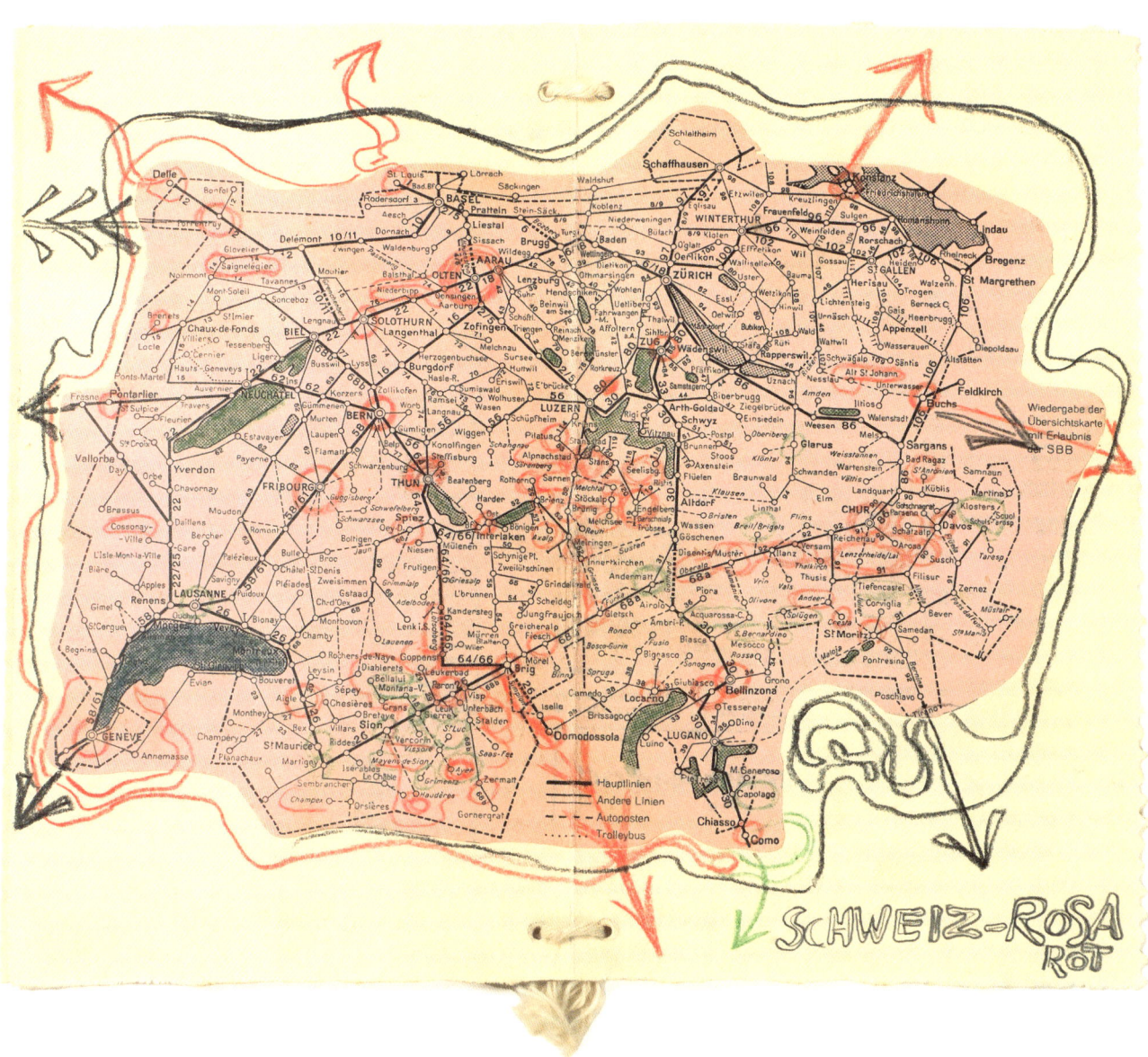

ANNEMARIE VON MATT
Helvetisches Verkehrs-NETZ in Rosarot, 1956

CASPAR WOLF, *Thunderstorm and Lightning Over the Lower Grindelwald Glacier*, 1774–1775

HENRY FUSELI
The Silence, c. 1795–1799

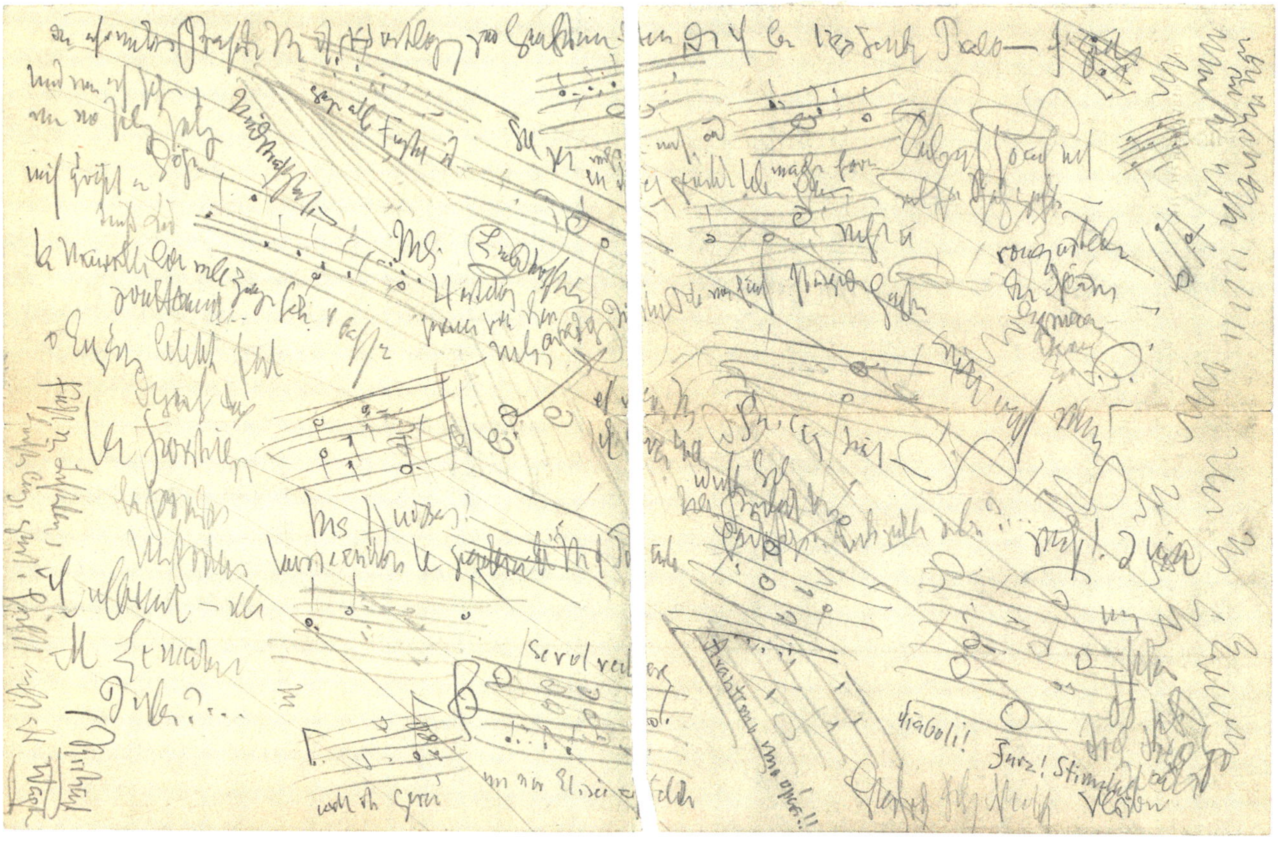

Composition,
Friedrich Nietzsche, 1889

Les Confessions
de J.J. Rousseau
Prémiére Partie.
Livre I.

J'ai remarqué souvent ~~dans les recherches que j'ai~~ que, même parmi ceux qui se piquent le plus de connoitre les hommes, chacun ne connoit guéres que soi, s'il est vrai même que quelqu'un se connoisse ; car comment bien déterminer un être ~~~~ par les seuls rapports qui sont en lui-même, et sans le comparer avec rien ? Cependant cette connoissance imparfaite qu'on a de soi est le seul moyen qu'on employe à connoitre les autres. On se fait la régle de tout, et voila précisément où nous attend la double illusion de l'amour-propre ; soit en prêtant faussement à ceux que nous jugeons les motifs qui nous auroient fait agir comme eux à leur place ; soit dans cette supposition même en nous abusant sur nos propres motifs, faute de savoir nous transporter assez dans une autre situation que celle où nous sommes.

J'ai fait ces observations surtout par rapport à moi, non dans les jugemens que j'ai portés ~~sur~~ des autres, m'étant senti bientôt une espéce d'être à part, mais dans ceux que les autres ont portés de moi ; jugemens presque toujours faux dans les raisons qu'ils rendoient de ma conduite, et d'autant plus faux pour l'ordinaire, que ceux qui les portoient

Les Confessions, Premier Manuscrit,
J.J. Rousseau, 1769–1771

THOMAS HIRSCHHORN
Nietzsche-Map, 2003

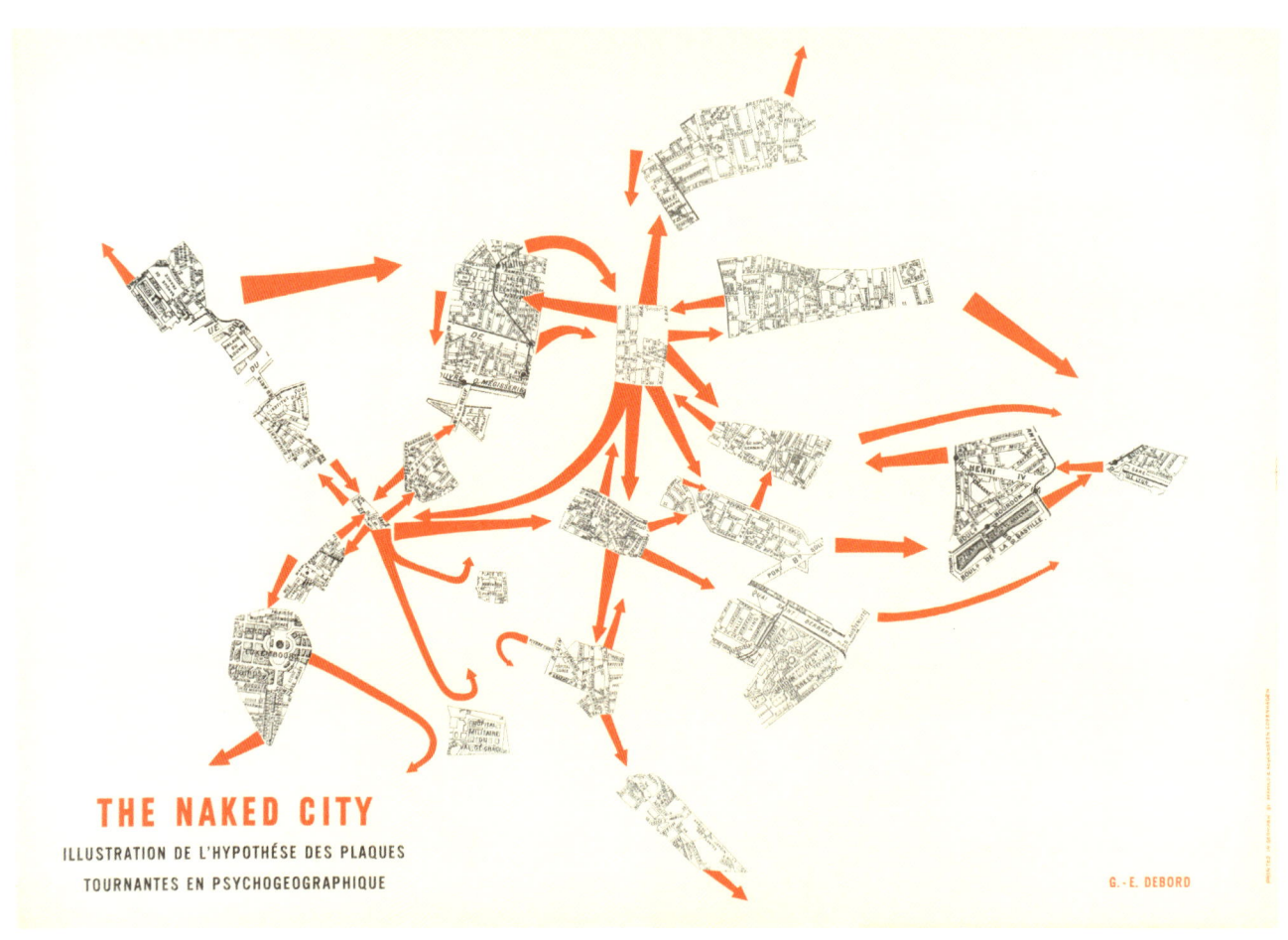

GUY DEBORD, *The Naked City.*
Guide psychogéographique de Paris, 1957

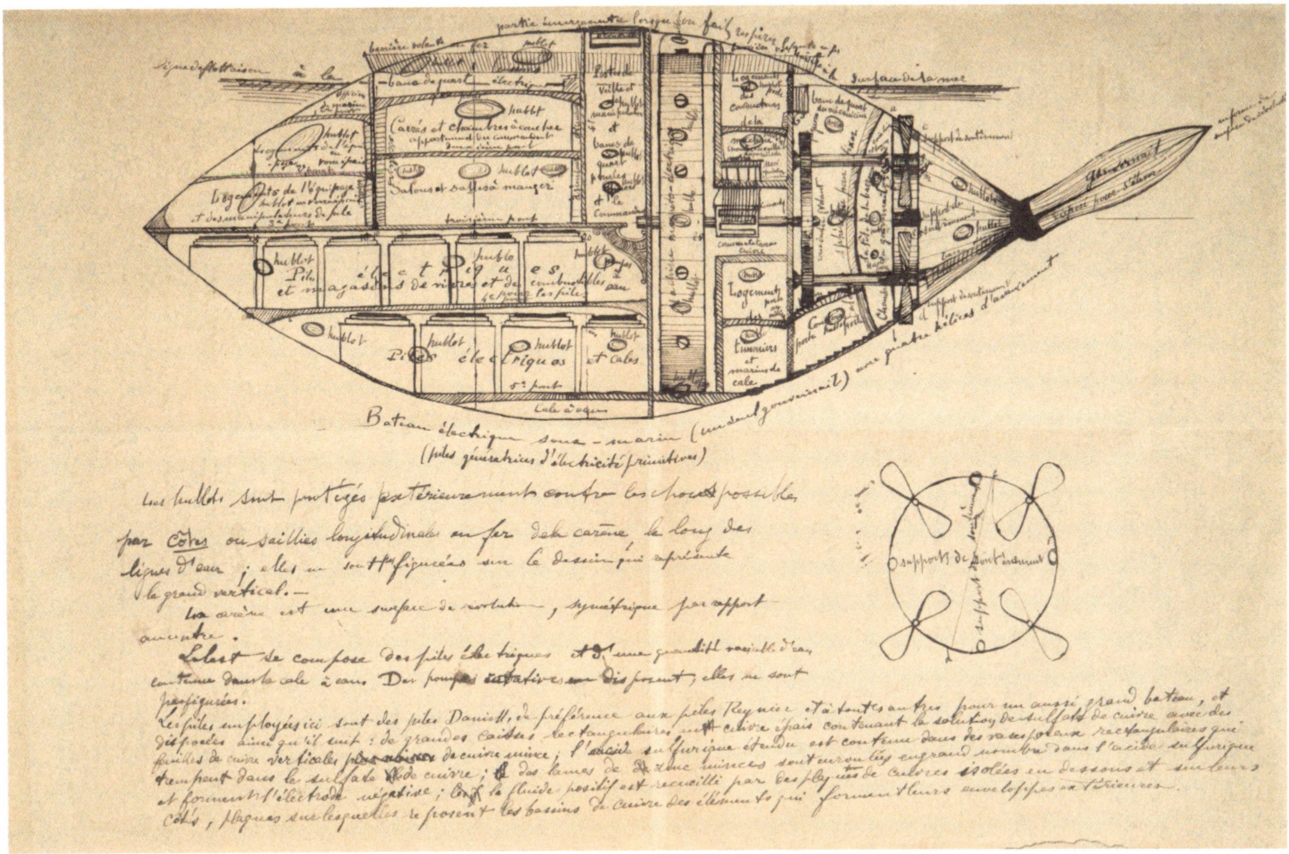

ALPHONSE G., *New electro-mechanical, rotating machine for steering a submarine*, 1886/1887

HENRY FUSELI
Satirical self-caricature of Fuseli entering Switzerland after his stay in Italy, 1778

C. G. JUNG
Female Half-Figure, c. 1920

C. G. JUNG
Spherical Vision III, 1919

HEIDI BUCHER
*The Parlour Office of Doctor Binswanger,
Bellevue Sanatorium*, 1988

From Freud's to Jung's

Stefan Zweifel

Psycho analysis

Analytical Psychology

Spaces are like shells or skins. They peel away one after another, shedding whatever is repressed, neglected, wasted, missed, buried, razed, eroded, inverted, diluted, forgotten, persecuted, or wounded.

Heidi Bucher

Anna O. and the Basic Concepts of Freudian Psychoanalysis

Floating aloft as the last image of *Landscape of the Soul* at the Swiss National Museum is a work by Swiss artist Heidi Bucher: *The Parlour Office of Doctor Binswanger*, an enigmatic work that takes its place in this catalog's line-up of illustrations on page 29. Not by chance does our preoccupation with Switzerland as a landscape of the mind lead us from the forest walks so beloved of J. J. Rousseau and through the realm of Jungian archetypes into the present, only to loop back to the luxury Bellevue Sanatorium on Lake Constance. After all, it was there that Ludwig Binswanger treated Europe's elite, and it was his consulting room that Heidi Bucher recently wrapped in latex, which she then stripped off and reworked as an installation; not as the scene of Binswanger's existential analysis but as the place where, in 1882, he set Anna O. on the path of opium withdrawal. Alone the anonymizing abbreviation used to identify Bertha Pappenheim, the future women's rights activist is enough to alert us to Bucher's critical view of the way women, as victims, were all too often silenced and forgotten.

In reality, it had been Anna O. herself who initiated the therapy and who had christened it the "talking cure." Plagued by deafness, blindness, and a speech impediment following her father's death, she consulted Josef Breuer and in dialog with him developed a "cathartic"—that is, "liberating"—course of treatment that consisted entirely of conversation. In the course of the more than one thousand hours that the two of them spent talking to each other, her symptoms slowly subsided—and then flared up again.

For Sigmund Freud, Breuer's report on Anna O. became the key that might unlock the mind. She herself referred to their sessions as "chimney sweeping," a term that for Freud was so full of sexual connotations that he even saw fit to correct his friend Breuer, who turned a deaf ear to such impulses, arguing that it was above all sexuality—an aspect of human experience that in the Victorian age had been radically suppressed—which led to tics and other disorders of the kind suffered by Anna O.

Women diagnosed as being hysterical like her had once had to "perform" their hysterics on stage in front of Jean-Martin Charcot, the Master Hypnotist of the Salpêtrière hospital in Paris, whose work Freud had once praised to the skies. Freud himself was not a gifted hypnotist and had in any case observed that the relief from symptoms brought about by hypnosis tended to be only temporary; hence his preference for scouring the conscious mind for a way into the unconscious.

After installing his patient—who in the early years of his practice was mostly a woman—on the couch, he let her give free rein to her feelings in a stream of consciousness that was to be as uncensored as possible by the rational mind. Seated behind the analysand in a cloud of cigar smoke was the analyst himself, who from time to time, waving the glowing tip of his cigar through the fog of the patient's personal history, would draw attention to significant omissions, forgotten details, and slips of the tongue—all of which he read as pointers to the primal urges and the resurfacing of things repressed.

The consulting room with couch thus expanded into a three-story house of the mind inhabited by the ego, the id, and the superego. This was how Freud conceived of the psyche. The conscious ego must serve two masters, he said: on the one hand the desires of the subconscious id, and on the other the commandments of the superego, as the advocate of moral and often religious concepts. Whatever we have repressed, he argued, can be inferred indirectly from our dreams, our jokes, or our failings, proving that the "ego is not the master of his own house."

When describing consciousness, Freud also used the metaphor of the *Wunderblock*, the child's writing and drawing toy that in the English-speaking world is known as a Magic Slate. While we can indeed record memories on a Magic Slate, its capacity is limited. It is therefore furnished with a slider that can be moved back and forth to wipe the slate clean. If the blunt stylus is pressed too hard, however, the upper layer of cellophane will tear. Such a "trauma," in the truest sense of the word, is bound to remain an obstacle so that whatever else is recorded has to follow the line of the tear. Only by unearthing and exposing past traumas could new paths and new lines be found to circumnavigate them. Not by chance is the Magic Slate a child's plaything; after all, our ego, too, remains forever a child, overlaid with countless layers, inscribed one on top of the other, with the new entries often following the lines of those already erased.

For Freud, however, who was writing at a time when girls and boys were bandaged to prevent them masturbating, children were not just sexual beings, but their sexuality was what he called "polymorphous perversity" that played out in three phases: an "anal," "oral," and "genital" phase. His idea that not all of the many accounts of sexual abuse suffered in childhood were true, and that some were perhaps merely imagined, led him to what was—and still is—a scandalous view: that such tales were often born of repressed desires.

His framing for the dangerous drives behind such desires was the myth of Oedipus. Cast out by his parents as a child, Oedipus returns to Thebes as a grown man, and there liberates the city from pestilence by solving the Riddle of the Sphinx. On his way to Thebes, however, Oedipus encounters, and slays, his own aged father without recognizing him; he then marries the widowed queen, his own mother, again without being cognizant of who she really is. Thus he fulfills those deep-seated desires that are present in all of us, argued Freud. Only by becoming aware of our neuroses can we heal them and ensure that the ego is once again master of its own house, free to love without being led astray by the unconscious. That, at any rate, is the theory behind the proverbial Oedipus Complex.

"I have always lived on the ground floor and in the basement of the building," wrote Freud in a letter to Binswanger, asserting that with his "existential analysis," Binswanger had fled to the philosophical-religious spheres higher up. "On changing one's viewpoint," Freud continued, "one can also see an upper floor housing such distinguished guests as religion, art, and others [...] In this respect you are the conservative, I the revolutionary."

Jung, too, having once caught a whiff of the "magical scents" of the occult, would turn away from Freud and later speak dismissively of that "infantile-perverse morass of dirty-joke psychology." Ultimately, Freud's thesis of infantile sexuality was roundly rejected by all his Swiss counterparts, most predictably of all by the parson and psychoanalyst Oskar Pfister, who when he gifted Freud a Matterhorn paperweight presumably did so without paying any heed to the symbolic form of that pointed peak...

That the grounds of psychopathological disorders were to be found in early childhood sexuality was a "shibboleth" of his theory, Freud insisted, even though the Swiss, and first and foremost among them was C. G. Jung, who chose not to follow him down that route.

Freud and Jung—A Friendship
with an Epilogue

Eugen Bleuler asked his young assistant C. G. Jung to give a talk on Freud's treatise *On the Interpretation of Dreams* as early as 1900, and Jung made a point of acknowledging his debt to the "brilliant discoveries of Freud" in the foreword to his psychiatric magnum opus *On the Psychology of Dementia Praecox,* published seven years later. Before long, Jung and his wife were paying regular visits to Vienna, where the first meeting between the two giants of psychoanalysis is said to have lasted a full thirteen hours! Freud returned the compliment in the late summer of 1908, when he spent three days as a guest of Jung, accommodated in his living quarters on the second floor of the Burghölzli hospital.

Freud was delighted to learn that his teachings were being institutionalized, and he saw Jung as the Joshua to his Moses, who would carry psychoanalysis into the Promised Land of psychiatry. "It was only by his appearance on the scene," he confided to another correspondent, "that psychoanalysis escaped the danger of becoming a Jewish national affair."

Freud's choice of crown prince was indeed inspired. At the Burghölzli, especially, there were many other key figures who played an important role in the early days of psychoanalysis, including Karl Abraham, Sándor Ferenczi, and Freud's English biographer Ernest Jones: "Most of the followers I have today came to me via Zurich," wrote Freud in 1914: "The representatives of the most prominent nations stream into Switzerland, which is so mentally active, and an infective lesion in this place was sure to become very important for the dissemination of the 'psychic epidemic,' as Hoche of Freiburg called it."

Freud, in this review, skates over the role played by women, especially Russian women. By then, female students had been admitted to institutions of higher education in Paris, Geneva, and Zurich, and around ten Russian women would go on to write doctoral dissertations in the new science before taking up employment at the Burghölzli and garnering international acclaim for their work there. Especially worthy of mention is Sabina Spielrein, whose insights into *Destruction as the Cause of Coming into Being* (1912) prompted Freud to change his view of sado-masochism and to posit the existence of a death wish . . .

By 1910, there were so many "infected" men and women in Zurich that Freud even considered making it the "center of the psychoanalytic movement." That made the break with Jung in their letters of 1912–13 all the more devastating. This correspondence, in which the sophisticated minds of both men shine through much as they would in a game of chess, and which is summarized in the excerpt "Estranged Intimacy," ended with Jung's pronouncement of January 6, 1913: "The rest is silence."

Except that it wasn't. In June 1933, just weeks after the Nazis' notorious book burning of May 10, when Freud's works had been tossed into the flames with cries of "*Against* the soul-shredding overestimation of the sex drives! *For* the nobility of the human soul!" Jung was appointed president of the Allgemeinen Ärztlichen Gesellschaft für Psychologie (German General Medical Society for Psychology, AÄGP) and co-editor of the journal *Zentralblatt für Psychotherapie.* It was there that his 1934 essay "On the State of Psychotherapy Today" was published, and with it the now notorious lines conflating his criticism of Freud with anti-Semitic tropes.

"The Aryan unconscious," opined Jung, "has a higher potential than the Jewish, which is the advantage and disadvantage of a youthfulness not yet fully weaned from barbarism. In my opinion it has been a grave error in medical psychology up till now to apply Jewish categories—which are not even binding on all Jews—indiscriminately to Germanic and Slavic Christendom. Because of this, the most precious secret of the Germanic peoples—their creative and intuitive depth of soul—has been explained as a morass of banal infantilism, while my own warning voice has for decades been suspected of anti-Semitism. This suspicion emanated from Freud."

And then, even more pointedly: "He did not understand the Germanic psyche any more than did his Germanic followers. Has the formidable phenomenon of National Socialism, on which the whole world gazes with astonished eyes, taught them better? Where was that unparalleled tension and energy while as yet no National Socialism existed? Deep in the Germanic psyche, in a pit that is anything but a garbage bin of unrealizable infantile wishes and unresolved family resentments."

This sparked a public debate, in the course of which, in February 1934, the psychoanalyst Gustav Bally published an essay in the *Neue Zürcher Zeitung NZZ* titled "Deutschstämmige Psychotherapie?" (Ethno-German Psychotherapy?). Jung felt he had been misunderstood, and in his letters of the coming weeks stressed that he was not "an opponent of the Jews, even if he was an opponent of Freud," as he put it in a letter to Dr. B. Cohen.

Yet the fact that Jung, as president of the AÄGP, had written the lines quoted above in part to hold a protective hand over the fate of psychotherapy in Germany, lent them a weight they might not otherwise have had. That from 1936 onwards he would be supported in this endeavor by Matthias Heinrich Göring, a cousin of Reich Minister Hermann Göring, was especially damning. Theirs was a balancing act, in the course of which Jung was at least able to thwart the publication of an article by Göring about the Nazi Alfred Rosenberg, since "I cannot let my name provide cover for such missteps."

Acting on the legal expertise of Wladimir Rosenbaum, moreover, he also took steps to ensure that all the other national chapters could send "non-Aryan" speakers to the society's international congresses, even if the Germans themselves did not. As he wrote to Erich Strauss in March 1938, "I cannot and shall not exclude non-Aryan speakers."

What is often forgotten is that Jung also wrote character references and letters for Jewish friends and pupils wishing to flee Germany and go into exile in Switzerland. Fritz Grünbaum, for example, wrote to him on August 9, 1938 as follows: "As you will have learned from the daily papers, Jewish physicians are to be stripped of their license to practice as of Sept. 30th, 38 and hence banned from doing any further work at all, whatever form it might take." Jung thereupon wrote him a reference letter, asserting that "Dr. Franz [sic] Grünbaum is one of my pupils."

That same development also prompted Fritz Meyer to appeal to him for help: "Today I am writing to you out of dire necessity, it having yesterday been announced that as of September 30th, Jewish doctors are to lose their license to practice. A married man and father of three children, I am to be deprived of all possibilitiy of making a living. In view of this shattering fact, I beseech you to once again let my fate be of some concern to you and to consider whether, given the wealth of connections you have at your disposal, dear Professor, you might not be able to find me a place as a psychotherapist or supervisor of drug patients in some country or other. Furthermore, both I myself and my wife, who for many years has been my best assistant, have undergone thorough training in respiratory gymnastics. I am thinking above all of Holland and America."

Three weeks later Jung sent him a letter of recommendation: "*To whom it may concern*. Mr. Fritz Meyer, M.D., from Berlin, is a competent psychotherapist of great practical experience. I know him personally. He enjoys a very good reputation as physician among his colleagues as well as among his patients. He has developed a special method of psychological treatment for toxicomania in all its different forms. Psychotherapist who are able to deal in an efficient way with the toxicomanic disposition are very rare. Dr. Meyer is known to be one of the few. I have published some of his articles in a scientific journal edited by myself. I warmly recommend Dr. Meyer."

Jung finally resigned from the AÄGP in the summer of 1939, his views having made the office of president untenable. The outbreak of war only widened the gulf between him and the society, prompting him, two years later, to refuse even the title of honorary president, whereupon his writings were banned in Germany and burned in France. Writing to Mrs. Goodrich on May 20, 1940, Jung made it quite clear that Switzerland was on the side of England: "If you lose the war," he told her, "we, too, will not escape the rule of the Antichrist."

In later interviews, Jung, with hindsight, described Hitler as a "rat-catcher of resentments." In a conversation with *Weltwoche*, moreover, he talked about the collective guilt of the Germans, even if he neatly side-stepped the complicity of other European nations, including the Swiss: "For psychologists, the question of collective guilt is [...] a fact, and getting Germans to acknowledge this guilt is set to become one of therapy's most important tasks!"

Jung's Active Imagination and the Self-Empowerment of Women

This ambivalence, as well as that in the relationship between Freud and Jung, is of course only one aspect of Jung's legacy. The exhibition therefore accords rather more space to the evolution of Jung's ideas after his publication of the *Red Book*, in which he began his inquiry into the collective unconscious, psychological types, and archetypes, and explained what he called his "analytical psychology." The essays about Jung presented here in this catalog explore the fundamentals of this psychology from several different angles. To avoid the repetition that would otherwise be inescapable, the following discussion of his contributions to both theory and practice will not be as wide-ranging as that of Freud's basic concepts (which the authors took as a given). That it should be prefaced with a source for the active imagination nevertheless seems only sensible: "The point is that you start with any image, for instance just with that yellow mass in your dream," wrote Jung in a letter to one "Mr. O" in May 1947. "Contemplate it and carefully observe how the picture begins to unfold or to change. Don't try to make it into something, just do nothing but observe what its spontaneous changes are. Any mental picture you contemplate in this way will sooner or later change through a spontaneous association that causes a slight alteration of the picture. You must carefully avoid impatient jumping from one subject to another. Hold fast to the one image you have chosen and wait until it changes by itself. Note all these changes and eventually step into the picture yourself, and if it is a speaking figure at all then say what you have to say to that figure and listen to what he or she has to say. Thus you can not only analyze your unconscious but you also give your unconscious a chance to analyze yourself, and therewith you gradually create a unity of conscious and unconscious without which there is no individuation at all."

Many artists embraced this advice as a kind of life philosophy. In connection with the exhibition and catalogue this might say much the same of a much less well-known text: Jung's discussion of a book by Hermann Graf Keyserling that was published in 1928 as "Die Bedeutung der schweizerischen Linie im Spektrum Europas" ("The Swiss Line in the European Spectrum"). Jung's interest in the influence of landscape on the psyche coincided with the Surrealists' nocturnal forays into Paris, which were part of their effort to fathom the impact of gardens and parks on the mind. Among them was Louis Aragon, who wrote about their findings in his book *Le Paysan de Paris*.

In this respect, the Surrealists were anticipating the Parisian Situationists centered around Guy Debord, who spent days and days tramping all over Paris in an attempt to sound out the city's "psychogeography." They recorded its psychogeographic hotspots and frontiers in their scribbled plans and notes, which in 1957 were published as the *Guide psychogéographique de Paris*. That work, in its turn, recalled the *Helvetisches Verkehrs-NETZ in Rosarot*, Annemarie von Matt's work of 1956, which might justifiably be dubbed this exhibition's very own *leitmotif*.

It goes without saying that the urbane modernism of the Surrealists was completely at odds with the "chthonic" quest in Jung's text. And whereas Jung would have regarded the Surrealists and Situationists with much the same misgivings as he had about Dada and Picasso, his active imagination method, indeed his work generally, for many artists got to the core of their creativity, as it still does today. Jung has also seeped into popular culture, extending even as far as Hollywood.

The potency of Jung's influence became apparent early on in the case of Hermann Hesse, who first encountered Jung's world in his sessions with "rogue" analyst Johannes Nohl at Monte Verità. Hesse soon switched to Bernhard Lang, Jung's scholar, with whom he underwent sixty hours of analysis in 1916 alone and would develop a deep and enduring friendship. It was Lang who advised him to draw and paint watercolors, which Hesse would henceforth do in parallel to writing his whole life long.

But it was above all the women who had sought out Jung as an analyst who created works of art. Among them was Erika Schlegel, whose series of 1917 turns on Marcel Janko's masks at the Cabaret Voltaire. As the sister of Sophie Taeuber-Arp, she was presumably the one who told the latter of Jung's collection of kachina dolls, which were the inspiration for Taeuber-Arp's famous Dada dance costume.

This transition from Dada to Surrealism would be reinforced in the works of Meret Oppenheim, who was just fourteen when her father, acting on Jung's advice, encouraged her to write down her dreams. Hesse, in his short story "Das schreibende Glas", describes how the circle of Hugo Ball, Emmy Hennings, and Lisa Wenger (to whom he was briefly married in the 1920s) was fascinated if not by "psychogeography" then certainly by "psychography:" "There was also talk of spiritistic techniques, of crystal balls, of psychography. Frau Lisa told of a very simple method of magnetic writing, similar to table tilting."

It was out of this world of the unconscious that Oppenheim, as a member of the Surrealist circle known for its fascination with *écriture automatique*, developed her world-famous fur-coated teacup, though she also translated her reading of Jung straight into paintings, as she acknowledged in a letter to him on November 30, 1954: "Dear Professor, Your book *On the Roots of Consciousness* contains talk of an 'inverted tree.' I remember how some time ago (aged 14), I made a picture, a 'collage' that depicted just such a tree, albeit somewhat altered. Its title, too, *Le paradis est dans la terre*, was eerily similar to the sentences in your book … it is rooted in the earth of paradise. And if paradise, in my picture, seems to be in the earth and not on the earth, then the 'earth' in which the tree is rooted is a pale blue sky [...] I first heard of this symbol in your book."

The liberating effect of Jung's theories can be felt in the rather less well-known works of artist Erna Schillig, who turned to him at a moment of personal crisis in 1947: "It was like this," she wrote: "Two years ago, a serious operation left me paralyzed. There was peripheral nerve damage, though my girlfriend, who is a doctor, suspected that the causes were psychogenic, especially as she knew that the hospital happened to put me in the same room as the one in which my lover died. At her urging, my family had me admitted for psychotherapeutic treatment. I am still weak, disturbed, confused. Why must mental anguish be healed through bitter acquaintance with oneself? This is the question I would like you to answer." As medical confidentiality blocks access to the greater part of the ensuing exchange of letters, Jung's answer can only be reconstructed from her later works.

Also worth rediscovering are the works of the aforementioned Annemarie von Matt, who shared her loneliness with the psychiatrist Jakob Wyrsch in Lucerne, who also worked at the Waldau hospital. Von Matt sought his closeness even while issuing dire warnings against psychiatry, making her a lone precursor of the anti-psychiatry movement of the 1970s: "Do not lock up paintings and sculptures in museums but leave them scattered in chapels and churches to enhance their impact," she wrote. "The same applies to disturbed but interesting people: Do not lock away the *per*turbed with Jakob Wyrsch. They should rather be scattered widely, undisturbed, and left to their own devices, even with their dependents."

This self-empowerment of women in the spirit of Jung makes for a stark contrast with the disempowerment that Heidi Bucher exposes in her installation in memory of Anna O. and her fate at the hands of Freudian psychoanalysis. Both exhibition and catalog explore the Freud/Jung dichotomy, broadening the scope of their inquiry through the inclusion, in words and pictures, of some all-too-often forgotten pioneers of psychoanalysis and analytical psychology and through dialog with all those artists who drew their poems, novels, paintings, sculptures, and installations from the psychic realm. Today, their works serve us viewers as a mirror in which to catch a glimpse—no, many different glimpses—of our own psyche.

Bibliography:
Jana Baumann and Jenni Sorkin (eds.), *Heidi Bucher: Metamorphosen*, Berlin 2021.
Sigmund Freud and C. G. Jung, *The Correspondence between Sigmund Freud and C. G. Jung*, edited by William McGuire, Princeton 1974.
C. G. Jung, *Letters*, edited by Gerhard Adler and Aniela Jaffé, translated by R. F. C. Hull, 2 volumes, Princeton 1973–1975.
Roman Kurzmeyer and Roger Perret (eds.), *Dunkelschwestern – Annemarie von Matt – Sonja Sekula*, Zurich 2008.
Doris Lier, "Vom Unsinn zum Ursinn – Dada-Anklänge im Bildarchiv" (on Erika Schlegel) in *Das Buch der Bilder – Schätze aus dem Archiv des C. G. Jung-Instituts Zürich*, edited by Ruth Ammann, Verena Kast, Ingrid Riedel, Ostfildern 2018.
Lisa Wenger and Martina Corgnati (eds.), *Meret Oppenheim—My Album. The autobiographical Album "From Childhood until 1943" and her handwritten biography*, expanded new edition, Zurich 2015.

Our loveliest mountain, which dominates Switzerland far and wide, is called the Jungfrau—the "Virgin." The Virgin Mary is the female patron saint of the Swiss. Of her Tertullian says: "... that virgin earth, not yet watered by the rains," and Augustine: "Truth has arisen from the earth, because Christ is born of a virgin." These are living reminders that the virgin mother is the earth. From olden times the astrological sign for Switzerland was either Virgo or Taurus; both are earth-signs, a sure indication that the earthy character of the Swiss had not escaped the old astrologers. From the earth-boundness of the Swiss come all their bad as well as their good qualities: their down-to-earthness, their limited outlook, their non-spirituality, their parsimony, stolidity, stubbornness, dislike of foreigners, mistrustfulness, as well as that awful Schwizerdütsch *and their refusal to be bothered, or to put it in political terms, their neutrality.*

Switzerland consists of numerous valleys, depressions in the earth's crust, in which the settlements of man are embedded. Nowhere are there measureless plains, where it is a matter of indifference where a man lives; nowhere is there a coast against which the ocean beats with its lore of distant lands. Buried deep in the backbone of the continent, sunk in the earth, the Alpine dweller lives like a troglodyte, surrounded by more powerful nations that are linked with the wide world, that expand into colonies or can grow rich on the treasures of their soil. The Swiss cling to what they have, for the others, the more powerful ones, have grabbed everything else. Under no circumstances will the Swiss be robbed of their own. Their country is small, their possessions limited. If they lose what they have, what is going to replace it?

There are two kinds of interference which cause the hackles of the Swiss to rise: political and spiritual. Everyone can understand why they should defend themselves to the utmost against political interference, and this utmost is the art of neutrality born of necessity. But why they should defend themselves against spiritual interference is rather more mysterious. It is, however, a fact, as I can confirm from my own experience. English, American, and German patients are far more open to new ideas than the Swiss. A new idea for the Swiss is always something of a risk; it is like an unknown, dangerous animal, which must if possible be circumvented or else approached with extreme caution. (This, I may add, accounts for the remarkably poor intuitive capacity of the Swiss.)

Thus far, I find everything quite as it should be. I believe that the spirit is a dangerous thing and I do not believe in its paramountcy. I believe only in the Word become flesh, in the spirit-filled body, where yang and yin are wedded into a living form.

The danger inherent in the spirit is that it will uproot man, bear him away from the earth and inspire him to Icarian flights, only to let him plunge into the bottomless sea. The chthonic man is rightly afraid of this and instinctively defends himself against it, but in the most unpleasant way-by his "resentment." Conversely, the man of the spirit fears and loathes the prison of the earth. It is, at bottom, the same kind of prejudice which the intuitive type has in regard to the sensation type: he confuses the latter with his own inferior sensation function. Naturally the sensation type has the same prejudice against the intuitive.

When the two clash, both are aggrieved, because they feel that their most essential values have been misunderstood. The "other" in us always seems alien and unacceptable; but if we let ourselves be aggrieved the feeling sinks in, and we are the richer for this little bit of self-knowledge.

The unpleasant reaction Keyserling has evoked in Switzerland is not a sign of repudiation—it merely proves that the cap fits. Everybody reads him, and his book is discussed at every social gathering. An influence like this is usually not unilateral.

Something emanating from Switzerland has had its effect on Keyserling, as every attentive reader will have observed; and this something is indigenous to Switzerland.

If it be true that we are the most backward, conservative, stiff-necked, self-righteous, smug, and churlish of all European nations, this would mean that in Switzerland the European is truly at home in his geographical and psychological centre.

There he is attached to the earth, unconcerned, self-reliant, conservative, and backward—in other words, still intimately connected with the past, occupying a neutral position between the fluctuating and contradictory aspirations and opinions of the other nations or functions. That wouldn't be a bad role for the Swiss: to act as Europe's centre of gravity.

I do not wish to evoke the impression that I am trying to turn our national vices into a virtue. I do not deny the ugly side of the earthbound character, but I take it as a given fact and am merely trying to discover what its meaning might be for Europe.

We need not be ashamed of ourselves as a nation, nor can we alter its character. Only the individual can alter or improve himself, provided he can outgrow his national prejudices in the course of his psychic development.

C. G. Jung, "The Swiss Line in the European Spectrum," 1928

A Grammar of the _____ in the

Alain de Botton

New Mind Swiss Spirit

STEFAN ZWEIFEL *According to Plato's allegory of the cave, the cave-dwellers mistake the shadows flickering on the cave wall for reality, although only to the point when they are guided outside and see the actual objects being carried past the mouth of the cave and casting their shadows on its interior. Eventually, they are able to look at the sun and see it as truth, beauty, and goodness.*

When reading your books, the reader gets the impression that you give each of us cave-dwellers a different guide with which to find our way into the bright light of consciousness: philosophers such as Socrates in The Consolations of Philosophy, *artists such as Da Vinci in* Art as Therapy *and, not least, psychoanalysts such as Sigmund Freud in* A Therapeutic Journey. *And in your first bestseller,* How Proust Can Change Your Life, *it was a writer. But why Proust?*

ALAIN DE BOTTON I think one of the strangest things about writers and writing is that sometimes we get the experience as readers that the writer has been inside our own minds, has known us better than we know ourselves. The writer's describing something that is completely at odds, really personal, but at the same time is also their experience. So the good writer provokes doubts about our own identity and its uniqueness. Proust is described as a classic, a great writer, a colossus of literature. So one immediately imagines that the things he'll be discussing are very far away. Maybe very impressive, but far away. And then one discovers that they are, in fact, extremely intimate. And it's almost as though he's describing you. Your personal life. And I think this hugely enriches one's sense of what art can be. It breaks loneliness. It clears up confusion.

SZ *When we read Proust, we share with him the taste of the madeleine and travel back in time not just to his childhood but to our own—much as we do in psychoanalysis.*

ADB The therapeutic premise is that there are things inside you which you both know and don't know, which is, in fact, exactly what Proust also reminds us of. Because when you read Proust, you think: Now I remember what I always knew. So Freud's psychoanalysis is very classical. It's very connected with a project that existed long before it came on the scene. It is only the most recent and vivid articulation of an ancient idea, which is that we should know more of ourselves because consciousness is only a tiny part of our mental experience.

What I can tell you now about me in this moment in time is a tiny and abbreviated version of who I actually am. And so it's a very humbling, fascinating idea that we are mostly strangers to ourselves and we can't understand ourselves directly.

SZ *Not by chance was the motto of the very first publication on psychoanalysis, the 1895 treatise* Über Hysterie, *identical with that of the Oracle at Delphi: "Know thyself—gnōthi seauton."*

ADB Yes. And now: What did Freud do that was different? For me, some of what's most impressive is not particularly the intellectual structure, but the practical structure. Freud suggested that we should lie on a couch. Very interesting. We know that our physical posture impacts our level of self-awareness. Also, that we should show up to the office of a psychoanalyst on a regular basis, that the psychoanalyst should speak, and more broadly should not speak in a very specific way. These are innovations at the level of practice. Freud built an institution, and we often forget this. He was a writer, but he was also the builder. You might want to call it a business. Psychoanalysis is a business. It has money coming in and money coming out. Freud was what we might nowadays call an entrepreneur, a psychological entrepreneur. And I think this is often missed and is something hugely important about him.

SZ *Lying on the couch really does change our perspective. We look up at the ceiling and see the shadows of our own desires and anxieties flickering by just like in Plato's cave... It is the start of a different life.*

ADB The premise of psychoanalysis is that people get unwell. People suffer because their understanding of themselves has not kept up with their reality: there are things about themselves that they can't bear to acknowledge, understand, or feel. Therefore a special technique is needed. And here, Freud is absolutely a quintessential Western philosopher in thinking that if there is self-knowledge, then there will be enlightenment and release and recovery. Seen this way, it's no coincidence that early psychoanalysis was written literally like a detective story. You know, you will learn why, you can't trust—and boom, you will be able to trust. By working through conflicts in the relationship with the psychoanalyst, you are able to take a more complete and judicious sense of reality out into the world beyond the psychoanalytic route.

sz *Which is what makes the relationship to an analyst completely different from a conversation with a friend.*

ADB Yes, exactly. People often say: Why don't you just talk to a friend? But that's rather like saying: Why do you go to a brain surgeon? Just get a friend to do it. Or why do you go to a trained pilot? You could just fly. It's true that sometimes an untrained person can fly a plane, but ninety-nine percent of the time they'll crash it. In other words, what we think of as friendship comprises a whole host of disciplines at which most people are very bad. Insofar as a friend is meant to listen to you and bring you comfort, this is a very complicated mission. And, as we all know, even the loveliest of friends just get this wrong. They give us advice after one second. They can't bear to listen because it's too sad. They tell us everything is fine. They have their own extreme prejudices: Never leave your partner. Always leave your partner. All kinds of personal prejudice emerge in that advice. So without wishing to dismiss the notion of a friend—we all have friends and we all rely on them—it is completely underestimating the technical skill and training of a psychoanalyst to say that a friend could do this.

sz *The potential of transference and countertransference to destabilize the analyst–client relationship made it a truly dangerous method in the early years of psychoanalysis, especially in C. G. Jung's first analyses of Otto Gross and Sabina Spielrein.*

ADB There are dangers. You know, I think one of the dangers is that you lead people to truths which are unbearable and then you leave them in the middle of something unbearable.

sz *The same problem afflicts the use of LSD today. As Freud discovered with hypnosis, it can open up something for which the consciousness is not prepared and is not ready, or even able, to process.*

ADB Toward the end of his life, Freud speculated on the fact that in the future there might be a substance that one could take, which would assist in the recovery of unconscious material. And we've been searching for that ever since. Your reference to psychedelics is extremely interesting. I mean, one can't fail to be interested in this if one is interested in the unconscious, because let's remember that human beings have always been interested in intoxicants, substances that will release parts of you that are not present in daily life. In the time of the ancient Greeks, one of the central gods was Dionysos. His magical potion was wine, which would lead to what we would call, nowadays, the recovery of unconscious thoughts. So it's sad that in the modern world we often look at intoxicating substances only as party drugs, something fun, and therefore miss the fascinating ways in which there could be tools to open up bits of the mind that otherwise stay closed.

sz *Free association attempts to open up the mind in a similar way, though obviously in much smaller doses. In analysis, the unconscious speaks through jokes, slips of the tongue, and dreams.*

ADB That's why Freud analyzed dreams. He analyzed jokes, he analyzed things that are forgotten. If you forget the keys, why did you forget them? If you were late, why is that? He understood that we constantly leak information about our unconscious selves, and that a good therapist should be picking them up. And there are other techniques, too.

sz *Like the Rorschach Test invented by the Swiss Hermann Rorschach, although this was just one of the many contributions to psychoanalysis to emanate from tiny little Switzerland. No less worthy of mention are the concepts of Ludwig Binswanger, Jean Piaget, and Sabina Spielrein—Switzerland has spawned so many different methods of exploring the unconscious.*

ADB It's completely remarkable, considering its size. One speculation: The word "hierarchy" comes to mind. The stronger the hierarchy, the more we need to follow the rules, to decide that some things are normal and acceptable and others are not. Switzerland didn't have an aristocracy, a traditional hierarchy. It was democratic, not only in its voting system but in its thinking system. And this was extremely helpful when it came to thinking about the mind, because it meant that all sorts of concepts would not have to be abided by. Psychoanalysis is an anarchic discipline in a way. Plato had this idea that the mind is like a horse with a rider on top, holding the reins. Well, psychoanalysis disagrees with this. Actually, the rider is not really in control of the horse. The horse is leading. And so it's inherently anti-hierarchical. And I think that has something to do with the Swiss spirit.

SZ *That began back in the eighteenth century with Fuseli's* The Nightmare, *and with Jean-Jacques Rousseau wandering through the forest and noting down how his peregrinations were affecting his mental state.*

ADB Again we're talking about the couch as a useful place to discover parts of you that you don't when sitting in a chair. I think Rousseau's discovery was that there are certain parts of you that appear when you're walking, and particularly when you're walking in nature. This is something that we intuitively know is correct. We know that there are some places where it's easier to think. For example, it's easier to think in bed or in the shower than at a desk.

Again, this is the idea that it's when you're not "supposed" to think that you think best. The mind needs to be a little bit distracted in order to think properly. And really, the bits of the mind that need to be distracted are the more hierarchical, normative, procedural bits of the brain that make us more stupid than we are. Every child is more intelligent than an adult in a way because they don't have that censorship. So children are permanently on a walk. Children are permanently in a "reverie," permanently on the couch. As we grow up, we censor everything. But sometimes, as on a walk, we think: I'm just on a walk. Then the mind is distracted enough by time. Trees and mountains and clouds. Boom. Some bit of the truth slips out. And that's what Rousseau was very good at capturing.

SZ *You like to illustrate your books with works of art, presumably because a stroll through a museum is much like a stroll through the countryside, in that it opens up new prospects for the mind.*

ADB Absolutely. And it's one of the tragedies—well, not really a tragedy, but it's inevitable when you look at a painting in a museum and you're there for five minutes, maximum. Or you might be there for twenty seconds. But works of art are not created to be seen in twenty seconds. If we think of the Zen Buddhist tradition... let's say the rock garden. You don't just look and then say: Okay, I've seen a rock and some gravel, and now I'll move on. You look inside. You look outside. The outside and the inside are helping each other. The outside is a gateway to certain inner pictures... You could look at a Mark Rothko or a Caspar David Friedrich in a similar way, as a kind of gateway to something inner. This is why I think the museum gift shop is very important, because you go buy the postcard, put it on your desk, and later can look at it and take a little journey.

SZ *When we met a few years ago in London to talk about Proust, you said: "The best thing I ever did was to read Proust," only to qualify your assertion by adding: "Until I went to therapy. That was best of all!"*

ADB I think we have to be careful here. Doing therapy takes time. It takes money. It's a privilege. And I don't want to say life is impossible without it. I also think that the relationship between a therapist and a client is very difficult to get right. It's a little bit like love. It all depends on whom you fall in love with. It could be a nightmare. And some people never fall in love. They never meet the person that they should be with who might make them happy. A therapist is not like a pilot. Every pilot who can fly is good. Not every therapist is going to be good for you. It's a very personal relationship. I think this is why many people have bad experiences with therapy and psychoanalysis. I believe there are some people who call themselves therapists and analysts who should not be in the profession. Not because they do anything wildly wrong or dangerous. But it's an art, not a science.

sz   *One of the arts of midwifery, as Socrates would say.*

ADB   Socrates thought that the way in which you get people to say what's really on their mind is to ask them lots of questions. Normally about words... like, are you using the word happiness, and what do you really mean by that? Or the word love: What do you mean by love? He thought we use language without properly understanding what we mean. So, if a philosopher such as Socrates gets more and more precise about what words mean, we also get more precise. But this is once again Freud's superior genius in this area, understanding the concept of the unconscious, and that there are things which the mind will not be able to say to somebody. What do you mean by love? They could give you an answer, but it might not be the correct one because the real truth might be hidden from them by unconscious processes, which is a fascinating and in a way rather depressing insight, but a very important one.

sz   *Freud handled this through recourse to the ancient myth of Oedipus.*

ADB   People tend to misunderstand this. They think of Freud as telling us that we want to have sex with our parents. It ends up very quickly in a sort of simplistic boxing match where someone says, yes, you do, no, you don't, etc. We need to start from a different place. I think what Freud was trying to tell us is that in order for a boy or a girl to grow up into a happy man or woman, it helps if there is a certain kind of relationship with a parent. A parent should acknowledge the attractiveness of their child. That's really what he meant. And the child should acknowledge or feel that they are being found attractive. But there are two enormous dangers. One is that this doesn't happen at all. And the danger there is that the child will not be able to make themselves comfortable with their own potency. They will become frightened of or cut off from it. And the other danger, of course, which we're aware of today, but of which Freud was also very aware, is that the parent will seduce that child and that would actually cross the boundary. So healthy development requires this sort of dance between two very dangerous extremes, not acknowledging the potency of the child and acknowledging it to not forcing one's own desire on a child. Both of these are kind of catastrophes. And by calling it "Oedipal," you're simply leaning on a Greek myth in order to say there can be something in the relationship between parents and children that involves desire and which needs to be handled very carefully. Otherwise you have a tragedy.

sz   *Whether ancient myth or dream—Freud's perspective is always highly individual, which is why archetypes are just as alien to him as Jung's notion of a collective unconscious.*

ADB   I'm more Freudian. It's never actually the psychoanalyst who analyzes the dreams. It's only ever the patient who is the analyst. It's always more interesting to ask the client to come up with their own dream dictionary. It always helps to say, if you have a dream about a black cat, what are black cats for you, not for an ancient Egyptian or a Persian you know, for you what is a black cat? It stands for more of a chance to get at something. Then to say all snakes are or all bridges are, etc... Jung's problem is that he literally thinks the unconscious is a language which is universal and which can be translated, and I think this doesn't respect the differences in experience and culture. There is a grammar to the unconscious, but it's not a dictionary. So this is the difference. Freud believed in a grammar, in grammatical rules, but Jung really believed in a dictionary. And I think that's going too far.

sz   *Not even single words can be said to have a universal validity. The German word "Seele," for example, means something rather different from the English word "soul."*

ADB   The genius of psychoanalysis is that it's a discipline that rests on universal assumptions about human nature. But at its best, it's done individually, so that every patient is a new person in psychoanalysis. And the good analyst will be ready for anything, ready for novelty, and will listen carefully. It should be two people in the room who don't know what's going to happen next. The danger is always to rely too much on a medical model where the doctor knows what's wrong with the patient. I think it's much better to proceed as if it's two explorers in an unknown landscape.

Dreaming is on the whole an act of regression to the earliest relationships of the dreamer, a resuscitation of his childhood, of the impulses which were then dominant and the modes of expression which were then available. Behind this childhood of the individual we are then promised an insight into the phylogenetic childhood, into the evolution of the human race, of which the development of the individual is only an abridged repetition influenced by the fortuitous circumstances of life.

We begin to suspect that Friedrich Nietzsche was right when he said that in a dream "there persists a primordial part of humanity which we can no longer reach by a direct path," and we are encouraged to expect, from the analysis of dreams, a knowledge of the archaic inheritance of man, a knowledge of psychical things in him that are innate. It would seem that dreams and neuroses have preserved for us more of the psychical antiquities than we suspected; so that psycho-analysis may claim a high rank among those sciences which endeavour to reconstruct the oldest and darkest phases of the beginnings of mankind. [...]

Personally, I have had no real anxiety dream for decades, but I recall one from my seventh or eighth year which I subjected to interpretation about thirty years later. The dream was very vivid, and showed me my beloved mother, with peculiarly calm sleeping countenance, carried into the room and laid on the bed by two (or three) persons with bird's beaks. I awoke crying and screaming, and disturbed my parents.

The very tall figures—draped in a peculiar manner—with beaks, I had taken from the illustrations of Philippson's bible; I believe they represented deities with heads of sparrowhawks from an Egyptian tomb relief. The analysis also introduced the reminiscence of a naughty janitor's boy, who used to play with us children on the meadow in front of the house; I would add that his name was Philip. I feel that I first heard from this boy the vulgar word signifying sexual intercourse, which is replaced among the educated by the Latin "coitus," but to which the dream distinctly alludes by the selection of the bird's heads. I must have suspected the sexual significance of the word from the facial expression of my worldly-wise teacher. My mother's features in the dream were copied from the countenance of my grandfather, whom I had seen a few days before his death snoring in the state of coma.

The interpretation of the secondary elaboration in the dream must therefore have been that my mother was dying; the tomb relief, too, agrees with this. In this anxiety I awoke, and could not calm myself until I had awakened my parents. I remember that I suddenly became calm on coming face to face with my mother, as if I needed the assurance that my mother was not dead. But this secondary interpretation of the dream had been effected only under the influence of the developed anxiety. I was not frightened because I dreamed that my mother was dying, but I interpreted the dream in this manner in the foreconscious elaboration because I was already under the domination of the anxiety. The latter, however, could be traced by means of the repression to an obscure obviously sexual desire, which had found its satisfying expression in the visual content of the dream. [...]

In the best interpreted dreams we must often leave one portion in obscurity because we observe in the interpretation that it represents the beginning of a tangle of dream thoughts which cannot be unravelled but which has furnished no new contribution to the dream content. This, then, is the keystone of the dream, the place at which it mounts into the unknown. For the dream thoughts which we come upon in the interpretation must generally remain without a termination, and merge in all directions into the net-like entanglement of our world of thoughts. It is from some denser portion of this texture that the dream-wish then arises like the mushroom from its mycelium. [...]

The dream gives us proof that the suppressed material continues to exist even in the normal person and remains capable of psychic activity. The dream itself is one of the manifestations of this suppressed material, [...] which in the waking state has been prevented from expression and cut off from internal perception by the antagonistic adjustment of the contradictions, finds ways and means of obtruding itself on consciousness during the night under the domination of the compromise formations.

Flectere si nequeo superos, Acheronta movebo.

At any rate the interpretation of dreams is the via regia to a knowledge of the unconscious in the psychic life.

Sigmund Freud, "The Navel of the Dream," 1900

Geneva: A Stage for Psycho

Michael Jakob

and "Gateway" analysis

From J. J. Rousseau to Sabina Spielrein and Beyond

The soul is private, personal, unique, indivisible, and incommunicable. Even if philosophers since antiquity have rhapsodized about the "soul of the world," nothing is more individual than the soul or conscious mind. Shielded from the outside world on the analyst's couch, the ego bares its inner workings, endlessly constructing and deconstructing its own world. Although both Sigmund Freud and Carl Gustav Jung, right from the start, had hopes of fathoming the universal mechanics of the psyche, the fact is that every ego, as the sum of all its conscious and unconscious acts, is bound to remain stubbornly special and unique.

Psychoanalysis, as the most authentic form of self-knowledge, entails what an anthropologist might call the physical encounter of two *non*-communicating individuals, whose very noncommunication is in fact what makes analysis possible to begin with. They are as if separated by an invisible wall, on one side the person being analyzed and on the other the person doing the analyzing. The analysand on the couch and the analyst seated behind it (Freud cited the historical importance of hypnosis to justify this setup) belong, as it were, to different worlds. The analysand is there to enhance the degree of self-perception to such an extent that ultimately (and ideally), he or she becomes his or her own analyst. The analyst's position, meanwhile, is one of neutrality and nonparticipation in the analytical process, as visualized by the couch setup. Perhaps this also explains why so many well-known analysts have adopted a neutral style of dress (even to the point of having multiples of the same outfit made for them) and dispensed altogether with the display of personal objects like wedding bands. Freud also noticed that this radical asymmetry was a necessary precondition for the analyst to be able to follow his or her own unconscious train of thought during analysis.

The analyst's curious status as one who stands apart, doomed to remain forever isolated from everyone else, is a crucial factor for anyone trying to understand the apparent contradiction of the desire to socialize that is so pronounced among psychoanalysts. This quest for company, as manifested in the countless circles, societies, associations, movements, and such in which psychoanalysts typically congregate, can be read as a response to the asymmetrical non-encounter of the analytic situation. Starting in 1902, the Psychoanalytische Mittwoch-Gesellschaft (the Wednesday Psychoanalytic Society) met for coffee and cake at 8.30 p.m. every Wednesday in the waiting room of Freud's own practice at Berggasse 19 in Vienna. The discussions at this first gathering of professional psychoanalysts turned on theoretical questions and individual cases as well as more general matters relating to art, society, and much more. By 1907, the group had seventeen members and a secretary (Otto Rank), and its meetings were becoming increasingly disputatious. The fellowship was dissolved on April 8, 1908 and promptly relaunched as the Vienna Analytic Society, which two years later was likewise dissolved, making way for the International Psychoanalytic Society.

The migration of psychoanalysis and psychoanalytic discourse from Freud's waiting room to the premises of the Vienna School of Medicine was accompanied by a revision of its "foreign affairs" and the consolidation of its many circles and societies (in Vienna, Budapest, Zurich, Brussels, etc.) at the Nuremberg Congress of 1910. With the psychiatric hospital known simply as the Burghölzli as its bastion and Ludwig Binswanger, C. G. Jung, and Karl Abraham among the many psychiatrists of renown who worked there, Zurich was a major research center that as a complementary—rather than opposite—pole helped further the differentiation of analytic practice and theory. Switzerland, of course, had been important to psychoanalysis from the start; yet there was more to Switzerland than just Zurich. No less momentous, in the first half of the twentieth century, was the ascendancy of psychoanalysis in the French-speaking cantons, first and foremost Geneva.

Geneva as the "Gateway" to France

As the seat of the famous Institut Jean-Jacques Rousseau, Geneva played an influential role in the early history of psychoanalysis, especially in the important first two decades of the twentieth century. Founded in 1912 by Édouard Claparède and Pierre Bovet, the institute rose to become an internationally acclaimed center of child psychology, though it also played a key role in both the pacifist movement of those years and the cult of childhood that extended far beyond purely academic or medical spheres.

That it was named after J. J. Rousseau is relevant in more ways than one. Founded in Geneva 300 years after the birth of one of the city's greatest sons (whom the city had never truly accepted as one of its own), the institute saw itself as belonging to the tradition of the philosopher's works *Emile; or On Education* and the social contract, the *Contrat social*. As a laboratory and academic mouthpiece rolled into one, the institute concerned itself with all the great issues of the day, one of which was the discipline and practice of psychoanalysis. Édouard Claparède, for example, followed the psychoanalysts' lively debates and theorizing even while remaining somewhat aloof from them, and translated many a text by Freud into French. Another interesting connection that has yet to be properly investigated but is especially relevant to the prehistory of psychoanalysis is Rousseau's own body of autobiographical writings, in which he engages in extremely self-referential explorations of himself. Both the *Confessions* and his *Rêveries du promeneur solitaire* show the author taking a stroll into the inner workings of his own soul. These variations on the theme of self-exploration became ever more extreme, eventually culminating in the almost paranoid polemic *Rousseau juge de Jean-Jacques*.

The "conquest" of Geneva and French-speaking Switzerland mattered a great deal to Freud and his circle, who regarded them as a "gateway" for their coming "assault" on France. Their success at winning over a coherent target group as allies might thus be said to constitute at least a partial victory. Fortunately for them, Geneva had long been home to scholars of international renown, a local moneyed elite, some who belonged to whole dynasties of Calvinist pastors. This was the milieu into which Georges de Morsier and the aforementioned Claparède were born, as were Claparède's no less important cousin Théodore Flournoy, Raymond de Saussure, Pierre Bovet, and countless others.

Théodore Flournoy (1854–1920) was a professor of psychology best known for his spiritualistic studies and his transcriptions of the visions of his medium "Hélène Smith." This work, published as *Des Indes à la planète Mars* is known to have intrigued Jung. It was in part Flournoy's studies rooted in experimental psychology that prompted Jung, unlike Freud, to investigate variants of the unconscious emanating from the occult and the fantastical. Flournoy's son, Henri Flournoy (1886–1955), whose brother-in-law was the psychoanalyst de Saussure, was the author of *L'enfant nerveux: conseils éducatifs* (1932) and one of the pioneers of psychotherapy in French-speaking Switzerland. He had himself been analyzed by both Jung and Freud and played a pivotal role in the institutionalization of psychoanalysis.

That the practice of psychoanalysis slowly but surely gained acceptance within society without degenerating into a passing fad was thanks in no small part to figures such as these. Just as important was their academic study of the discipline. Their publications and lectures addressed all the great questions of the day, which became topics of heated debate both in professional circles and among interested members of the public, especially after Freud and Jung went their separate ways. It was Flournoy's public lectures on psychoanalysis of 1913 and 1916, for example, that caught the attention of the young Jean Piaget, who would go on to work at the Institut Jean-Jacques Rousseau in the 1920s.

That psychoanalysis was becoming ever more institutionalized and gaining recognition even among those outside the discipline, as can be inferred from the 1924 founding of the Institut International de Psychagogie et de Psychothérapie, an organization that counted not just Freud, Jung, and Flournoy but also the philosophers Mircea Eliade and Gaston Bachelard among its members.

At the same time the Geneva scene had another function, in that it reinforced the role of Protestantism in the reception of psychoanalysis. Not only was Jung the son of a pastor and Oskar Pfister himself a minister of the Swiss Reformed Church in Zurich, who by corresponding with Freud helped bridge the divide between religion and "Freudism," but almost all the members of the first generation of psychoanalysts in Geneva had roots in the city's Calvinist nomenclature. Many Swiss Freudians, moreover, dreamt about (and not all of them unconsciously) liberating psychoanalytic theory and practice from the assumed

"Jewish dominance," and even entertained the idea of initiating a new so-called "Reformed" psychoanalysis. Instead of focusing on sexuality, this new discipline would have given prominence to noble ideals (see Jung) and spirituality, that is, to categories more compatible with religious discourse.

The Dream Eater and Sabrina Spielrein

The sheer novelty of psychoanalysis and the communication skills of those who disseminated it in intellectual circles in the early 1920s made it more and more of a talking point in everyday discourse. To analyze or not to analyze, that was the question, and it was a question that was being asked outside medical circles, too. The new discipline's dialog with philosophical theories (see Binswanger), its admission to the bastions of psychiatry, the animus it aroused in its conservative detractors, the media parodies—all of the above served to enhance its visibility.

The play *Le mangeur de rêves* (*The Dream Eater*) premiered at Geneva's famous Théâtre Pitoëff on January 11, 1922. This drama by Henri-René Lenormand, a much-admired playwright at the time, turns on the love affair between an analyst, Luc de Bronte, and his patient, Jeannine. The avant-garde writer Lenormand, whose later affiliation with the Vichy regime is one reason why he is largely forgotten today, attended several meetings of Claparède's Geneva Psychotherapy Society and was an early practitioner of Freud's theories. The premiere of his play saw the part of Jeannine played by the playwright's wife, the famous Dutch actress Marie Kalff, and Georges Pitoëff himself in the part of the cynical psychologist. The tale of the tragic love affair between patient and doctor was inspired in part by Lenormand's own love affair with Rose Vallerest, a young woman he had met in 1916 at the Hotel Victoria in Davos (where he also met the playwright August Strindberg and Freud). The relationship between the amateur analyst and Rose lasted nearly ten years and ended only when the latter was interned in Küsnacht and most likely entrusted to the care of Jung.

Alongside the love triangle of Lenormand (Luc), Maria Kalff (Jeannine) and Rose Vallerest (Jeannine), Lenormand's play in nine acts (maybe unconsciously) lends expression to another relationship of some significance; for sitting in the audience on the opening night at the Théâtre Pitoëff was Sabina Spielrein, Claparède's young assistant at the Institut Jean-Jacques Rousseau. Evidently incensed by what she saw that night, she wrote an article about it entitled "Qui est l'auteur du crime?" which was published in the *Journal de Genève*.

Spielrein's verdict on Luc the analyst was damning: "Although interested in psychology, he is not a true psychoanalyst and is unequal to the situation. To be a psychoanalyst," she continued, "one first has to be able to master one's own instincts by freeing oneself from one's own ego." Yet it was precisely here that Luc had been found wanting, his behavior ultimately precipitating Jeannine's suicide. Another famous love affair that must also have sprung to mind on that momentous occasion, at least among spectators familiar with Switzerland's psychoanalytic scene, is that between C. G. Jung and Spielrein.

The miraculous unearthing of an important part of Sabina Spielrein's estate in 1977 (with more to come in 1982), along with the revelations of the many scholars, journalists, and artists who have since then studied her, have resulted in a number of fascinating discoveries. The relationship between Spielrein and Jung, for example, now belongs to the pantheon of history's great asymmetrical pairings, not unlike that between Hannah Arendt and Martin Heidegger. What makes their relationship so noteworthy, however, is not just the triangle of Spielrein-Jung-Freud, but also the quality of the dialog among the three protagonists and the important role that Spielrein is now known to have played in the development of key psychoanalytic categories (from countertransference and the death wish to the conception of the anima).

Legend has it that the neurologist Georges de Morsier found the precious suitcase containing Spielrein's diary and correspondence at the Palais Wilson in Geneva, the former premises of the Institut Jean-Jacques Rousseau. It was that find, and the interpretation of the material it contained by the Italian Jungian Aldo Carotenuto, that suddenly brought Spielrein and her work to the forefront of the story of how psychoanalysis took root in French-speaking Switzerland.

A Russian Jew by birth, Spielrein attended medical school in Zurich and, after submitting her dissertation there in 1911, moved first to Munich and then to Vienna, where she attended Freud's Wednesday Psychoanalytic Society. On returning to Switzerland in 1914, she lived first in Lausanne and later in Geneva, where she worked at the Rousseau Institute. She spent many years in French-speaking Switzerland and during her time there gave lectures on the interpretation of dreams, repression, and psychoanalysis in general. "Mademoiselle Spielrein," as Bovet liked to call her, was an extremely active member of the Geneva Psychoanalytic Society and, as an analyst, numbered Piaget, Bovet, and Claparède among her patients, the former for eight months, the latter two only briefly. As a female analyst, a Jew, and a hyperactive scientist with an interest in linguistics (then an immensely important field in Geneva), Spielrein attracted critics as well as friends and was frequently caught in the crossfire between the divergent positions and methods.

The woman who, as a member of the audience at the Théâtre Pitoëff in 1922, "discovered" there a drama that turned on the patient–doctor relationship and hence on the status of analysis and its role in the history of culture, was thus an ideal spectator. By then she had already turned her back on Jung, both theoretically and in her own practice as an analyst and was in the process of outing herself as an adherent of the Freudian school.

Her astonishing career took her to several European countries and eventually back to her native Rostow in Russia, where she settled in 1924. This final act in Spielrein's own personal drama, which played out at a time when psychoanalysis had already triumphed and won acceptance even in psychiatric circles, was to prove tragic. She moved into a house that still stands and there continued practicing as an analyst in a room without windows—until Stalin declared psychoanalysis a bourgeois activity and banned it altogether.

Among the women who played a formative role in the history of psychoanalysis in French-speaking Switzerland one important figure was Marguerite Sechehaye, who like Spielrein was Claparède's assistant at the Institut Jean-Jacques Rousseau. Analyzed by Raymond de Saussure, she also practiced as an analyst in her own right and is widely regarded as the initiator of the psychoanalytic treatment of schizophrenia. Her famous *Journal d'une schizophrène,* in which the words of both the analyzed patient and her doctor are treated as sources of equal value, is seen as anticipating antipsychiatry.

No less important and original is the career of Marcelle Spira, a Swiss who was inducted into psychoanalysis while in exile in Argentina and who, with de Saussure's support, opened a practice of her own in 1955. Spira would go on to spend twenty-five years in Geneva, and is perhaps best known as a champion of the theories of Melanie Klein. After this period of deep involvement in psychoanalysis, she spent the last twenty-five years of her life living in seclusion on the Isola del Giglio in Tuscany.

Viewing all these cases together, it quickly becomes apparent that the story of how psychoanalysis developed is almost impossible to pin down, even within a clearly delimited region such as French-speaking Switzerland. The difficulty lies partially with the protagonists, who were constantly moving from one city, one country, one practice to another. Following the discipline's own internal logic, the things that really matter all happen in the palimpsest-like construct of the analyzed mind.

Bibliography:
Mireille Cifali, "Le fameux couteau de Lichtenberg" in *Le Bloc-Notes de la psychanalyse*, 4 (1984), pp. 171–188; "Les débuts de la psychanalyse en Suisse" in *Nervure: Journal de Psychiatrie*, 8 (1995), pp. 10–17; "Sabina Spielrein in Genf" in *Sabina Spielrein/Ausgewählte Schriften*, edited by Günter Bose and Erich Brinkmann, Berlin: Brinkmann u. Bose Verlag, pp. 255–258; online: mireillecifali.ch (accessed January 17, 2025).
Annick Ohayon, "Un auteur dramatique et ses fantômes: Henri-René Lenormand, mangeur de rêves" in *Revista Culturas Psi/Psy Cultures*, 8 (April 2017), pp. 5–18.
Alain de Mijolla (ed.), "La Suisse Romande" in *Dictionnaire international de la psychanalyse*, Paris 2002, pp. 1747–1749.

I shall never, during my whole life, lose the recollection of a herbalizing I one day made on the side of the Robaila, a mountain belonging to the Justicier Clere. I was alone, exploring the hollows and chasms of this mountain, from wood to wood, from rock to rock, when, at length, I discovered a retreat so truly concealed, that never in my life did I behold so wild and romantic a scene. Black firs were mingled with prodigious beech trees, several of which had fallen with age, and crossing each other, shut up this retreat as with an impenetrable barrier. Through some opening of this dreary enclosure, the eye was presented with craggy peaked rocks and horrible precipices, which I dared not cast a look at, without laying down with my face to the ground. The horned owl, the raven, and the spray, screamed from the clefts of this mountain, while some small birds, scarce but familiar, tempered the horror of the solitude. There I found the notched heptaphyllos, the cicclamen, the nidus avis, the greater laserpitium, and some other plants, which delighted and amused me for some time; but insensibly governed by the forcible impression made on me by so many striking objects, I forgot my botany, and seating myself on a bed of lycopodium and moss, began to contemplate at my ease, supposing I was in a retreat unknown to the whole world, and where my persecutors could never find me. A sentiment of pride was mingled with this reverie; I compared myself to those great voyagers who discover desert islands, and said, with self-complacency, "doubtless, I am the first mortal whoever penetrated this retreat," regarding myself as another Columbus. While I was indulging this idea, I heard, at some small distance, a kind of clattering noise, which seemed familiar to me; I listen—the noise is repeated and increased. Surprised, and curious, I rose hastily, and crept through the bushes, on that side from which the found proceeded; when, in a thicket, not twenty paces distant from that retreat which I thought no one but myself had ever discovered, I perceived—a stocking manufactory!

I cannot express the confused and contradictory agitation I felt in my heart on this discovery. My first sensation was an involuntary joy at again finding myself among mortals, when I had supposed myself totally alone; but this emotion, more rapid than lightening, soon gave place to a melancholy and more lasting reflection, which was, that I could not possibly hide myself, even among the cliffs of the Alps, from the cruel search of men, who would delight to torment me; [. . .]

But who would have expected to find a manufactory on the edge of a precipice? Indeed, there is no spot in the world which exhibits such a mixture of uncultivated nature and human industry, as Switzerland; the whole country, to use the expression, is nothing but one great city, whose streets, longer and wider than those of St. Antoine, are adorned by forests, or separated by mountains, and whose straggling lonely dwellings, only communicate by a kind of English gardens. [...] A single trait of this kind throws a greater light on Switzerland than all the descriptions of travellers. [...]

[In the Middle of the Lake of Bienne]
Everything fluctuates on earth; nothing remains in a constant and lasting form, and those affections which are attached to external things necessarily change with their object. We are ever looking forward or backward, ruminating on what is past, and can return no more, or anticipating the future, which may never arrive; there is nothing solid to which the heart can attach, itself, neither have we here below any pleasures that are lasting. Permanent, happiness is, I fear, unknown, and scarcely is there an instant in our most lively enjoyments when the heart can truly say, May this moment last forever!!! How then can such a fugitive state be called happiness, which leaves an uneasy void in the heart, which ever prompts us to regret something that is past, or desire something for the future?

But if there is a state where the soul can find a hold strong enough to lean on securely, to attach its whole being to, without a single wish to recall the past or anticipate the future, where time appears avoid, and the present is extended without our noticing its duration, or tracing its successions without any idea of privation or enjoyment, pleasure or pain, desire, fear, or sensation, except of our existence, that sentiment alone employing it, while this state lasts, the person who feels it may call himself happy; not possessing an imperfect happiness, poor and dependent, but a complete felicity, perfect and full, which leaves no wish or void in the soul.

Such is the state in which I frequently found myself in the island of Saint Pierre, in my solitary reveries; whether stretched in a boat which I let float to the will of the waters, seated on the banks of the agitated Lake, on the borders of a beautiful river, or by a brook murmuring over its pebbled bottom.

J.J. Rousseau, "Psychogeographic Reveries," 1776–1778

Sigmund Freud, in his *Interpretation of Dreams*, published in 1900, opened a door to the psyche that enabled him to explore the power of sexuality, as manifested in fetishes (for example, in the works of the artist Henry Fuseli) or suppressed by religion. The Victorian practice of applying antimasturbation bandages to thwart infantile sexuality made Freud's bold theories all the more scandalous; but even if we have long since overcome such prudery, Oedipal tensions in the nuclear family remain as explosive as ever—as visualized in the works by artist Marlene Dumas. Louise Bourgeois also grappled with Freudian concepts both in her own psychoanalysis and in her works of art. Her piece *La Fillette,* for example, can be read as a profound commentary on Freud's Oedipus Complex and the notion of penis envy.

    The ethnopsychoanalysts Paul Parin, Fritz Morgenthaler, and Goldy Parin-Matthèy wanted to find out whether Freud's Oedipus Complex was "universal" and true, for example, of the Dogon of Africa. Among the tools they used in the field was the Rorschach Test. If they broadened the scope of Freud's theories, so did Jung's former patient and lover, Sabina Spielrein. She became one of the earliest pioneers of psychoanalysis and it was her studies of destruction that prompted Freud to posit the existence of a death wish.

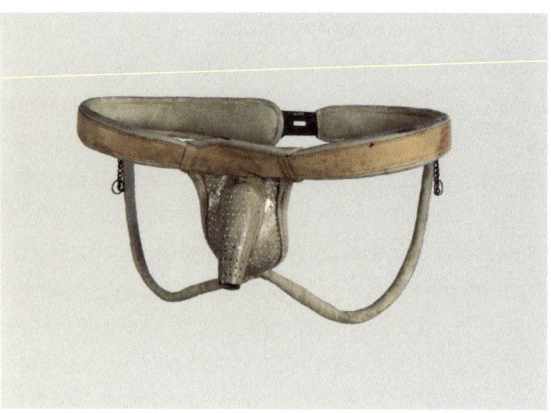

Masturbation bandage,
nineteenth century

LOUISE BOURGEOIS
Fillette (Sweeter Version), 1968

MARLENE DUMAS
Nuclear Family, 2013

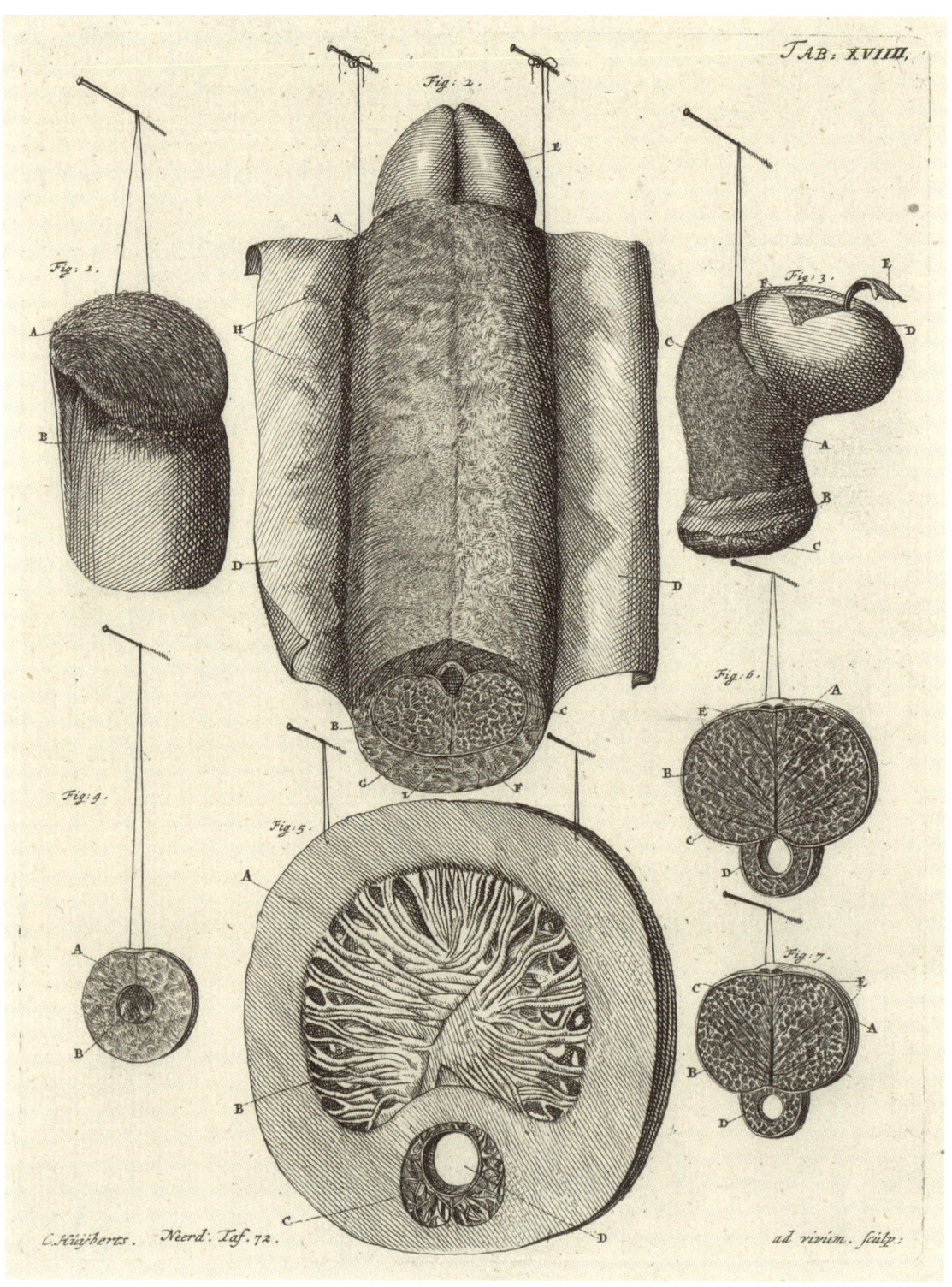

CORNELIS HUIJBERTS, *Sezierter und mehrfach quergeschnittener menschlicher Penis,* before 1744

KERIM SEILER
Holotypes (LA), 2007

Goldy Parin-Matthèy among the Dogon,
photographed by Paul Parin, 1959–1960

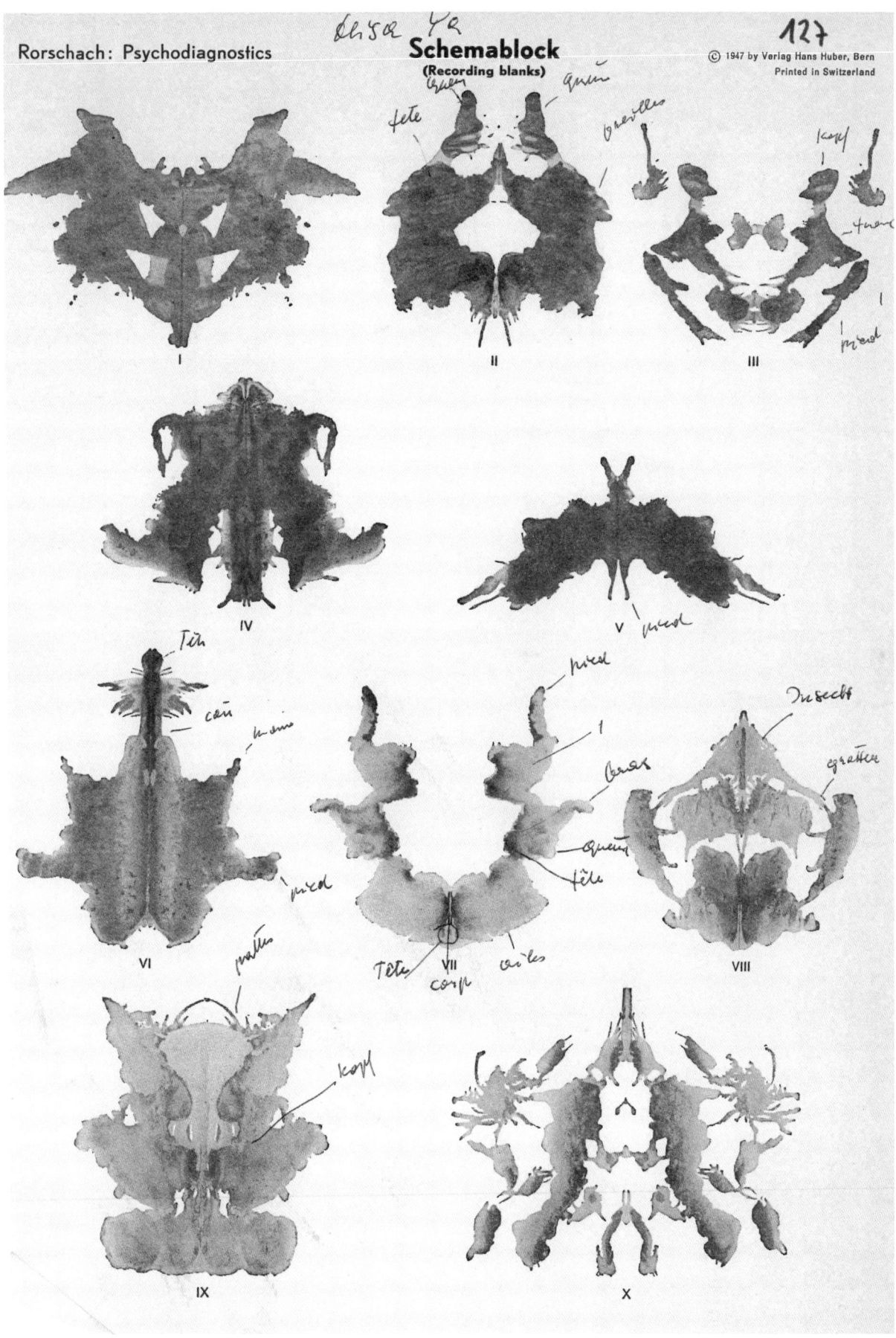

Spricht französisch   Mlle Elisa Ajé ca 17 Jahre   24.3.1966

Meine Analysepatientin, letzte Stunde.
Sie hat dieses Versinken sehr ausgesprochen. Sie sitzt da, und blickt in Richtung der Tafel, wie wenn sie sie in ihrer Hand vergessen hätte. Sie hält die Tafel (wie viele) so, als ob die T. mehrere Kilo schwer wäre, und ihr Handgelenk ermüden würde, so dass der obere Rand der Tafel, die sie am unteren Rand hält, sich nach hinten zum Tisch neigt, tiefer liegt, als dort, wo sie sie hält.

	a G	(dreht brav) Hm! Einige Wolken, manchmal sind die Wolken so am Himmel	G	HdF	Wolken
	c G	Ein Tier, das ist so (wie?) Ich kann nicht sagen (lächelt mich bittend an)	G	F+	T

Regression in Verbalen
Zuwendung VL

I	a G	2 Tiere Elefant	G	F±	T
	a rot.oben	(wie?) der Schwanz		S-g	Absurd
	a lat.schw.Ausl.	Ohren (hält T. nach hinten gekippt)			
	a Schw.Seite oben	Wildschwein (zeigt) Kopf	D	F-	T
	a rot oben	das ist der Schwanz (versinkt mit fernem Blick vergisst T. in ihrer Hand 1½')			Absurd
,30					

II		(nimmt T. selbst) (schaut genau)			
	a Kellner	2 Tiere 2 Affen (wie?) Sie haben Früchte in der Hand	DG,	6F+	T/Frucht
	a schw.Mitte – G Kellner	(zeigt) Kopf Leib Bein (wieder das Versinken mit der T. in Hand, bis sie ablegt)			Absurd
,20					

| | | (nimmt T. selbst, lässt sie nach hinten kippen und blickt 2Min. leer darauf) Das kenne ich nicht (hält mir T. hin, Ich: Du hast alle Zeit) No madame, (versinkt, bekommt einen Angstblick) Madame, das kenne ich nicht! (legt ab) | | | Absurd Zuwend z VL |
| 50 | | | | | |

| | a G | (wartet bis ich T. gebe) Insekt, das fliegt (zeigt) Kopf Flügel Füsse (legt ab) | G | F+ | T |

		(dreht, hält T. nah zu sich, schaut auf mich) Ich kann nicht! (Ich: man kann raten) (2Min.)			Zuwend z VL
	a ObT	Hier sehe ich einen Kopf Hals	G S-g	F+	M
	a HptT.ob.seit.Ausl.	Hand			
30	" " seit.Ausl	Fuss			

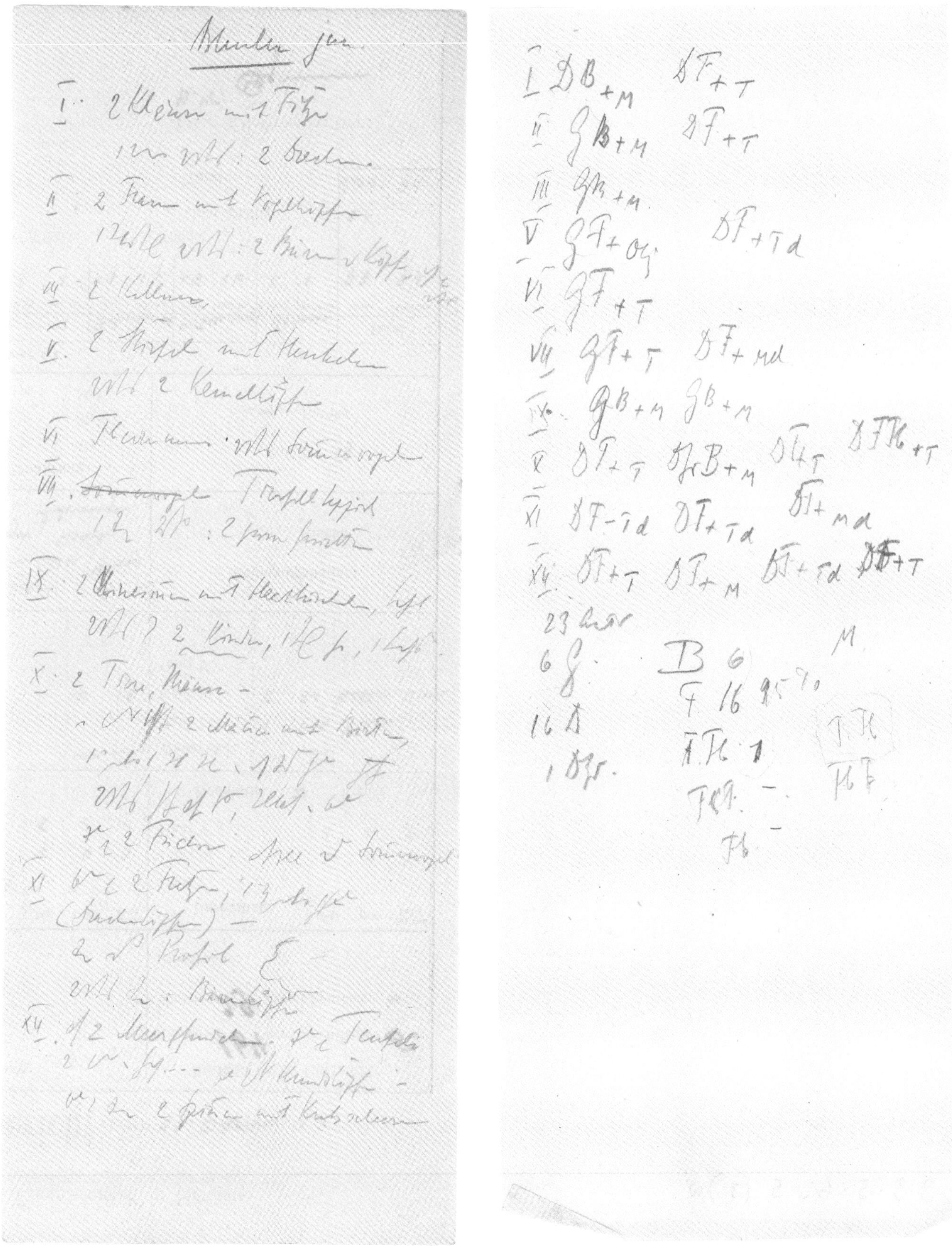

Evaluation by Hermann Rorschach of
Eugen Bleuler's Rorschach Test, c. 1920

Preliminary drawing of the second Rorschach plate,
Hermann Rorschach, 1917–1918

C. G. Jung sitting in his study
photographed by Yousuf Karsh, 1958

MAX POLLAK
Portrait of Sigmund Freud at his desk, 1914

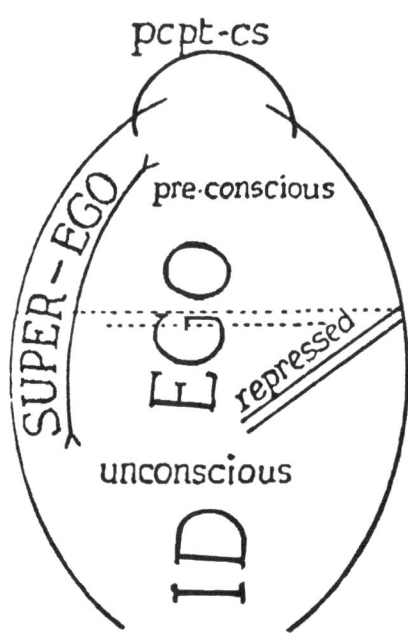

Sigmund Freud's model of the soul:
ego, id and superego, 1923

Internationale Psychoanalytische Vereinigung

Dr. C. G. Jung
Präsident

Küsnach=Zürich, 6.I.13.

Lieber Herr Professor!

Ich werde mich Ihrem Wunsche, die persönliche Beziehung aufzugeben, fügen, denn ich dränge meine Freundschaft niemals auf. Im Übrigen werden Sie wohl am besten selber wissen, was dieser Moment für Sie bedeutet. „Der Rest ist Schweigen."

Ich bin Ihnen dankbar, dass Sie Burrow's Arbeit gütigst angenommen haben.

Ihr ergebener
Jung.

Letter from C. G. Jung to Sigmund Freud, January 6, 1913

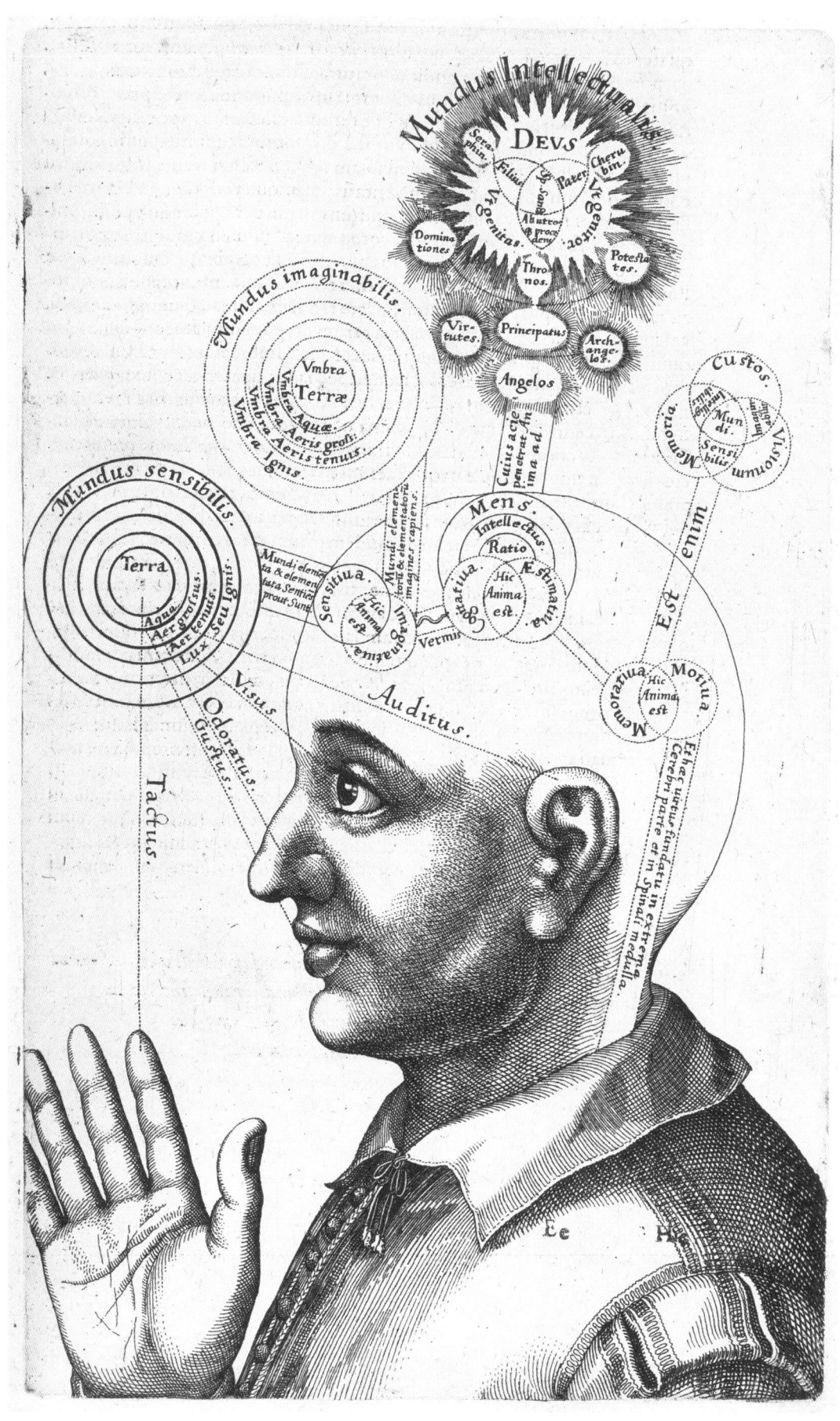

ROBERT FLUDD
Tomus secundus, 1619–1621

FISCHLI / WEISS, *Jacques Lacan at the Age of Two Recognizes His Image in the Mirror for the First Time*, 1981–2012

SOPHIE TAEUBER-ARP
Dr. Komplex, 1918

SOPHIE TAEUBER-ARP
Freudanalytikus, 1918

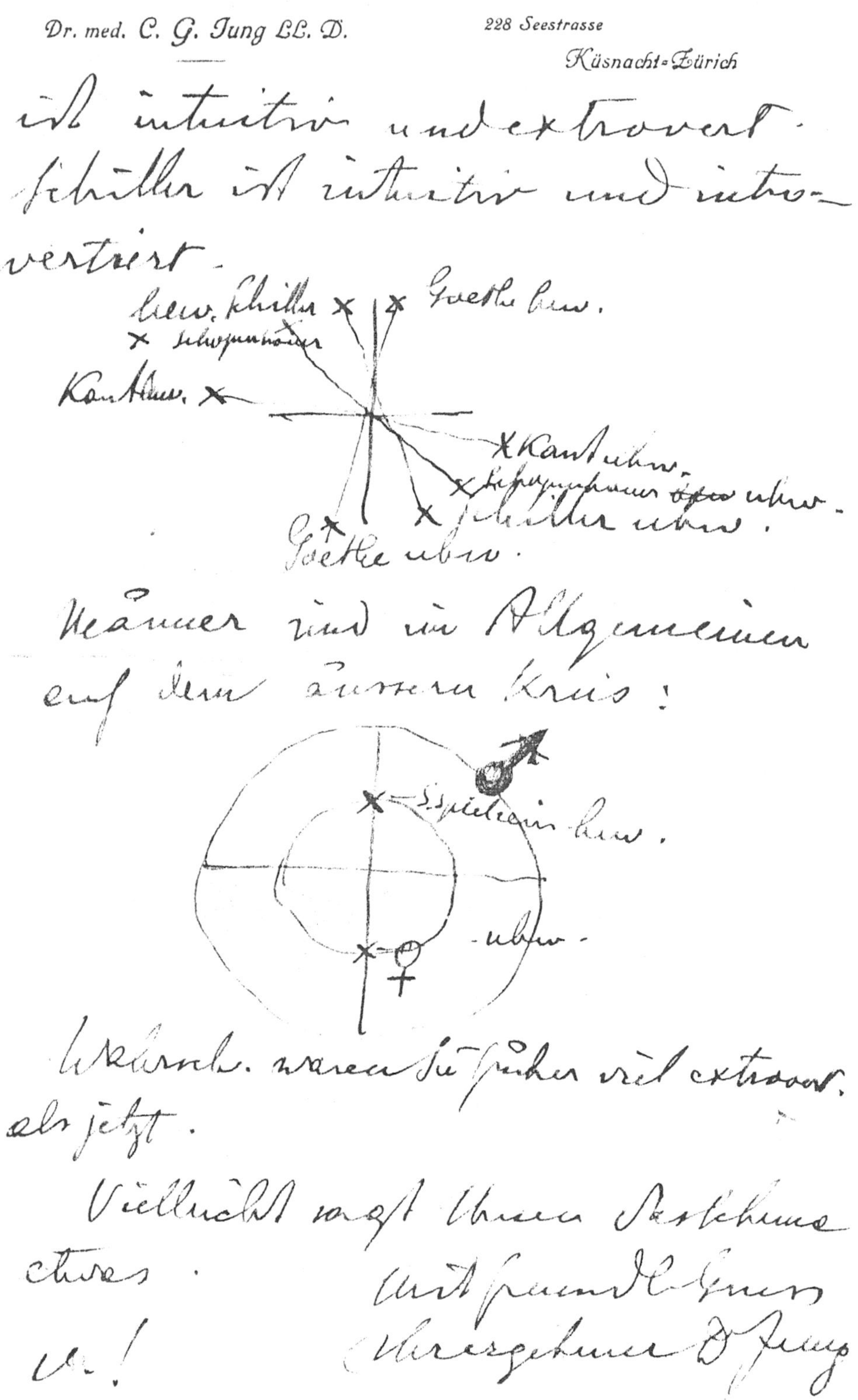

Dr. med. C. G. Jung LL. D.

228 Seestrasse
Küsnacht-Zürich

ist intuitiv und extrovert. Schiller ist intuitiv und introvertiert.

bew. Schiller ×
× Goethe bew.
× Schopenhauer
Kant bew. ×
× Kant unbew.
× Schopenhauer unbew.
× Schiller unbew.
Goethe unbew.

Männer sind im Allgemeinen auf dem äussern Kreis!

× Spielrein bew.
unbew.

Wahrscheinl. waren Sie früher viel extravert. als jetzt.

Vielleicht sagt Ihnen Astrologie etwas.

Mit freundl. Grüssen
Ihr ergebener Dr Jung

u.!

Letter from C. G. Jung to Sabina Spielrein
with diagram, 20.12.1917

Sonderabdruck aus dem Jahrbuch für psychoanalytische
und psychopathologische Forschungen. Band IV.

Die Destruktion als Ursache des Werdens.

Von Dr. **Sabina Spielrein** (Wien).

Destruction as the Cause of Coming into Being,
Sabina Spielrein, 1911

Sabrina Spielrein (fifth from the left)
at the Rousseau Institute, 1921

The Last Turn?

in Zurich in the

Peter Schneider

Ethnopsychoanalysis 1980s

*An Eyewitness Account
and Rather Daring Hypothesis
Forged with Hindsight*

When I traveled to Zurich for my first meeting with Paul Parin in the fall of 1982, the Swiss customs officer asked what my business was in Switzerland. Not without some pride, I told him of my intention to commence psychoanalysis and to train as a psychoanalyst there. "The Zurich School?" he muttered—no!—and then turned his attention to what I might have hidden in the cladding of my car. Finding nothing suspicious, he wished me a safe journey and waved me through.

Paul Parin, who together with his wife Goldy Parin-Matthèy and their mutual friend Fritz Morgenthaler had a practice at Utoquai 41 in Zurich (the address had an almost magical pulling power among psychoanalysts back then), felt that he was too old to take on any new patients and suggested that I try my luck with Emil Grütter, Arno von Blarer, or Mario Erdheim.

My analysis with Mario Erdheim began in May 1983. Even then, psychoanalysis was nowhere near as popular as it had been previously—in 1909, say, when Sigmund Freud, sailing across the Atlantic on his first and last trip to the USA, was accosted by the ship's steward who wanted to talk to him about his book *Zur Psychopathologie des Alltagslebens* (*The Psychopathology of Everyday Life*); or in the 1950s and 1960s, when psychoanalysis was still a fixture of psychiatry in both Europe and America; or even later still, in the 1970s, when psychoanalysis as social critique still carried some weight in public discourse. By the 1980s, however, the tide had turned and the practice was in decline—though not yet in Zurich.

The Psychoanalytische Seminar Zürich (PSZ), which in 1976 had splintered off from the Ausbildungsinstitut der Schweizer Gesellschaft für Psychoanalyse (formerly the PSZ and after that the Freud Institute), was a liberal, left-leaning, anti-authoritarian, grassroots (you name it) (anti-)institution, which had no wish to deviate from the highly eclectic curricula of the International Psychoanalytic Association, even if it did take issue with the heavily hierarchical form of its psychoanalytic training programs. Students at the new PSZ were required to attend theoretical courses and to undergo psychoanalysis themselves before they could be entrusted with conducting "clarifying" conversations with "real" patients. And if they were then deemed sufficiently competent, they could open their own practice and have their work supervised by a more experienced colleague. This very liberal handling of psychoanalytic training had been rendered possible by a decades-old legal vacuum that no one had thought fit to fill. Both the PSZ and, later, the Freud Institute, had long been lax about requiring all new applicants to have a professional qualification as a physician or psychologist, and this laissez-faire attitude had made Switzerland one of the best places in the world to train as a psychoanalyst, including for people like me, who had only a Masters in Philosophy. The PSZ's secession from the Schweizer Gesellschaft für Psychoanalyse was more than just an institutional schism; it also reset the compass of the training program, which henceforth would be less hierarchical and focused more on the collective generation and dissemination of knowledge.

Parin, Parin-Matthèy, and Morgenthaler published the two great classics of second-wave ethnopsychoanalysis in the mid-1960s: *Die Weissen denken zuviel. Psychoanalytische Untersuchungen bei den Dogon in Westafrika* (*White People Think too Much: Psychoanalytic Investigations among the Dogon of West Africa*) and *Fürchte deinen Nächsten wie dich selbst. Psychoanalyse und Gesellschaft am Modell der Agni in Westafrika* (*Fear Thy Neighbor as Thyself: Psychoanalysis and Society Among the Anyi of West Africa*). Many of the early ethnopsychoanalytic works published during Freud's own lifetime had set out to prove the universality of the Oedipus Complex through fieldwork; after all, Freud's own *Totem and Taboo: Resemblances between the Psychic Lives of Savages and Neurotics* was the work of an armchair anthropologist and lacked empirical foundations. The Parins and Morgenthaler, by contrast, proceeded by applying the psychoanalytic method in the field in hopes of better understanding the connection between subjectivity and societal structure and of describing more accurately what, at least from the Western perspective, were alien alternative social orders. Their works put Zurich on the map as an important center for the "progressive" application of psychoanalysis.

The third wave of ethnopsychoanalysis that broke in the 1980s reinforced this reputation.

Mario Erdheim's book *Die gesellschaftliche Produktion von Unbewusstheit. Eine Einführung in den ethnopsychoanalytischen Prozess*, which as a habilitation thesis was rejected in Zurich but accepted in Frankfurt, shows the Zurich-based psychoanalyst broadening the psychoanalytical-ethnological approach of the 1960s and 1970s to a more general theory of culture extending beyond the mere description of alien ethnicities. It was published in the autumn of 1982, two years after the "opera house riots" that so upset the extremely staid bourgeoisie of Switzerland's largest city. Among those to profit from the change of climate ushered in by that youthful uprising were academia's ethnology departments (as reflected in the steady rise in enrollments throughout the 1980s). It was also then that feminist and postcolonial theory took root in academia.

Erdheim's book can be read as recounting the convergence of different epistemological cultures and the merger of ethnological and psychoanalytic practices in the service of a new form of knowledge generation. Still a long best-seller for Suhrkamp-Verlag, even today, the book cannot possibly be reduced to any single descriptor. It is more like Oxo, which according to the proverbial advertising slogan "makes all meat dishes." Writing in his foreword to the paperback edition, Erdheim admitted: "Any summary of all the many different subjects that this book is about, is bound to sound at once improbable and random: Epistemological theory and history both come up for discussion; but I also tell of old Vienna, the Aztecs, the Sun King and Versailles, of human sacrifice and Fascism, and of philosophy and the history of medicine, of cruel coming-of-age rituals and the current situation at a Zurich high school." What captivated me most about the book was its history of science. This was partly due to another book that I had chanced upon around the same time, namely *Entstehung und Entwicklung einer wissenschaftlichen Tatsache* (1935; *The Genesis and Development of a Scientific Fact*, 1979) by Ludwik Fleck, whose theory of the "thought collective" I would return to repeatedly over the coming decades.

The history of psychoanalysis must include the history of the many different ways in which it has built on other academic disciplines. At first it was archaeology, prehistory, ethnology, linguistics, and such like that were brought to bear, either to prove that psychoanalysis was right or to broaden its scope. Later there were several epistemological turns, each of which re-interpreted psychoanalysis from the outside: as a social science, as structural linguistics, as neuroscience, and so on.

Psychoanalysis as ethnopsychoanalysis was just such a turn, even if the aim, in this case, was not to re-interpret it from the outside—as a sub-discipline of ethnology, as it were—but to lay the groundwork for the establishment of psychoanalysis as a theory of cultural development that did not rest on essentialist-anthropological premises ("Humans have always...").

Needless to say, there was a less glorious side to the 1980s that was to become apparent only later on. The psychoanalysis then being practiced at the PSZ seemed torn between critique (of ego psychology and the societal conformism of American psychoanalysis) and idealizing self-legitimation (psychoanalysis as both a defender of the drives and social critique rolled into one). This gave rise to a stance that repelled anything and everything that in those days might be decried as "arbitrary postmodernism." The promising Zurich turn was eventually undone by what could be called "complacent rebelliousness" coupled with the desire for a return to serious, left-leaning institutionalization. Imagining its resilience to be an essential aspect of its identity, the PSZ became so smug that it walked straight into the trap of "old left" normativity and nostalgia, which brings us to the springboard for my rather daring hypothesis.

The "ethnopsychoanalytic process," to use Erdheim's terminology, was different in that it would have made psychoanalysis itself at once an object of the "science of science," also known as "science studies," and a method of the more modern variant of science studies that in 1980s was only just beginning to gain traction.

Science studies is not about how science *should* proceed in pursuit of the truth but rather about how the various scientific disciplines *actually* manufacture knowledge, and, even more important, how they themselves bring forth those same objects of study about which they then proceed to make assertions.

Ethnopsychoanalysis entails not just psychoanalyzing alien cultures but also taking a psychoanalytic view of the analysts' own society, as if it, too, were an alien tribe. The "Frankfurt Project" of psychoanalytically enlightened, social critique had been slowly but surely gathering dust when, in the 1980s, some researchers from Zurich breathed new life into it. Erdheim's followers wanted to know what stabilizes societies, how progress and authority work, and how conflicts are resolved, dealt with, or suppressed. The fieldwork for this could be done in front of—and behind!—their own front door, even if the attempts to apply (ethno-) psychoanalysis to the analysts' own ethnicities and practices remained at best episodic and anecdotal.

Whereas the attitude of classical epistemologists towards scientific practice was not unlike that of Christian missionaries towards savages, modern epistemologists regarded themselves as modern ethnologists having a particular interest in a wide range of epistemological practices. In this they were inspired by Paul Feyerabend's "Epistemological Anarchism," though without his polemicizing.

Science studies undermines the question of whether something is ontological or epistemological. After all, asserting that an object can be at once real *and* a construct is not a contradiction in terms as such, though it is certainly an all too often disregarded triviality. Science studies examines how science "prepares" its objects of study. (The term "preparing" is perhaps preferable to "constructing" in that it carries less of the stain of arbitrary constructivism.) While the act of preparing does indeed serve the object, it also lends it a form that it would not otherwise have, if left as is. It is like opening a dialog between object and subject, in the course of which something new will emerge.

The 1960s saw the publication of *Die Struktur wissenschaftlicher Revolutionen (The Structure of Scientific Revolutions)* in which the physicist and philosopher Thomas S. Kuhn coined two of the most influential terms in the history and theory of science: that of the "paradigm" and that of the "paradigm shift." Kuhn was drawing on Fleck's studies of "thought style" and the "thought collective" of the 1930s that had led him to emphasize the social character of knowledge.

What makes a paradigm inadequate? What brings about the overthrow of an old paradigm and its replacement by a new one? A paradigm is thrown into crisis if newly discovered facts or newly surfaced lines of inquiry break the mold of the academic hypotheses, methods, and models hitherto applied. An existing paradigm can also fail on grounds of its intrinsic contradictions and/or inadequacies, as can a regime in a political revolution. When grassroots empiricism revolts against an all too rigid theoretical framework, it creates a new one—at least for a while. The shift from the old paradigm to the new is not a regulated process, since the new paradigm is not simply standing by like a new wineskin into which the old wine can be decanted and which promises to be a better receptacle for all present and future wines, too. On the contrary, all kinds of battles have to be fought before the new paradigm is accepted as a legitimate cognitive framework. The main target of Kuhn's widely read work was Karl Popper's rational understanding of science as highly methodical hypothesizing. Kuhn, by contrast, emphasized the influence of social, historical, and even irrational factors, and hence was criticized both for his excessively broad definition of "paradigm" and his unsystematic application of the same. Another charge laid at his door was his imperfect grasp of science's working methods and hierarchical structures, and the external factors (political and economic) that have a bearing on it. One of Kuhn's principal critics in this respect was Imre Lakatos, who tried to reconcile Popper's and Kuhn's respective approaches. Kuhn responded to the criticisms in his afterword to the 1969 edition of his book, though the alternatives to the "paradigm" concept that he proposed there never really caught on.

Those familiar with Fleck's musings on "thought style" will find it hard to resist applying the term to psychoanalysis, most likely in a variant that credits the field with a dominant "thought style" with room for many different, even conflicting, competitors that have not yet led to what Kuhn called a "paradigm shift." The dialectic of normality and crisis, in other words, seems not to play out in psychoanalysis as it does in physics, say, whose history Kuhn was investigating.

Yet there does seem to be another mechanism at work, one that I once proposed should be called "paradigm exhaustion"—an admittedly rather lofty term for what is actually a rather banal phenomenon: trivialization.

In a rather curious lecture of 1910 entitled "Future Opportunities for Psychoanalytic Therapy," Freud argued that advances in psychoanalytic theory and the refinement of psychoanalytic methods would translate into ever more and ever better opportunities for its application. After all, the more successful it became, the more authoritative it would become. And even if society, being naturally recalcitrant, was not exactly rushing to accord psychoanalysis the authority due to it, Freud was confident that reason would triumph eventually. His third point concerned the "general effect" of psychoanalytic work, which was a reference to the idea that shedding light on the meaning of neurotic symptoms would render the production of such symptoms impossible. The ultimate vindication of psychoanalysis, in other words, would be its self-abolition. While this line of argument is depressingly self-referential and steeped in a profound misconception of what psychoanalytic work can actually accomplish, it does at least expose the one fatal flaw that has haunted psychoanalysis since its inception: the fact that its persuasiveness depends in no small measure on the readiness of analysands to apprehend their own subjectivity in psychoanalytic terms and, once bound by the psychoanalytic "thought style," to view themselves both productively and dispassionately as at once alien and surprising. While it is easy enough to understand how suggestion and transference on the one hand and resistance on the other both have an impact on the theoretical and therapeutic work of psychoanalysis, there can also be no doubt that the normalization of the psychoanalytic "thought style" had a far more serious and corrosive impact than did any external opposition to its tenets.

Viewed from the outside, psychoanalysis seems not to have any more surprises in store for us. It counters whatever internal and external opposition it still encounters by either broadening its own scope in order to ingratiate itself or by adopting ever more esoteric distinctions. Sterile hypersensitivity and crude activism are two of the less satisfactory escape routes from such an exhausted, impoverished-looking psychoanalysis.

Zurich's ethnopsychoanalysis of the 1980s might have offered a different escape route. By ethnologizing, culturalizing, and historicizing psychoanalysis, and viewing it from a healthy distance, this approach might have been able to keep it up to date, rather than having to join Marcuse in lamenting—and at the same time celebrating—its obsolescence ("What a terrible thing for society that psychoanalytic theory no longer fits.")

For me, the heyday of ethnopsychoanalysis in Zurich remains a period of intense intellectual engagement through which I acquired a deeper understanding of how knowledge is not just produced but also shaped and circumscribed by the cultures in which it emerges. Ethnopsychoanalysis is itself a shining example of how the transformation of knowledge within different cultures takes place, and how that transformation brings with it both opportunities and limitations. The story is by no means over, however, and the lessons to be learned from Zurich's ethnopsychoanalysis of the 1980s might one day become relevant again, if and when new networks and constellations arise to refashion and perpetuate its legacy.

In 1944, Goldy Matthèy, Fritz Morgenthaler and myself worked as doctors in a hospital supporting the partisans in their fight against Fascism. When we arrived back in Zurich we decided to train as psychoanalysts—it was an attempt to change the world from the bottom up, because you can't change what's happening at the top. Goldy always said: Psychoanalysis is a continuation of the guerrilla fight by other means. We wanted to help individuals free themselves and thereby change society from the ground up, starting with the individual.

Psychoanalysis explores people's souls. It explores how very early experiences define a person's later life—especially when you forget those experiences. Psychoanalysis helps us recall things we have forgotten, so that we don't blindly keep doing the same again. This unknown land of the soul is like Africa. We think it has been explored, but when we go there, we see that everything is different. There is no such thing as an African, just as there is no such thing as a Swiss. There are only individual people, nestled within a family, a tribe. And in every tribe there are different fears.

When we set off over fifty years ago, driving away in the Jeep from the Café Sélect in Zurich, we had studied piles of maps. We had taken the Jeep apart in a garage several times, to make sure we'd be able to fix it ourselves in the desert—in a sandstorm, among Fata Morganas that had us believe we were seeing lakes and palm trees.

We read everything about Africa we could lay our hands on. We thought we knew what it would be like there. And as we knew everything about the human soul thanks to psychoanalysis, we also thought we knew how we could help the people there. But we were wrong. We knew nothing about their soul.

We were full of prejudice, beset by the misapprehension that African people lived in a magical world and didn't think rationally. When I met a rainmaker, I asked him whether he could make rain. And he said: Of course, I know all the dances and songs that are needed to make rain. But when I asked him whether he could make rain now, he looked at me with surprise, as if I was crazy. He pointed at the sky: How do expect me to make rain now, in the middle of the desert, when there's not a single cloud in the sky?

We traveled with open ears and listened to the Dogon people. We talked to them about their fears and wishes, just on a rock in a cave instead of here on a couch in the practice. And we realized how different they were—they didn't live separately by themselves like we do here, more in groups. And there's nothing indecent about sex, for instance. It's only improper if done in secret, as long as others are told it's not indecent.

The village elder Ogobara wanted to talk to me about his soul. But then he experienced me as an analyst, not as a friend. He felt misunderstood. He grabbed a passing chicken and wrung its neck—instead of mine.

Another Dogon said to us: White people think too much, then they make new things and earn money. For fear of losing their money they think even more and make even more money. That's why they aren't happy.

The "other"—in our case Africa—is like a mirror held up to us. So it wasn't surprising that a repressed drive also surfaced in me while I was there. I hadn't fired a gun for many years, only at the fun fair shooting stall, because Goldy liked those artificial flowers so much. But when I bought a second hand gun for 800 francs in preparation for Africa and was choosing a gun sight, I was suddenly gripped with hunting fever. That ritual was all it took to rekindle a forgotten, repressed drive. Most hunters say they hunt to keep the game population under control. That's a rationalization. They hunt because we carry a desire to kill in us. Hunting is killing for pleasure, and I have done such killing for pleasure.

We brought a lot of new knowledge back from our visits to Africa. And once a monkey. On the banana boat, Fritz Morgenthaler hid it under his shirt, and when it howled as we went through customs, he pretended to be having a coughing fit. This monkey was like a child to us. It loved Goldy so much. It loved to clutch onto her short hair. It lived with Fritz for three years. We draped the walls with wet towels to recreate the damp feel of the rain forest for it. And I showed it how to catch grasshoppers, crawling on all fours by the forest edge.

Humans are free, they can choose to have a monkey for a child, or live in a large tribe—or live in a small flat, uptight and inhibited. We had to travel to Africa; you already learn about different cultures at school. Who knows, perhaps you're much freer than we were.

Paul Parin, "A Brief Ethno-Psychoanalysis for Children," 2008

Leading Women

A Short Guide

Ita Grosz-Ganzoni

in Psychoanalysis

Lou Andreas-Salomé
Sabina Spielrein
Marguerite Sechehaye
Marcelle Spira
Marie Langer
Goldy Parin-Matthèy
Alice Miller
Ilka von Zeppelin
Judith Valk
Margret Tönnesmann
Judith Le Soldat
Margarete Mitscherlich
Christa Rohde-Dachser
Sophinette Becker

Women have always played an important role in the history of psychoanalysis—as clinicians and theorists, and as founders of psychoanalytical groups. Unlike other high-status qualified professions, Sigmund Freud's psychoanalytical movement was open to women from the start. Their wide-ranging contributions to both theory and practice are recognized across the world.

In the following, some of the women who in my view played an important role in inspiring, disseminating, and also criticizing Freud's theories are introduced in short "biographemes," which also provide a snapshot of the twentieth century with all its tragic upheavals and fates of persecution and exile.

Two women remain widely known today with regard to the founding of the first psychoanalytical groups in Vienna and Zurich respectively: Lou Andreas-Salomé and Sabina Spielrein.

Lou Andreas-Salomé
1861–1937

Born in St. Petersburg in 1861, Lou Salomé grew up in an aristocratic family and took an interest in philosophy early on. At the age of nineteen, she moved to Switzerland with her mother to study philosophy, art history, and religion at the University of Zurich, which was one of the few universities in Europe that admitted women to study at the time. Due to a lung condition, she had to give up her studies. Lou Andreas-Salomé was a highly unconventional woman, she was widely perceived as a scintillating "femme fatale." At the same time, she was an inspiring thinker who greatly influenced Friedrich Nietzsche—with whom she was also involved romantically—and the young Rainer Maria Rilke.

Lou Andreas-Salomé had already been a well-known author for many years when she discovered psychoanalysis at age fifty and became one of the first women to join the young movement. Her correspondence with Freud began in 1912 and was to last almost two decades—a written dialog about personal and scientific matters conducted with fondness and respect. Sadly Lou Andreas-Salomé's writing on psychoanalysis remains little known to this day, even though Inge Weber and Brigitte Rempp published the anthology *Das zweideutige Lächeln der Erotik* in 1990.

This ultimately also applies to the theoretical texts of Sabina Spielrein, who became known above all for her personal story, portrayed in films such as David Cronenberg's *A Dangerous Method* (2011). This lack of scientific recognition persists despite a detailed and enthralling biography written by the Zurich-based psychoanalyst and author Sabine Richebächer: *Sabina Spielrein. Eine fast grausame Liebe zur Wissenschaft*, about which the critic Sabina Meier in the *Neue Zürcher Zeitung* of September 11, 2005 rightly commented: "Sabine Richebächer's biography finally lifts Sabina Spielrein out of the shadows cast by her affair with Jung—Spielrein is elevated from the obscurity of academic footnotes and is presented as an independent and extraordinarily talented scholar who advanced from patient to pioneer of psychoanalysis."

Sabina Spielrein
1885–1942

Sabina Spielrein came to Switzerland with her family in 1904, aged eighteen, and was hospitalized at her own request for psychiatric help. Diagnosed with "hysteria," she was admitted to the Burghölzli, the cantonal psychiatric hospital in Zurich, and came under the care of C. G. Jung, then a senior physician. Jung was in charge of her therapy from 1905 to 1907, during which time he partly followed Sigmund Freud's psychoanalytical approach. This being new for him, he also corresponded with Freud about what he referred to as the "Spielrein case."

The therapy was successful and Spielrein, talented and hungry for knowledge, began studying medicine at the University of Zurich while still residing at the clinic. Over time, an intimate love affair developed between Jung and Spielrein, which was eventually ended with the terminating of her treatment by the doctor. Thus the still nascent science of psychoanalysis had its first scandal.

In 1911, Spielrein was the first woman to receive a doctorate with a dissertation on psychoanalysis, entitled *Über den psychologischen Inhalt eines Falles von Schizophrenie.* Wanting to meet Freud, she traveled to Vienna, where she joined his weekly psychoanalytical working group. In 1914, Spielrein married the Russian Jewish physician Pawel Naumowitsch Scheftel in Rostov-on-Don and the couple went on to have two daughters. From 1915 to 1921, Spielrein lived in Lausanne and later in Geneva, where she taught at the Institut Jean-Jacques Rousseau and was a very active member of the Geneva Psychoanalytical Society. Her clients included Jean Piaget, who saw her for a period of eight months and went on to become a famous biologist, epistemologist, and child psychologist. Spielrein was herself a pioneer in researching childhood development of the psyche and became a talented child analyst. Her article "Contributions to the Knowledge of the Child's Soul," published in 1912, was the first work on child analysis in psychoanalytic history.

Spielrein returned to Russia in 1923, which was now part of the Soviet Union. When Stalin outlawed psychoanalysis in 1929 for being "idealist," she was at least given permission to work as a medical doctor, and she continued to publish essays in Western psychoanalytical journals. Her paper "Die Destruktion als Ursache des Werdens" (1912; "Destruction as the Cause of Coming Into Being," 1994) influenced one of Freud's central theses—the death drive. In 1942 Spielrein—then aged fifty-six—and her two daughters Renata and Eva, were shot by a Nazi murder squad at the infamous Zmievskaya Balka ravine, together with around 25,000 other Jews living in Rostov.

Marguerite Sechehaye
1887–1964

Marguerite Sechehaye is another figure who illustrates the great influence psychoanalysis had from the start in the French-speaking part of Switzerland—mainly Geneva. As early as 1900, the neurologist and psychologist Théodore Flournoy spoke about Freud's recently publicized dream interpretation at the University of Geneva. Among his students was Éduard Claparède, who later became Sechehaye's training analyst. In 1912, Claparède and Pierre Bovet founded the famous Institut Jean-Jacques Rousseau. The institute became an internationally recognized center for child psychology, where—as mentioned—Sabina Spielrein also worked.

Sechehaye was one of the Swiss women psychoanalysts who engaged in an intensive cross-border exchange with analysts predominantly specializing in child psychiatry: Melanie Klein, René A. Spitz, Anna Freud, and Donald W. Winnicott. Sechehaye's psychoanalytical specialty was in the treatment of schizophrenics. She was among the first therapists in Switzerland to take a psychoanalytical approach to psychoses and seek to understand the schizophrenic experience. In her book *Renée,* published in 1947, she describes the successful decade-long treatment of a young girl diagnosed with schizophrenia. Her well-known second work *Journal d'une Schizophrène* (1950; *Autobiography of a schizophrenic girl,* 1951) was translated into many languages and even made into a film in 1968. But it wasn't until 1986—twenty-two years after Sechehaye's death—that the book was published in German (*Tagebuch einer Schizophrenen*). In it, the patient "Renée" describes her experiences during the therapy and Sechehaye comments the statements.

Marguerite Sechehaye adopted "Renée," whose actual name was Louisa Düss (1912–2002), after her recovery. Düss went on to become a psychoanalyst herself, and in 1940 developed a method for using fables in providing psychoanalysis for small children. The "fable test" is still being used today.

From 1951 to 1952, Sechehaye and Düss gave a series of lectures at the psychiatric university clinic Burghölzli in Zurich, which were published in 1954 under the title *Introduction à une psychothérapie des schizophrènes*.

Marcelle Spira
1910–2006

Marcelle Spira returned from Argentina to French-speaking Switzerland in 1955 and went on to become a well-known psychoanalyst. Originally from La Chaux-de-Fonds, and a psychologist by profession, she emigrated to Buenos Aires at the beginning of the Second World War. There she came into contact with the leading exponents of the psychoanalytical movement after Melanie Klein, in particular Marie Langer, her own psychoanalyst. Spira trained extensively as a child and adult analyst, taking advantage of the rapid advancement that psychoanalysis was undergoing in Argentina at the time. Back in Switzerland, Spira settled in Geneva and was accepted into the Swiss Society for Psychoanalysis (SGP). She became a pioneer in the dissemination of Melanie Klein's theories and founded her own group for this purpose. Spira knew Klein personally. In 2013, the book *Melanie Klein, lettres à Marcelle Spira* was published, edited by Jean-Michel Quinodoz. It contains forty-five letters that Klein wrote to Spira; a very precious find, as there are still hardly any letters from her to other psychoanalysts. The first analyst to lecture favorably on the teachings of Klein at the Psychoanalytical Seminar Zurich (PSZ) was Marie Langer. She did this at a time when the response to Klein's theories was generally negative.

Marie Langer
1910–1987

For many colleagues of my generation, Marie ("Mimi") Langer was a role model—as a professional woman with a dramatic life story, as a proponent of progressive psychoanalysis, as a feminist, and as the mother of five children. She was also beautiful, a chain smoker—like many back then—and full of wit and charm.

The feminist criticism of Sigmund Freud's theories on femininity that was being voiced in the 1970s was not openly discussed at the PSZ for many years. It was Langer who explicitly criticized Freud's theories on femininity in one of her talks. She regarded it as an absolute error to define women as "deficient and suffering from penis envy."

She pointed to Karen Horney (1885–1952) as one of the most well-known protagonists of the early femininity debate in the 1920s and 1930s. Following her emigration to the US, Horney had successfully championed her own theories and founded a psychoanalytical institute.

Marie Langer was born in Vienna in 1910 and died in Buenos Aires in 1987. She studied medicine, joined the Communist Party, and started training as a psychoanalyst shortly after. In 1936, she and her husband went to Spain to support the International Brigades against the fascists in the Spanish Civil War. After the annexation of Austria by the German Reich, the couple fled first to Uruguay and eventually to Argentina in 1942. In Buenos Aires, Langer soon gained a name as a psychoanalyst, became a founding member of the Argentine Psychoanalytic Association, and was appointed head of the psychosomatic service in the city hospital's gynecology department. Psychosomatics and psychoanalysis for women were among her specialties. Later she was a member of a left-wing international platform (Plataforma Internacional) founded in 1969, which was critical of society and institutions within the International Psychoanalytical Association (IPA). The platform had members in Europe and South America and also at the Psychoanalytical Seminar Zurich.

Langer regularly traveled to Austria and Switzerland to give talks and provide supervision, especially after she was expelled from Argentina in 1974, persecuted by the infamous Alianza Anticomunista Argentina (AAA) anti-communist terror organization who had her on its death list. She fled to Mexico, where she was given asylum, and worked there in her own practice and at the university.

The psychoanalytical congresses Langer helped to organize in Havana (Cuba), during the 1980s and 1990s, are one of her unforgettable legacies. They were the first official conventions for psychoanalysts and psychologists to take place in a socialist state. At the first congress in 1987, Fidel Castro delivered the welcome speech—and then asked Langer for the recipe for apple strudel. Mimi felt both flattered and angered at once. Shortly before her death she returned to Buenos Aires.

We have Vera Saller, psychoanalyst and lecturer at the PSZ, to thank for making Langer's principal work known in German-speaking countries, where it has been intensively discussed. This happened, however, only decades later: *Madernidad y Sexo* was published in 1953 and didn't appear in German until 1988 as *Mutterschaft und Sexus. Körper und Psyche der Frau* (*Motherhood and Sexuality*, 1992).

Goldy Parin-Matthèy
1911–1997

Elisabeth Charlotte (Goldy) Matthèy-Guenet was born in Graz, into a wealthy Swiss family of Huguenot descent. During the 1930s she was an active member of a Graz-based anti-fascist group, and travelled to Spain in 1937 to join the civil war against Franco, working for the International Brigades' medical service. Following the Fascist victory and the annexation of Austria by Nazi Germany, Matthèy lived in Zurich, where she ran a laboratory for blood analysis.

There she met Paul Parin (1916–2009), who was concluding his medical studies. Matthèy and Parin traveled to Yugoslavia as volunteers in 1944, together with five other Swiss doctors. There the group assisted Tito's partisans at their central hospital. In 1946, Goldy and her colleague Fritz Morgenthaler joined others in setting up the Prijedor outpatient clinic in Northern Bosnia. Following the Second World War, Goldy began training as a psychoanalyst in Zurich and subsequently became a member of the Swiss Society for Psychoanalysis (SGP). In 1952, Matthèy, Parin, and Morgenthaler opened their legendary psychoanalytical group practice at Utoquai 41 in Zurich.

Goldy and Paul Parin married in 1955. Together with Morgenthaler, the couple embarked on six expeditions to Western Africa between 1954 and 1971, where they researched the spiritual life of the Dogon and Agni peoples through psychoanalytical conversation techniques. With their internationally successful works *Die Weissen denken zuviel* (1963; *White People Think Too Much*, 2023) and *Fürchte deinen Nächsten wie dich selbst* (1971; *Fear Thy Neighbor as Thyself*, 1980) they became the founders of German-speaking ethno-psychoanalysis, a science that considers psychoanalysis together with ethnology. An important source of data for the field research material is the participants' own experience, processed using psychoanalytical techniques.

For Parin-Matthèy, who described herself as a "moral anarchist," psychoanalysis was a "guerrilla fight by different means." She put forward this controversial thesis mainly in private discussions. There is very little written work by her. Instead, she participated in Parin's psychoanalytical and political publications. Even when writing his stories, she was his most important critic, but also a source of encouragement. He always insisted that he wouldn't have been able to write anything without Goldy.

Alice Miller
1923–2010

Alice Miller was the eldest daughter of a wealthy Orthodox Jewish family. When Poland was occupied by Nazi Germany in 1939, the family was sent to a ghetto. Alice was able to flee, and, by using false papers, she lived in Warsaw and was later able to rescue most of her family. Her father died in the ghetto.

Her first book, *Das Drama des begabten Kindes* (1980; *The Drama of the Gifted Child*,

1981), became an international bestseller and was translated into many languages. Alice Miller then gave up her psychoanalytical practice and teaching role in Zurich. Further successful books followed in quick succession—with catchy titles and on similar subjects. Miller had become a radical critic of Freud and psychoanalysis in general. Her understanding of the power of repressed childhood trauma influenced generations. She became internationally famous as a childhood researcher, but critics accused her of false psychological conclusions, undifferentiated claims, and simplifications. In 2013, her son Martin Miller published *Das wahre Drama des begabten Kindes* (*The True Drama of the Gifted Child*, 2018), an autobiographical account of his mother's tragic life and the resulting cruelty he suffered as a child. He described her as unempathetic and destructive, and unable or unwilling to protect her young son from the violent outbursts and beatings of his father. The book was received with consternation within the psychoanalytical community, but also with surprisingly little discussion.

Ilka von Zeppelin
1936–2009

Following her studies in psychology in Freiburg, Germany, Ilka von Zeppelin came to Zurich in 1961, where she worked as a lecturer in clinical psychology. She became an academic associate of Ulrich Moser.

She got her doctorate in 1965 and went on to train as a psychoanalyst at the Psychoanalytical Seminar Zurich. Moser was the first psychoanalyst to be ordained in Zurich, where he held the Chair of Clinical Psychology from 1962 to 1990. Von Zeppelin had a great influence on a whole generation of young psychologists. With her empathetic presence and critical, precise thinking she was a great role model for us youngsters, and she was also very popular and valued as a practicing psychoanalyst, supervisor, and lecturer. She was also one of the initiators of the previously mentioned platform group.

Moser and Zeppelin developed what they called a "dream-generating model" through which the visual dream sequence—as opposed to the narrated dream—is interpreted as the outcome of a cognitive-affective controlled regulation process. Their publication on the topic, *Der geträumte Traum*, appeared in 1996. In 2005, von Zeppelin also published a slim volume she had been working on for many years. In *Dieses Gefühl, dass etwas nicht stimmte: eine Kindheit zwischen 1940 und 1948* the reader is confronted with the world as seen through the eyes of a child, and shares her experiences, thoughts and feelings. The moving quality of this short autobiographical work is not least the result of von Zeppelin's reserved style.

Judith Valk
1929–2014

Born in Budapest, Judith Valk, (née Weiszberg), was the daughter of a bourgeois Jewish family. When Hungary was occupied by Nazi Germany she and her family were interned in the Bergen-Belsen concentration camp. In 1944, they were among those Jews taken to Switzerland in a special transport. From there they emigrated to Palestine. Valk lived in a kibbutz near Tel Aviv for two years and became a primary school teacher. It was through her Israeli husband that she first came into contact with psychoanalysis. She moved to Zurich in 1954, studied psychology, and then completed her psychoanalytical training at the PSZ. Valk was an accomplished host and bridge builder. The platform group discussion evenings at her large practice are well remembered by those who attended. She played a lively and pro-active role in PSZ activities, was a friend of Marie Langer's, and supported her work for the *Salud Mental* project in Nicaragua. In 2005 she edited Fritz Morgenthaler's *Psychoanalyse, Traum, Ethnologie*.

Margret Tönnesmann
1924–2014

Originally from Düsseldorf, Margret Tönnesmann moved to London. where she trained in psychoanalysis and qualified as a psychiatrist. As a member of the so-called "Middle Group" or "Independents" (British psychoanalysts who did not support either Melanie Klein or Anna Freud) and the British Psychoanalytical Society, she specialized in object relations theory and its techniques, subscribing in particular to the teachings of Donald W. Winnicott and Michael Balint. For over twenty years, Tönnesmann traveled to Frankfurt, Darmstadt, Düsseldorf, and Zurich to teach at training weekends. In her unique, humorous, and impressive way, she succeeded in combining theory and practice, along with meta-level and historical aspects of psychoanalysis; laced with amusing anecdotes about personalities within the British psychoanalysis circles.

Judith Le Soldat
1947–2008

Born in Budapest, Judith Le Soldat (née Szatmary) studied in Zurich and received her doctorate under Professor Ulrich Moser in 1978. After completing her training in psychoanalysis at the PSZ she worked as a lecturer, supervisor, and analyst. Her research focus was on new approaches on homosexuality, a topic widely debated within psychoanalytical circles today. Since 2015 Monika Gsell, a Zurich-based gender researcher and psychoanalyst, has been working on the publication of Le Soldat's collected works.

Margarete Mitscherlich
1917–2012

Christa Rohde-Dachser
*1937

Margarete Mitscherlich and Christa Rohde-Dachser are both psychoanalysts who have had considerable influence on the discussion in German-speaking countries around Freudian theories on femininity denounced by feminists. Mitscherlich questioned, among other things, Freud's myth of the vaginal orgasm, which was hotly debated among men and women during her time and dispelled the myth of the naturally peaceful woman in her book *Die friedfertige Frau* (1987), Rohde-Dachser achieved recognition in 1991 with the widely-discussed bestseller *Expedition in den dunklen Kontinent. Weiblichkeit im Diskurs der Psychoanalyse*. In this work, Rohde-Dachser submits the theories of Freud and his successors to a systematic feminist ideological critique.

Sophinette Becker
1950–2019

A collection of Sophinette Becker's writings, edited by Anna Koellreuter and Margret Hauch, was published shortly after her death under the title *Leidenschaftlich analytisch*. Becker was a charismatic sexologist, psychotherapist, and critical thinker from Frankfurt. In her seminars and articles she successfully underpinned even taboo topics and theories with her wealth of clinical experience. Her final work *Geschlecht und sexuelle Orientierung in Auflösung—was bleibt?* (2018) addresses the highly topical and often controversial manifestations of sexuality in modern society. Becker represents a contemporary, socio-critical psychoanalysis which continues to be as alive and relevant as ever.

PREFACE   The diary entries from April to June 1921 by Anna Guggenbühl form a unique document in which one can virtually follow Sigmund Freud's analytic practice "live," with experiences of early childhood sexuality already coming to light in the very first session. Anna Guggenbühl was unwilling to consent to the proposed marriage with Richard. After the three-month analysis, she would call off the wedding, travel to Paris, and there meet her future husband. At the end of her analysis, Freud observed in a letter to Oskar Pfister, who had referred her to him: "Little G is now completely transparent." The document was annotated by Anna Koellreuter and translated into English by Ernst Falzeder and Kristina Pia Hofer.

Diary of an analysis, April 1921

Guggenbühl:
When I was four years old, in Strasbourg, there was my little cousin, a fat baby. I pinched her, and when I was alone I always bullied her until she cried. Once I pulled out all the saplings on the balcony, I thought they were weeds. Incidentally, I discovered masturbation there by pressing myself against a cornice.

Freud:
This is a very remarkable memory. Did you also badger your little brother?

Guggenbühl:
I turned him on his back, for instance, so that he could no longer get up.

Freud:
You started to masturbate when you felt lonely. You were no longer loved' as much as when you were as a single child. So you took revenge on the little child and on the symbol, the sapling.

Guggenbühl:
When my brother Walter was born, I asked when I saw him: Why doesn't he cry?

Freud:
So you would have liked to see him in a crying state, just like your cousin? One can clearly see three levels in your life: The uppermost one is your present conflict with R[ichard] etc. The one in the middle concerns your relation to your brother.

You are still quite unconscious of the deepest level, which is connected with your parents, and which is the most important one. It is from this that the relation to the brother is derived.

Guggenbühl:
Later. I tell Freud: When I went to grammar school, I thought I would like to love a young man who was immensely sad, and I would make life possible for him, and he then would be happy.

Freud:
Like with your brother.

Guggenbühl:
Then I thought later I would like to have seven children; I did not think of the father.

Freud:
Seven men, actually. Seven?

Guggenbühl:
Adam had seven sons. Papedöne hangs his seven sons. "Der Hungerueli Isegrind frisst sini 7 chline Chind." I believe male cats devour their offspring.

Freud:
You are coming so near the secret of the deepest level that I can break it you.
    You loved your father, and never forgave him his betrayal with the mother. You wanted to be the mother of the child. So you wished the mother, who took the lover away from you for herself, dead. Bit by bit you will produce evidence for this, and the riddle of why you cannot get away from your brother will be solved.
    Three layers are easily recognisable in your life, the present one, which concerns the brothers; and the deepest one, which is connected with the parents. What is pathological is the long-lasting indecision whether or not you should marry Richard. The fact that no decision is reached proves that something else must lie behind it, something that is, as you recognise yourself, connected with the brothers and the parents. [. . .]

25. April

Guggenbühl:
When Goethe was pretty old he wanted to marry a girl. In the past I thought that she, of course, did not like the idea, but now I see quite well that one might want to marry someone older. So this means I might perhaps want to marry you, I really like you very much.

Freud:
Now this is the transference of the old love and infatuation you had for the father, onto me. Al the painf.[ul] disappointment, jealousy etc. will come to light later, too.

26 April, 21

Guggenbühl:
In the waiting room I heard the pat.[ient] who comes before me say the word "chlorophyll." I thought I could never come up with such an association. I am so terribly ignorant. I lack all humanistic education, and I haven't absorbed the scientific education either.

Freud:
So you want to belittle yourself intellectually. Other women usually do it in physical matters. They might for instance say they've got haemorrhoids, etc.

Pause

Guggenbühl:
Nothing comes to mind.

Freud:
So this is a spec.[ial] resistance that has to do with transference.

Guggenbühl:
I cannot tell you how much I like you; I think I've never loved anybody this way before.

Freud:
This love for your father was so enormous that everything that came later paled in comparison. People have no idea of the intensity of the love of children, it only exists in potential form, after all, and is not put into action.

Guggenbühl:
When I was a child I always thought: Let me never experience unhappy love, for my love is greater than that of other people.

Freud:
You are able to think all that only because you had already experienced disappointment at one time, which you did not remember consciously. When you belittle yourself you do so to spoil your love for me, just like e.g. the lady with the haemorrhoids...

Guggenbühl:
But why does a neurosis then develop in me, is it not so that all human beings experience such disappointment.

Freud:
First of all, the force of passion varies in different persons. There is a degree of passion that can no longer be dealt with by the child, secondly, the other party's behaviour can be a cause.

Anna Guggenbühl, "In Freud's Practice," 1921

C. G. Jung first began studying dreams and visions during a personal crisis in 1913. That experience gave rise to *The Red Book*, a kind of *Gesamtkunstwerk* comprising not just his own psychological musings and the literary explorations of his own mind, but also calligraphic and figurative works of art. Jung and his wife Emma, who had been among the women to speak at the International Psychoanalytic Congress in Weimar in 1911, sought to fathom the psyche following lines of inquiry that echoed Jung's *Wandlungen und Symbole der Libido* (*Transformations and Symbols of the Libido*, 1912)—and took them away from the ideas of Freud.

Jung worked on the premise of a collective unconscious, in which were manifested the archetypes that he believed to be universal to every individual psyche. Guided by his concept of an *anima* and *animus*, he took the view that the female-connoted *anima* played an important part in the mental life of men, just as the *animus* did in the mental life of women. Building on what he called active imagination, Jung encouraged his patients to visualize their own minds as mandalas and to raise them to the level of consciousness where they could be interpreted.

C. G. JUNG, *The Red Book – Liber Novus*, 1913–1930

C. G. JUNG, *The Red Book – Liber Novus*,
1913–1930

C. G. JUNG, *The Red Book – Liber Novus*, 1913–1930

Patient image 016. APAJ
from the Collection of C. G. Jung, 1929

Patient image 039. BMAX
from the Collection of C. G. Jung, 1928

OLGA FRÖBE-KAPTEYN
Untitled (Visions – Final Series – #5), 1937

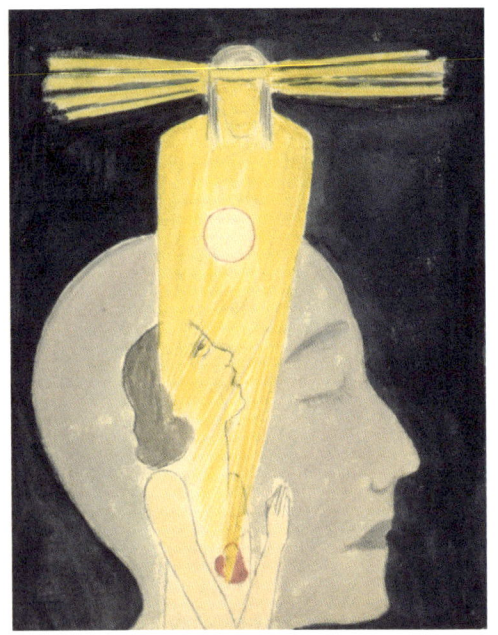 

Patient image 002. ABHG
from the Collection of C. G. Jung

Patient image 002. ABAB
from the Collection of C. G. Jung

Patient image 009. AIBH
from the Collection of C. G. Jung, 1929

Patient image 021. AUAC
from the Collection of C. G. Jung

Patient image 006. AFAI
from the Collection of C. G. Jung

HÉLÈNE SMITH
Drawing of a transmission, c. 1908

Patient images 009. AIAK, 009. AIAL,
009. AIAR and 009. AIAS from
the Collection of C. G. Jung, May 22, 1917

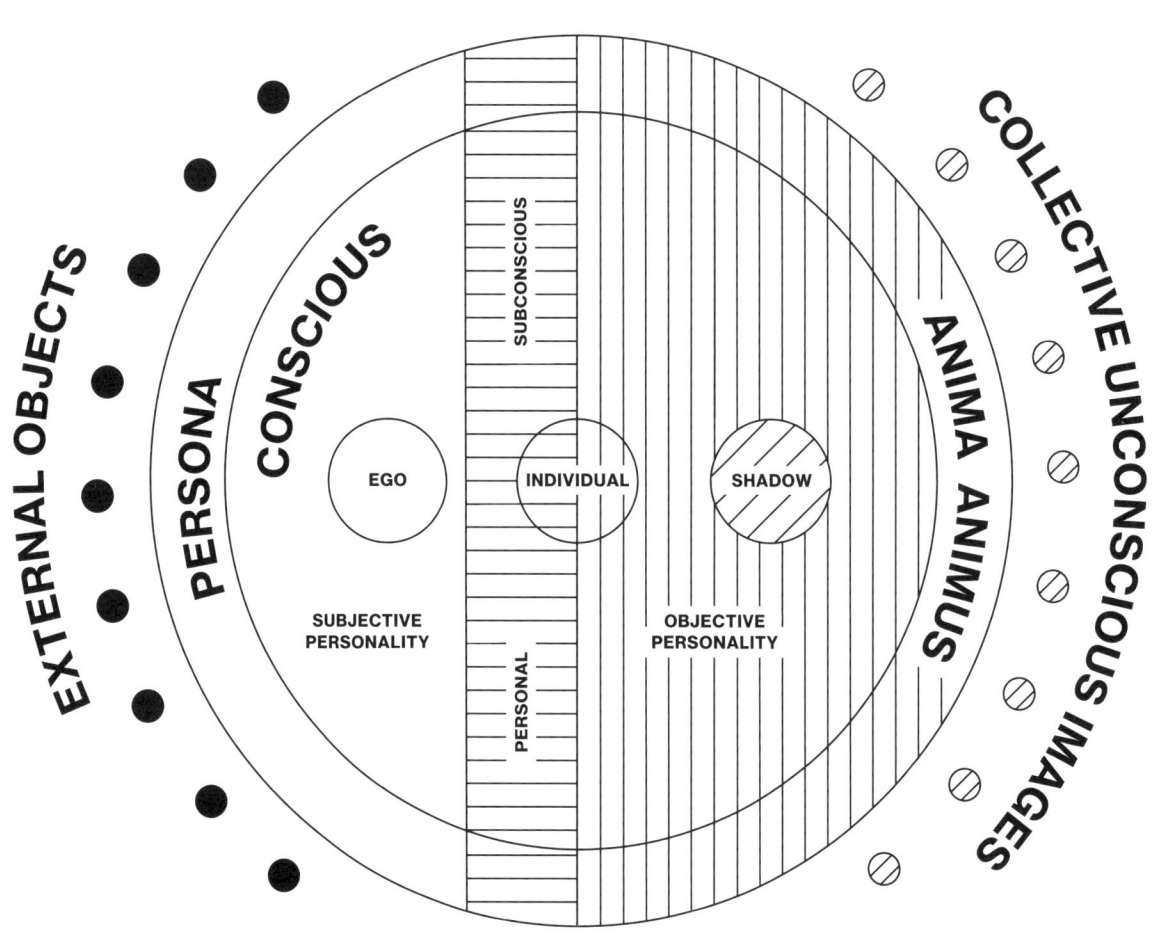

Soul model
by C. G. Jung, 1925

C. G. Jung
photographed by Henri Cartier-Bresson,
c. 1959

Emma Jung
photographed by Camille Ruf,
1905

Manuscript *Red Book*,
C. G. Jung, c. 1930

Küsnacht, d. 10. September

Verehrter Herr Professor,

Soeben sind die Separata des II. Teiles der "Wandlungen und Symbole" erschienen und zu allererst muss ich Ihnen eins davon schicken. Von Jones, den ich bei Gelegenheit des hiesigen Congresses sah, hörte ich,

Letter from Emma Jung
to Sigmund Freud, 1912

Synthesis of Emma Jung's cosmology
in a picture painted by her, c. 1919

Third International Psychoanalytic Congress in Weimar in 1911, C. G. Jung (sixth from right, second row from bottom), Sigmund Freud (seventh from right, second row from bottom); Emma Jung (fifth from right, bottom), Lou Andreas-Salomé (seventh from right, bottom), photograph: Franz Vältl

"Libido" in dem ihr ursprünglich eigenen Sinne des Sexualtriebes, des Sexualbegehrens enger gefasst. Die Erfahrung nöthigt zur Annahme einer Verlagerungsfähigkeit der Libido, indem zweifellos Functionen oder Localisationen nicht sexueller Triebkräfte fähig sind, einen gewissen Betrag an Sexualtriebkraft, einen "libidinösen Zuschuss" aufzunehmen. (a.) Es können dadurch Functionen oder Objecte Sexualwerth erhalten, die unter normalen Umständen und eigentlich nichts mit Sexualität zu thun haben.¹⁾ (z.B. Schulstechnisums etc.) Aus dieser Thatsache ergibt sich der Freud'sche Vergleich der Libido mit einem Strom, der theilbar ist, der sich stauen lässt, der in Collateralen überfliesst etc.²⁾ Freud's ursprüngliche Auffassung erklärt also nicht "Alles sexuell" wie unsere Gegner zu behaupten belieben, sondern anerkennt die Existenz besonderer in ihrer Natur noch nicht bekannter Triebkräfte, denen Freud aber, gedrängt durch die offenkundigsten Thatsachen, die jedem Laien einleuchten, die Fähigkeit zuschreiben musste, "libidinöse Zuschüsse" zu empfangen. Das grundliegende

a.) Freud (sexuellen unterschei einem R als eroge Erregung

1.) Freud (l.c. ungen, die der sexuellen Werthe nicht dem Wesen ungeacht bil

2.) Siehe Freud. l.c. p. 28.

...handlungen. 1. Aufl. p. 26): „Ueber einen an sich nicht
motorischen Impuls quellen stammenden Trieb"
...an — den Partialtrieben — einen Beitrag von
...nehmenden Organ (Haut etc.) Letzteres soll hier
...one bezeichnet werden, als jenes Organ, dem
...ib den sexuellen Character verleiht."

...ung..., p. 12 [Aufl.], „Eine bestimmte dieser Berüh-
...tigen hypnoschleimhaut, Art als Kuss — einen hohen
..., obwohl sie dabei in Betracht kommenden Körpertheile
...pparat angehören, sondern den Eingangspunkt der...

C. G. Jung

and

Murray Stein

as Thinker

Author

C. G. Jung, it has been claimed, was the most famous Swiss physician since Paracelsus. He would have been pleased with this pronouncement, which associates him with the medically innovative sixteenth century son of Switzerland from Einsiedeln. When Jung was invited to help celebrate the 400th anniversary of Paracelsus's death in 1941, he participated enthusiastically with two brilliant lectures, one to the Swiss Society for the History of Medicine in Basel and the other in Einsiedeln at the official Paracelsus Celebrations. The two Swiss physicians share many features in common, including an insistence on the freedom to think for themselves and not bowing to the established authorities, and a tendency to write works that are difficult to classify according to genre.

Depending on the text, Jung's writing can be read as psychiatric and psychological research, as psychoanalytic theory, religious studies, and moral philosophy, or as belonging to still other academic disciplines—from ethnology, literary studies, theology, and sociology to physics and the history of science—but none of these categorizations captures his writing adequately because genres are often mixed. Jung also builds bridges from modern psychological studies to ancient traditions of reflection on the human soul. His studies in alchemy more or less single-handedly revolutionized the understanding of this ancient hermetical tradition, which reaches back to late antiquity's Zosimos of Panopolis and forward to Paracelsus and brought it into the field of modern depth psychology. His thought also anticipates new developments in science and world culture. Like Paracelsus, who was known as "the wild ass of Einsiedeln," Jung broke through fences that separated the sciences and the humanities and showed the way to a different kind of thinking.

Cartography of the Soul

Jung's self-chosen mission was to understand the human soul empirically. To his critics he wrote in his essay, "The Philosophical Tree": "[…] I speak of the facts of the living psyche and have no use for philosophical acrobatics." The tools he used for this project were psychological concepts and theories put together from the works of thinkers like Kant, Schopenhauer, Eduard von Hartmann, Nietzsche, C. G. Carus, William James, and Sigmund Freud. From these he forged his own original concepts. He did not insist on the absolute truth of these instruments, but rather thought of them as serviceable means to investigate and name the features of the human mind as they became manifest in his research. It was a scientific endeavor. In a sense, he was an explorer, mapping a new continent, the inner world of subjectivity. And the maps he created continue to serve psychoanalysts who practice psychotherapy with patients. They also help scholars in many other fields to understand more profoundly their relationship to the subjects that engage them.

Jung used these psychological concepts to collect and assimilate cultural materials from many sources—from Ancient Greece, Gnosticism, alchemy, Eastern religions, myths of all kinds and locations, and from his own religious tradition, Christianity. These would be used for his core project, the exploration of the heights and depths of the psyche. He could draw imaginatively from many cultural traditions, but he understood and used them by employing the concepts and theories of analytical psychology.

These acts of assimilation did not amount to psychological reductionism, despite what his critics said. Jung's thinking was in the service of scientific investigation and the hermeneutical retrieval of meaning. It was a complex project. With respect to his own religious tradition, he felt the distance, typical of the modern intellectual, but he also had a strong desire to retrieve the meaning of Christian symbols on a psychological level. Thus, he wrote about the Holy Trinity, Catholic mass, the ritual of baptism, the figure of Jesus Christ, and about many other biblical and traditional religious figures by using an interpretive lens grounded in the workshop of his "psychological laboratory." In making these interpretations, he was able to recover spiritual meaning from religious symbols for "modern man in search of a soul," which is the title of one of his most popular books. His interpretive writings were in part an exercise in finding meaning for himself as a modern person living in the twentieth century, but in a larger sense they were also an effort to assist all of his contemporaries in creating a connection back to their lost spiritual ancestry. Historians of culture and religion can tell us about the past, while Jung's thought can help us to *re-experience* the past as spiritually meaningful for ourselves today.

The Authority of Writing

Jung was convinced that human beings need a sense of higher meaning, an *Übersinn*, in order to live well. When deprived of the guidance offered by religious traditions, the human being loses spiritual orientation and the soul eventually withers and dies. This is a dangerous condition. People become not only mentally ill, but unconsciously suicidal. Thus, Jung advocated for the importance of experiencing the unconscious, that is, the non-rational dimensions of the psyche. From these experiences, which would include contact with the numinous and eternal features of the psyche, a person could create a *Weltanschauung* that would satisfy the soul's needs for transcendent meaning.

Once when Jung was traveling with his friend, Fowler McCormick, in some remote mountainous region of Switzerland, they stepped into a country store where an aged woman recognized Jung and greeted him. He was surprised and asked if she had read his books. "Those are not books! That is bread!" she exclaimed. She had tasted the spirit in his writings and found reading his works nourishing as soul food. Jung is a baker of spiritual bread.

What is the yeast in this bread? In his essay, "The Spirit Mercurius," Jung comments on the works of Gerhard Dorn, the sixteenth century alchemical philosopher: "But man, and through him the unconscious, expresses a great deal that is not necessarily conscious in all its implications." It is the spirit of the unconscious that slips the yeast of the spirit into the dough. There is a spirit in Jung's works that extends beyond the words on the page. It is this unknown spirit, a *genius* in the Latin sense of the word, that constitutes an essential part of Jung's legacy as a thinker and author.

In November 1932, the City of Zurich surprised Jung by awarding him its Literature Prize. As he joked in a letter to a friend: "There are great news happening here. Last week I got the 'Literaturpreis der Stadt Zurich,' which means that I'm no longer a prophet in my own country. A sad end to a hopeful young prophet's career. It is always sad when one loses a perfectly good reason for grumbling." Jung was not without a sense of humor, and he was now accepted as a true son of Switzerland through and through. But he was also a man for the ages and a citizen of the world. A friend and colleague of mine whose home was in the Caribbean once commented that Jung should have won the Nobel Peace Prize for his work, *Psychological Types* (1921/1971). "It is the greatest treatise ever written on the topic of tolerance!" he exclaimed. He had a point. With Jung's perspective, as often expressed in his writings, one can accept and tolerate the many cultural and individual differences that one experiences so readily in the world today. Jung's writings can build a bridge for the increase of tolerance among the peoples of the Earth.

Writing was an essential creative activity for Jung, and through it he established himself as an author with authority. The English word "author" derives from the Latin *auctor*, meaning "enlarger, founder" and "one who causes to grow." A true author is a writer who is original, who enlarges a field, and whose writings cause ideas to grow. Jung belongs to a very small company of modern thinkers who have created a body of work that founded a field which has consistently provoked modern consciousness to grow. Authors in this sense get and hold authority. Their ideas as expressed in their writings have force. Their works change people.

Diversity in Unity and Unity in Diversity

For true authors, moreover, creating written work is non-negotiable. Jung spoke of the *daimon* that compelled him to author his works. Of this compulsion to write, Jung told his friend, the Dominican priest, Father Victor White: "Not very long after I have written to you, I simply had to write a new essay I did not know about what. It occurred to me I could discuss some of the finer points about Anima, Animus, Shadow and last not least the Self. I was against it, because I wanted to rest my head.

Lately I had suffered from severe sleeplessness and I wanted to keep away from all mental exertions. In spite of all I felt forced to write on blindly, not seeing at all, what I was driving at. Only after I had written about 25 pages in folio, it began to dawn on me, that Christ—not the man but the divine being—was my secret goal. It came to me as a shock, as I felt utterly unequal to such a task."

From this compulsion flowed Jung's critical interpretation of the Christ symbol in his book, *Aion* (1951/1968) and shortly thereafter his incandescent interpretation of the Bible, *Answer to Job* (1952/1969).

In the act of writing, Jung discovered his thoughts. To him, they were often a revelation, unexpected and sometimes disturbing. His writings are stamped with his energetic personality and are not only expository, entertaining, or academic. They are often also passionate, sometimes delivered with inspirational overtones, and often in the voice of a prophet-like critic. Everything Jung published bears the imprint of his forceful personality. It may be that he identified somewhat with Friedrich Nietzsche. Like Nietzsche, Jung is driven by a daimon whose vision he articulates with all his available energy. Jung's works continue to be read by people in many walks of life. Their generative effects do not diminish with time. They do not become stale and outdated. Today, the field of analytical psychology has global reach and is authorized by Jung's writings, which provide the authoritative charter for its enterprises.

Jung's legacy can be summarized as "diversity-in-unity and unity-in-diversity." This is the essence of his master concept of psychological wholeness. This concept affirms the value of the individual while also establishing each individual's profound connections to the whole human collective. While our experience tells us that there is enormous diversity in the world within and without, there is also a hidden fundamental unity in this diversity. This unity is revealed in image, process, and events. As image, Jung's preferred symbol was the mandala, which despite its many distinct elements and inherent opposing tendencies is an image of oneness. As process, unity is revealed in the universality of individuation, the lifelong psychological and spiritual development inherent in the unconscious of every human being. As event, unity is expressed in synchronicity, which suggests a common source behind the experienced division between subject and object. And in Jung's concept of the multi-level psyche, the collective unconscious is common to all human beings.

Bibliography:
C. G. Jung, *Letters*, edited by Gerhard Adler and Aniela Jaffé, translated by R. F. C. Hull, 2 volumes, Princeton 1973–1975.
Ann Conrad Lammers (ed.), *The Jung–White Letters*, London 2005.
C. G. Jung, *The Collected Works of C. G. Jung*, edited by Sir H. Read, M. Fordham, G. Adler and W. McGuire, 20 volumes, Princeton 1953–1983.
In particular:
"Psychological Types," vol. 6, (1921/1971).
"Paracelsus the Physician," vol. 15, (1942/1966).
"Paracelsus as a Spiritual Phenomenon," vol. 13, (1942/1967).
"The Spirit Mercurius," vol. 13, (1948/1967).
"Aion," vol. 9$_{II}$, (1951/1968).
"Answer to Job," vol. 11, (1952/1969).
"The Philosophical Tree," vol. 13, (1954/1967).

In the following night, the air was filled with many voices. A loud voice called, "I am falling." Others cried out confused and excited during this: "Where to? What do you want?" Should I entrust myself to this confusion? I shuddered. It is a dreadful deep. Do you want me to leave myself to chance, to the madness of my own darkness? Wither? Wither? You fall, and I want to fall with you, whoever you are.

The spirit of the depths opened my eyes and I caught a glimpse of the inner things, the world of my soul, the many-formed and changing.

I see a gray rock face along which I sink into great depths. I stand in black dirt up to my ankles in a dark cave. Shadows sweep over me. I am seized by fear, but I know I must go in. I crawl through a narrow crack in the rock and reach an inner cave whose bottom is covered with black water. But beyond this I catch a glimpse of a luminous red stone which I must reach. I wade through the muddy water. The cave is full of the frightful noise of shrieking voices. I take the stone, it covers a dark opening in the rock. I hold the stone in my hand, peering around inquiringly. I do not want to listen to the voices, they keep me away. But I want to know. Here something wants to be uttered. I place my ear to the opening. I hear the flow of underground waters. I see the bloody head of a man on the dark stream. Someone wounded, someone slain floats there. I take in this image for a long time, shuddering. I see a large black scarab floating past on the dark stream.

In the deepest reach of the stream shines a red sun, radiating through the dark water. There I see—and a terror seizes me—small serpents on the dark rock walls, striving toward the depths, where the sun shines. A thousand serpents crowd around, veiling the sun. Deep night falls. A red stream of blood, thick red blood springs up, surging for a long time, then ebbing. I am seized by fear. What did I see?

Heal the wounds that doubt inflicts on me, my soul. That too is to be overcome, so that I can recognize your supreme meaning. How far away everything is, and how I have turned back! My spirit is a spirit of torment, it tears asunder my contemplation, it would dismantle everything and rip it apart. I am still a victim of my thinking. When can I order my thinking to be quiet, so that my thoughts, those unruly hounds, will crawl to my feet? How can I ever hope to hear your voice louder, to see your face clearer, when all my thoughts howl?

I am stunned, but I want to be stunned, since I have sworn to you, my soul, to trust you even if you lead me through madness. How shall I ever walk under your sun if I do not drink the bitter draught of slumber to the lees?

Help me so that I do not choke on my own knowledge. The fullness of my knowledge threatens to fall in on me. My knowledge has a thousand voices, an army roaring like lions; the air trembles when they speak, and I am their defenseless sacrifice. Keep it far from me, science that clever knower, that bad prison master who binds the soul and imprisons it in a lightless cell. But above all protect me from the serpent of judgment, which only appears to be a healing serpent, yet in your depths is infernal poison and agonizing death. I want to go down cleansed into your depths with white garments and not rush in like some thief, seizing whatever I can and fleeing breathlessly. Let me persist in divine astonishment, so that I am ready to behold your wonders. Let me lay my head on a stone before your door, so that I am prepared to receive your light.

When the desert begins to bloom, it brings forth strange plants. You will consider yourself mad, and in a certain sense you will in fact be mad. To the extent that the Christianity of this time lacks madness, it lacks divine life. Take note of what the ancients taught us in images: madness is divine. But because the ancients lived this image concretely in events, it became a deception for us, since we became masters of the reality of the world. It is unquestionable: if you enter into the world of the soul, you are like a madman, and a doctor would consider you to be sick. What I say here can be seen as sickness, but no one can see it as sickness more than I do. This is how I overcome madness. [. . .]

Blood shone at me from the red light of the crystal, and when I picked it up to discover its mystery, there lay the horror uncovered before me: in the depths of what is to come lay murder. The blond hero lay slain. The black beetle is the death that is necessary for renewal; and so thereafter, a new sun glowed, the sun of the depths, full of riddles, a sun of the night. And as the rising sun of spring quickens the dead earth, so the sun of the depths quickened the dead, and thus began the terrible struggle between light and darkness. Out of that burst the powerful and ever unvanquished source of blood. This was what was to come, which you now experience in your life, and it is even more than that. (I had this vision on the night of 12 December 1913.)

C. G. Jung, "Descent into Hell in the Future," 1913–1928

The Domestic as the Scene Unconscious

Lothar Müller

Interior of Work on the

*The Desks of
C. G. Jung and Sigmund Freud*

Domestic interiors, furnishings, and house dreams generally all play a noteworthy role in those passages of C. G. Jung's autobiographical work, *Memories, Dreams, Reflections* (1962) in which the author ruminates on his relations with Sigmund Freud. Jung's dream of a two-story house that appears to be at once unfamiliar and his own takes him swiftly from the upstairs salon "furnished with fine old pieces in rococo style," to a ground floor dating from the fifteenth or sixteenth century, whose "furnishings were medieval." From there, a stone stairway leads down into the cellar, where yet another descent, flanked by what appear to be Roman walls, ends in a "low cave cut into the rock" containing "scattered bones and broken pottery, like remains of a primitive culture," as well as two "very old and half-disintegrated" human skulls.

Here, the younger man's rivalry with Freud as an interpreter of dreams plays out in the domain of archaeology, a key metaphor of psychoanalysis, and in a tour of a house. "Consciousness was represented by the salon," declares Jung, while the ground floor "stood for the first level of the unconscious." Contrary to Freud, who insists on reading the skulls in the cave as "secret death-wishes," Jung believes they tell of his discovery of the "world of the primitive man within myself," and with it one of the supporting pillars of his own theories.

Jung and Freud were exchanging these rival interpretations of dreams while sailing to the United States in the late summer of 1909. Yet their coming rift had been presaged even prior to that in the same year, when, on one of Jung's visit to Freud at his home in Vienna, they had both been witness to a seemingly occult phenomenon. They were discoursing on precognition and parapsychology when they suddenly heard a loud crash coming from one of Freud's bookcases. Jung wasted no time in declaring this unexpected interjection a "catalytic exteriorization phenomenon."

Freud's laconic reply to Jung's statement—"utter nonsense"—stands in marked contrast to the detailed account of "poltergeist phenomena" contained in the letter he wrote to Jung from his home in Vienna on April 16, 1909. There, Freud admits that the "continual creaking noises" coming from the oak bookcase containing two heavy Egyptian steles are easily enough explained, whereas in the "second room, where we heard the crash, such noises are very rare. At first I was inclined to ascribe some meaning to it," he continues, "as if the noise we heard so frequently when you were here were never heard again after your departure. But since then, it has happened over and over again, yet never in connection with my thoughts and never when I was considering you or your special problem."

The letter in which Freud ponders this question—of whether Jung has somehow "infected" his home with occultism—is not just any letter. On the contrary, it contains his "adoption" of Jung as an eldest son and his "anointing" of him as "my successor and crown prince." The ink had not yet dried on that ennoblement when the thought that Jung, through his presence at Berggasse 19 in Vienna, might have conjured a poltergeist as empirical evidence of occultism, pointed Freud in a direction that would mark a momentous turn in their relations. The magnitude of the fault line is evident from Freud's paraphrasing of Schiller's poem *Die Götter Griechenlandes* (1788): "I confront the despiritualized furniture as the poet confronted undeified Nature after the gods of Greece had passed away."

Writing Scenes

The desk at which Freud wrote this letter has survived and is one of the most prominent exhibits at the Freud Museum in London. It is topped with red felt and underneath the desktop are three heavy drawers on either side and one shallow drawer in the middle. It was built by the Atelier Siegmund Spitz in Vienna, and although undoubtedly a piece of fine furniture, is an object of use, not a showpiece. The family resemblance with the desks in the home of C. G. Jung and Emma Jung-Rauschenbach in Küsnacht, which have likewise become museum pieces, arises out of their being products of the same epoch.

Jung's desk might more fittingly be described as a "writing ensemble," since it comprises not just the relatively dainty desk in the smaller study, which doubles as a library, but also the larger desk in the "real" library, as well as the lectern at which Jung is known to have written his *Red Book*. For

Jung, as for Freud, the desks were embedded not just in the real interiors that they themselves inhabited but also in their everyday worlds and their respective biographies.

It was also in 1909, just when Jung, in his dreams, was envisioning the psyche as the interior of various houses, that he and his wife moved into their new house, which in dialog with the architect Jung had had a hand in designing. The smaller study as it currently stands contains copies of both the glass paintings of the Scourging, Crucifixion and Entombment of Christ that Jung had installed in the windows and the portraits of his ancestors that he hung on the walls. The larger desk in the "real" library, whose curved legs mark it out as a product of the latter days of Jugendstil, has a desk lamp that Jung dimmed by the simple expedient of putting a cap on it.

Jung's altercations with Freud are reflected in various writing scenes. When he sat down to pen the manuscript of "The Sacrifice," a chapter of his *Transformations and Symbolisms of the Libido* (1912), he knew that "it would cost me my friendship with Freud," and afterwards, he "could not so much as touch a pen for a full two months." His desk had been a silent witness to the rift that the letters had been opening up: "I sat at my desk and once again thought over my fears, and then I let go."

For Jung, as for Freud, the desk and the dreams, the desk and the library, the desk and the interior in which it stands, the carpet on which it stands, and even the pictures on the walls around it, all belong together. The abundance of trays and filing compartments on and alongside both desks is striking. Jung worked under the watchful eyes of his ancestors, whose portraits adorned the walls. In Freud's interior, by contrast, it is his hero Jean-Martin Charcot who, in an etching after André Brouillet's oil painting *Une leçon clinique à la Salpêtrière* (1887), takes pride of place above the couch.

Writing Staging

The fact that both desks served not just for writing but also for reading and reflection greatly adds to the dense tissue of associations in which they are enmeshed, as is apparent from the letter openers, magnifying glasses, and photographs on the desktop. Looking up from his writing, Jung would have seen a portrait of his wife. Meanwhile, the desk drawers hidden from view might well have contained something other than manuscripts. Besides attesting to their owners' work as authors, the desks also tell of their personal habits, as is demonstrated by the accoutrements of Jung the pipe smoker and Freud the cigar smoker. Jung's wooden tamper looks almost like a borrowing from one of the ethnographic museums of that era, though the archaic-looking figure embellishing it might also be a carving by the owner himself. These small tools of authorship in a scholarly library, compounded by vases, souvenirs, and the general paraphernalia of everyday life, together form a coherent ensemble.

Writing to Wilhelm Fliess in July 1899, Freud opines that "There are still some old gods, and I recently received a few of them, among them a stone Janus who looks at me disdainfully with his two faces." Presumably the Janus figure was standing on Freud's own desk when he wrote that. What this passage also tells us is that Freud had begun collecting antiquities even while putting the finishing touches on his *Interpretation of Dreams*. Knowing that the collection would have to fit inside his study, he chose to focus on small figurines. Yet it did not take long before these had outgrown the glass cases and shelves and spilled over onto the desktop, which thereupon became an exhibition space for a rapidly growing collection. The interior in which Freud lived, and the works that he wrote at his desk, were indeed inextricably bound up with each other. Thanks to his collection, that same ancient mythology that had come to play such a crucial role in his writings as both a referential space for psychoanalysis and a terminological resource was now laid out before him in the figures of Athena, Artemis, Hermes, and Mars.

Freud took care to keep his growing collection of ancient objects separate from the family area and housed it exclusively in the study and treatment room at Berggasse 19. In this respect he was following both the Humanist tradition of keeping books and objects of study close together, and the tradition of the Renaissance *studiolo*, which was itself modeled on the ancient practice of treating the room for work and the room for repose as two halves of a whole. Whereas absolute silence was preferred in the room for work, in this case the study-cum-library, the room for repose, or rather the treatment room with a couch in lieu of a daybed, admitted of at least two voices: the duet "sung" by the doctor and his patient. This arrangement excluded not just the family, moreover, but all forms of company—indeed the whole life of the salon.

A widely circulated etching by Max Pollak dating from 1914 shows Freud at his desk, seemingly transfixed by the figurines in front of him. It was an image that confirmed the public perception of Freud as one who wrote in the presence of "the old gods." Hugo Heller, the Viennese bookseller entrusted with the distribution of the work, knew Freud well, and besides being a member of the Wednesday Psychoanalytic Society was also the publisher of *Schriften zur angewandten Seelenkunde*. Heller's advertisement for the portrait also featured in the March 28 edition of Karl Kraus's *Fackel*, where in a column headed "Of the Contemplative and the Industrious" Kraus glossed it with a caustic commentary of his own in which he parodied Goethe's "appropriation" of *Faust* and associated Freud with esotericism. It was the quote in Heller's advertisement that prompted Kraus, as always, to pour scorn on it: "Max Pollak portrays the researcher in his study, sitting at his desk," he wrote. "The foreground is strangely animated by the ancient and archaic figures arranged on the desk. Boldly offset against the chiaroscuro of the study is the cerebral head of the scholar, wearing precisely that contemplative, to a certain extent i n w a r d - l o o k i n g, gaze that is the mark of all intellectually creative work."

Freud's Things

Not all the treatment that Freud provided as a practicing psychoanalyst was administered on the couch. His analysis might also extend into his own study with the glass cases and desk. Among the female patients he escorted into this room was the American author Hilda Doolittle, who published under the initials H. D. and who, like Freud, was knowledgeable about ancient mythology.

When Freud analyzed her in 1933–34, he used the objects in his collection and the books in his library as prompts for conversations and trains of association. "The room beyond may appear very dark or there may be broken light and shadow," she later wrote in her *Tribute to Freud*. "Or even bodily, one may walk into that room, as the Professor invited me to do one day, to look at the things on his table." Freud, in other words, was certainly not a white wall onto which his patients could project their innermost selves. Caught amid the lines of sight and fields of vision afforded by his own study and treatment room, the doctor was utterly inseparable from the collector and scholar.

H. D. also recounts how she was visiting Vienna's Kunsthistorisches Museum one Sunday when she noticed a painting by Titian showing a Renaissance man standing at a table with small statues and was instantly reminded of Pollak's etching of Freud "with his row of little images before him on the table." She also recalls a dream she had of "my little bottle of smelling-salts," which for her was a transference symbol that she associated with Freud and with her crisis as a writer. "In my dream, I am *salting* my typewriter. So I presume I would salt my savorless writing with the salt of the earth, Sigmund Freud's least utterance." The dream continues the next day, when the bottles become the objects standing on the desk in Pollak's etching: "In my dream I suddenly associate the Professor's semicircle of little images with bottles."

Memorializing the Lacunae

Like Freud's, Jung's desk also tells us that its owner was a collector, for whom ethnological, zoological, and anthropological objects were an integral part of his writing ensemble. But there is no iconic portrait of him as a learned author and collector sitting at his desk as there is of Freud, still less a work of art, which is what Pollak's etching was being marketed as. What we do have is a photograph of Jung's study in Küsnacht taken as early as 1909, the year he moved in. It shows his desk, the armchair in which his analysands sat, and, next to it, a couch, which unlike in Freud's study is not the centerpiece of the room. Jung himself, however, is nowhere to be seen. The only possible contender for an iconic image to equal Pollak's etching of Freud is a photograph of Jung as an old man, pipe in hand, legs crossed, sitting at his desk but turning to stare back at the camera as if receiving a visitor. It is not a writing scene, in other words, and the desk cut off at the right in the photograph plays only a secondary role.

Photography, and portrait photography in particular, had become a key medium for the creation of memorializing images even in the nineteenth century. When the Freud family was forced to leave Vienna in 1938, the analyst August Aichhorn commissioned the young photographer Edmund Engelman to take photographs of the "birthplace of psychoanalysis" so, that a "museum can be created once the storm of these years is over". Engelman, with Freud's permission, photographed not just his private apartment on the mezzanine floor of Berggasse 19 but also the stairwell and the facade of the building, which by then had a swastika flag hanging from its cornice and a swastika awning spanning the lintel of the front door.

According to the terms of his brief, the photographer was not to use flash or floodlights, nor was he to photograph such private spaces as the bedrooms and bathrooms. His portraits of Freud, his wife Martha and daughter Anna were also to be kept separate from his record of their home. In retrospect, therefore, the rooms look strangely empty, as if their occupants had already left. Especially prominent among them are the images of the study and treatment room. When Engelman's photographs were first published in 1976, they linked the view of his desk to the break in his biography that marks the beginning of his exile.

The removal of the desk left a lacuna that was to become central to the concept of the Freud-Museum in Vienna. However, that same desk became part of the inventory of the Freud Museum in London, as did a small collection of photographs showing the exiled Freud himself working at it. Indeed, the photographs of both Jung and Freud have outlived the individuals portrayed and are now exhibited alongside the desks belonging to their respective estates at the museums in Küsnacht and London.

Bibliography:
Hilda Doolittle, *Tribute to Freud*, New York 1974.
Edmund Engelman, *Sigmund Freud, Wien IX, Berggasse 19*, Vienna 1998.
Sigmund Freud, *Briefe an Wilhelm Fliess. 1887–1904*, edited by Jeffrey Moussaieff Masson, Frankfurt am Main 1986.
Sigmund Freud, *Letters of Sigmund Freud*, selected and edited by Ernst L. Freud, translation by Tania and James Stern, New York 1992.
Sigmund Freud and C. G. Jung, *The Freud/Jung Letters, The Correspondence between Sigmund Freud and C. G. Jung*, edited by William McGuire, translation by Ralph Manheim and R. F. C. Hull, Princeton 1974.
C. G. Jung, *Memories, Dreams, Reflections*, recorded and edited by Aniela Jaffé, translation by Richard and Clara Winston, New York 1989.
Karl Kraus, "Von den Nachdenklichen und den Betriebsame" in *Die Fackel XV*, nos. 395/396/397, Vienna, March 28, 1914.

Jung to Freud, 5.10.1906:
Bleuler is now completely converted.

Jung, 23.10.1906:
At the risk of boring you, I must abreact my most recent experience. I am currently treating an hysteric with your method. Difficult case, a 20-year-old Russian girl [Sabina Spielrein], student, ill for 6 years.

First trauma between the 3rd and 4th year. Saw her father spanking her older brother on the bare bottom. Powerful impression. Couldn't help thinking afterwards that she had defecated on her father's hand. From the 4th–7th year convulsive attempts to defecate on her own feet, in the following manner: she sat on the floor with one foot beneath her, pressed her heel against her anus and tried to defecate and at the same time to prevent defecation. Often retained the stool for 2 weeks in this way! Has no idea how she hit upon this peculiar business; says it was completely instinctive, and accompanied by blissfully shuddersome feelings. Later this phenomenon was superseded by vigorous masturbation.

I should be extremely grateful if you would tell me in a few words what you think of this story.

Freud, 27.10.1906:
The defecation story is nice and suggests numerous analogies. Perhaps you remember my contention in my "Theory of Sexuality" that even infants derive pleasure from the retention of faeces. The third to fourth year is the most significant period for those sexual activities which later belong to the pathogenic ones (ibid.). The sight of a brother being spanked arouses a memory trace from the first to second year, or a fantasy transposed into that period. It is quite unusual for babies to soil the hands of those who are carrying them. Why should that not have happened in her case? And this awakens a memory of her father's caresses during her infancy. Infantile fixation of the libido on the father the typical choice of object; anal autoerotism.

Jung, 4.12.1906:
Personally I am enthusiastic about your therapy and well able to appreciate its signal merits. Altogether, your theory has already brought us the very greatest increase in knowledge and opened up a new era with endless perspectives.

Freud, 1.1.1907:
The future belongs to us.

Jung to Freud, 31.3.1907:
The last shreds were dispelled by my stay in Vienna, which for me was an event of the first importance.

Freud, 7.4.1907:
Your visit was most delightful and gratifying; I should like to repeat in writing various things that I confided to you by word of mouth, in particular, that you have inspired me with confidence for the future, that I now realize that I am as replaceable as everyone else and that I could hope for no one better than yourself, as I have come to know you, to continue and complete my work.

Jung, 24.5.1907:
The continuation of the great "Freud battle" is guaranteed.

Jung, 6.7.1907:
Vienna has produced 3 anthropological-medical reformers: Mesmer, Gall, Freud. Mesmer and Gall felt cramped in Vienna, Freud (in keeping with the times) went unrecognized. Mesmer and Gall then moved to Paris. [...] Freud first met with clinical recognition in Zurich.

Jung, 25.9.1907:
Dr. Gross tells me that he puts a quick stop to the transference by turning people into sexual immoralists. He says the transference to the analyst and its persistent fixation are mere monogamy symbols and as such symptomatic of repression. The truly healthy state for the neurotic is sexual immorality. Hence he associates you with Nietzsche.

Freud, 19.4.1908:
Otto Gross urgently needs your medical help; what a pity, such a gifted, resolute man. He is addicted to cocaine and probably in the early phase of toxic cocaine paranoia. I feel great sympathy for his wife: one of the few Teutonic women I have ever liked.

Jung, 19.6.1908:
The day before yesterday Gross, unguarded for a moment, jumped over the garden wall. [...] For me this experience is one of the harshest in my life, for in Gross I discovered many aspects of my own nature, so, that he often seemed like my twin brother-but for the Dementia praecox.

Freud, 17.1.1909:
If I am Moses, then you are Joshua and will take possession of the promised land of psychiatry, which I shall only be able to glimpse from afar.

Jung, 4.6.1909:
Gross and Spielrein are bitter experiences.

Freud, 18.6.1909:
In view of the kind of matter we work with, it will never be possible to avoid little laboratory explosions. Maybe we didn't slant the test tube enough, or we heated it too quickly. In this way we learn what part of the danger lies in the matter and what part in our way of handling it.

Freud, 19.12.1909:
I long for mythologists, linguists, and historians of religions; if they won't come to our help, we shall have to do all that ourselves.

Jung, 25.12.1909:
It has become quite clear to me that we shall not solve the ultimate secrets of neurosis and psychosis without mythology and the history of civilization.

Jung, 11.2.1910:
At present I am sitting so precariously on the fence between the Dionysian and the Apollinian that I wonder whether it might not be worthwhile to reintroduce a few of the older cultural stupidities such as the monasteries. That is, I really don't know which is the lesser evil. Do you think this fraternity could have any practical use? [...]

I imagine a far finer and more comprehensive task for PSA than alliance with an ethical fraternity. I think we must give it time to infiltrate into people from many centres, to revivify among intellectuals a feeling for symbol and myth, ever so gently to transform Christ back into the soothsaying god of the vine, which he was, and in this way absorb those ecstatic instinctual forces of Christianity for the one purpose of making the cult and the sacred myth what they once were—a drunken feast of joy where man regained the ethos and holiness of an animal.

Jung, 17.4.1910:
At present I am pursuing my mythological dreams with almost autoerotic pleasure, dropping only meagre hints to my friends.
[. . .] I often feel I am wandering alone through a strange country, seeing wonderful things that no one has seen before and no one needs to see. It was like that when the psychology of Dementia praecox dawned upon me. Only, I don't yet know what will come of it. I must just let myself be carried along, trusting to God that in the end I shall make a landfall somewhere.

Freud, 22.4.1910:
I am overjoyed to hear that mythology is again giving you the "fairytale forest feeling" that comes of a sound conception. Autoerotic enjoyment is sure to be followed by exhibition—a development that I am eagerly awaiting.

Jung, 8.5.1911:
Occultism is another field we shall have to conquer—with the aid of the libido theory, it seems to me. At the moment I am looking into astrology, which seems indispensable for a proper understanding of mythology. There are strange and wondrous things in these lands of darkness. Please don't worry about my wanderings in these infinitudes. I shall return laden with rich booty for our knowledge of the human psyche. For a while longer I must intoxicate myself on magic perfumes in order to fathom the secrets that lie hidden in the abysses of the unconscious.

Freud, 12.5.1911:
I am aware that you are driven by innermost inclination to the study of the occult and I am sure you will return home richly laden. I cannot argue with that, it is always right to go where your impulses lead. You will be accused of mysticism, but the reputation you won with the Dementia will hold up for quite some time against that. Just don't stay in the tropical colonies too long; you must reign at home.

Freud, 12.11.1911:
The reading for my psychology of religion is going slowly. One of the nicest works I have read (again), is that of a wellknown author on the "Transformations and Symbols of the Libido." In it many things are so well-expressed that they seem to have taken on definitive form and in this form impress themselves on the memory. [...]

Why in God's name did I allow myself to follow you into this field? You must give me some suggestions. But probably my tunnels will be far more subterranean than your shafts and we shall pass each other by, but every time I rise to the surface I shall be able to greet you.

Freud, 30.11.1911:
I am afraid there is a misunderstanding between us, the same sort of thing as when you once said in an article that to my way of thinking libido is identical with any kind of desire, whereas in reality I hold very simply that there are two basic drives and that only the power behind the sexual drive can be termed libido.

Jung, 3.3.1912:
Let Zarathustra speak for me: "One repays a teacher badly if one remains only a pupil."

Jung, 11.11.1912:
I found that my version of PSA won over many people who until now had been put off by the problem of sexuality in neurosis.

Jung, 18.12.1912:
I would, however, point out that your technique of treating your pupils like patients is a blunder. In that way you produce either slavish sons or impudent puppies.

[...] You go around sniffing out all the symptomatic actions in your vicinity, thus reducing everyone to the level of sons and daughters who blushingly admit the existence of their faults. Meanwhile you remain on top as the father, sitting pretty.

For sheer obsequiousness nobody dares to pluck the prophet by the beard and inquire for once what you would say to a patient with a tendency to analyse the analyst instead of himself. You would certainly ask him: "Who's got the neurosis?"

Jung, 6.1.1913:
I accede to your wish that we abandon our personal relations, for I never thrust my friendship on anyone. You yourself are the best judge of what this moment means to you. "The rest is silence."

"Estranged Intimacy," correspondance between Sigmund Freud and C. G. Jung

Imagi

Creativity, and

Arche

nation,

Elizabeth Leuenberger
& Verena Kast

types

Elizabeth Leuenberger

The C. G. Jung Institute Picture Archive: An Active Treasury of the Imagination

The pictures stored in the picture archive of the C. G. Jung-Institute Zurich in Küsnacht, are as diverse, personal and complex, and as expressive and universal as the countless patients that created them. Scenes of anguished suffering with streams of blood sit alongside images of heavenly embraces. The collection also includes many mandalas, ranging in style from stark simplicity to sophisticated complexity, with some of breathtaking artistic beauty. Threatening storms, ominous crosses, and snakes as well as colorful flowers and verdant trees are depicted in other pictures, reflecting not just deep despair but also heightened inner experiences such as encounters with the Virgin Mary, Christ, or Buddha. They all mirror the soul and bear witness to the power and transformative potential of the images in our human psyche.

The self-experience that plays such a central role in the training of Jungian analysts requires them to creatively engage with their dreams and fantasies as they learn to recognize inner images (images from the subconscious) as tools for personal development and self-awareness—known as active imagination within the Jungian school.

From around 1913, at a time of inner and outer conflicts, as the collective psyche steered towards the First World War, and as personal as well as theoretical differences culminated in the bitter end of his collaboration with Freud, C. G. Jung engaged in extensive self-experimentation. Overwhelmed by disconcerting dreams and visions, he sought to understand what was happening in him by immersing himself in his own images and fantasies. Conversations with inner figures, which he recognized as personifications of archetypes and personal complexes, were rendered in both writings and elaborate, complex drawings.

The publication of *The Red Book* made these works accessible to the public, opening to scrutiny what Jung termed his "confrontation with the unconscious" in all its vividness. He described this time both as a period of inner turmoil as well as the source of his entire future understanding and work. On discovering the transformative effect of this creative engagement with the images of his unconscious, Jung applied the insights to his work with his patients. He encouraged them, as well as other analysts, to engage with their inner images in a similar way.

With the founding of a training institute in 1948, Jolande Jacobi (1890–1973) began collecting such artworks, which were created while working with patients in analysis, recognizing its potential for teaching and research. She cataloged the pictures and expanded the collection with detailed symbol and subject indexes. Together with Jung's endowment of his own collection of works painted by patients in the 1950s, the picture archive of the C. G. Jung-Institute Zurich was established.

The core collection of the archive comprises four parts: around 4,500 pictures made by patients from the Jung collection; about 6,000 from the Jacobi collection; as well as three photographic collections of archetypal and alchemical symbolism (i. e. images of archetypes such as "the hero" or "the Great Mother" from universal myths and archetypes, and symbols from the ancient discipline of natural philosophy such as "the philosopher's stone" which Jung associated with inner transformation and spiritual processes). These three collections go back to C. G. Jung, Jolande Jacobi, and the "Eranos" collection, started by Olga Fröbe-Kapteyn.

Since its beginnings, the archive has been continually expanded with relevant films, artworks, photographs, correspondence, and other historic documents, while analysts continue to curate, exhibit, and modernize the collection on an ongoing basis. Its main purpose is not only to document the development of Jungian psychology while preserving this historic selection of individual creative encounters with the unconscious; but the archive remains a valuable and growing resource for Jungian art- and image-based research, for training and for the development of creative methods for working with symbols and images of the unconscious.

Verena Kast

Developing our Creative Seeds

According to C. G. Jung there is a creative principle that pervades all of nature as well as the rest of the world. Humans need to be connected to this principle, which is of course also active within all of us, both physically and psychologically. This enables us to live with a creative attitude and thereby remain connected to our important resources—and it allows our self-healing powers to function as they should.

If a therapy centered on thinking, talking, and explaining doesn't result in satisfactory benefits, then we should let nature take the lead, said Jung. "[...] and what the physician then does is not so much providing treatment, but simply developing the creative seeds that reside within the patient." (Jung, GW 16, para 82) These "creative seeds" indicate what really matters in the relevant person's life; it's about developing a person's creative fantasy and imagination.

The Power of Imagination

"Imagination is the reproductive or creative activity of the mind overall, without being a particular capacity," writes Jung. "For me, fantasy as an imaginative activity is simply the intuitive expression of a person's vital psychological function, of the mental energy that is presented to the conscious mind in the form of images or content [...]" (Jung, GW 6, para 792).

The capacity for imagination is something that is unique to humans. It's hard to picture what life would be like without this basic ability. The world that we perceive is presented to us in imaginations and images composed of the elements provided by all our sensory modalities. We are also able to reconstruct situations from our memory, thereby creating representations from within. The projection never ceases while we're awake, and continues in our sleep as we dream.

This definition of imagination is also found in the history of philosophy, especially in the writings of Kant and Sartre, but many others too. And in all contexts, a connection is made between those inner images and our emotions.

Since around the year 2000, affective neuroscience has also taken a close interest in "self-generated thoughts" or daydreams. When we aren't focusing on something in particular, fantasies, daydreams, and thoughts arise—we indulge in reminiscences, we construct the future in our heads. As we do so, our experience of the external word influences our inner images, and the inner images influence how we view the external world. Our memories stem from our personal history, but also from the history of humanity, from literature and films. When we map out our future as a space of possibilities space and a means for problem solving.

The results of affective neuroscience correspond with the underlying idea and experience of Jungian analytical psychology and provide further evidence that the psyche undergoes change for the purpose of self-regulation: The psyche is creative in order to move away from imbalance, perpetually seeking to regain a dynamic balance while adapting to the demands of both the external and internal world. Quintessentially and therapeutically pivotal, Jung illustrates this by reference to complex imagination and the associated "transcendental function," as he termed it, which allows us to endure contradictions resulting in the formation of new symbols (Jung, GW 6, para 833). These creative processes occur as part of the dialog between consciousness and the unconscious, between the archetypal structures, complexes, and our emotional conflicts. The creative process develops between two poles. It develops when we include the other, the counterpart, the you—and thus the constructive contradiction. It develops in dialog.

A Treasure Trove of Collective Ideas

C. G. Jung saw our imaginations as "intuitions" from our inner world, as creative ideas. Something new occurs that also connects us to the past. Through retrospection and introspection "[...] a person penetrates into the sphere of the collective unconscious, where they discover first the treasure trove of collective ideas and then their own creative powers [...]" (Jung, GW 16, para 64).

Jung described the archetypes as the "a priori determinants of imagination and behavior" (Jung, *Briefe III*, letter of 9/2/1956). They have their basis in the structure of the brain, so have a biological root, but in the encounter of the human with the world they also display an "intellectual" aspect—and today we would add, a social side. It was Jung's life work to study myths, dreams, and literature, finding in them the creative fantasies that correspond to the archetypal constellations. The biological aspect of the archetypes, which is of great interest in the context of todays neuroscientific discourse, is something he frequently referred to. The archetypes—neuronal patterns for typical concepts that don't originate from a person's own history—serve to induce experiences and behavioral patterns typical for all people in their interaction with the world, and to connect these experiences with each other to give meaning to an experience (such as the experience of death).

In the creative process, the archetype shaped by a person's life history is translated into the language of the present. The creative result provides access to intellectual repositories that would otherwise remain buried and inaccessible to the individual—and these are significant mental resources. For Jung, this is also where the social significance of art lies. By participating in the production of art, people with less creative talent are equally able to engage with the archetypal subjects created within them and make use of this resource for themselves. This applies to all creative output that people have engaged in. Everyone has experienced how a sentence by an author of philosopher, a picture, a sculpture, a fairytale, or a text can touch us, speak to us and stay in our mind. And how, if we emotionally and cognitively engage with these works, they enrich us and give us ideas for our own life, for whatever we are currently dealing with. Our problems enter into a resonant relationship with problem solving suggestions from the history of humanity.

Translating Emotions into Images

Jung repeatedly referred to the process of active imagination, a special form of internal dialog. These references can be understood as relating to all forms of imagining, of focusing the mind on one's inner images and the developments that result from it. In that sense, all imagination is "active." When we talk about fantasies, however, we mean the images that arise spontaneously, the ones we aren't yet fully focused on—the raw material for our imagination.

Therapeutically effective guidance involves the regulation of emotions, allowing difficult, but also positive affects to be dealt with in a constructive and creative manner. In recollection of his emotional crisis in 1913 and the overwhelming feelings it triggered C. G. Jung wrote: "The more I was able to translate emotions into images, i. e. to find the images that were hidden within them, the greater was my sense of inner calm [...] My experiment provided insight into how helpful [...] it is to become consciously aware of the images that lie behind our emotions." (Jung in Jaffé, p. 181).

Jung focused on his emotions, which enabled him to access the other aspect of imagination, namely, the representations associated with them. With this method, he was able to regulate his own emotions and discover which conflicts had triggered them—and learn what representations of the future, were associated with them.

These internal images should also be defined and shaped, as they are generally somewhat vague. They are potentialities. By defining them we make them recognizable to other people, and by talking about them we make them specific—the issue becomes clear. Through this, we also come to realize that these inner images are always in motion, that they change even as they are being shaped and thus correspond with a perpetual process of development. By being creative, a person shapes themselves. If this dynamic has come to a standstill, it is seen as a "psychological problem," which should be addressed so that life can run its course again.

The method for creatively working through an emotion can take different forms. A person might first immerse themselves in their imagination and then paint or otherwise represent an important aspect of what was seen, or alternatively the painting process itself may be treated as active imagination. The picture archive of the C. G. Jung-Institute Zurich contains countless works resulting from this endeavor. It is indeed, as Jung put it, a treasure trove of active imagination.

Bibliography:
K. C. R. Fox, K. Christoff, M. L. Dixon, "Affective neuroscience of self-generated Thought" in *Annals of the New York Academy of Sciences*, May 2018, (uploaded October 15, 2018).
C. G. Jung, *The Collected Works of C. G. Jung*, edited by Sir H. Read, M. Fordham, G. Adler and W. McGuire, 20 volumes, Princeton 1953–1983.
C. G. Jung, *Memories, Dreams, Reflections*, recorded and edited by Aniela Jaffé, translation by Richard and Clara Winston, New York 1989.

In 1942, her grandmother, Lisa Wenger, whom M. O. had loved dearly and who had always been a great support, dies aged 82. [...] M. O. made a drawing of L. W. on her deathbed.

She continues to work but few pieces survive. She is constantly blocked by periods of deep depression. A feeling of "having her hands tied"—the drawing Geneviève (1942, a project for a sculpture) is like an illustration of her situation. [It's] a sort of thick plank cut symmetrically on the right and left, [onto which] some broken rods were attached: the arms.

It isn't until 1970, when she actually produces the sculpture, that she realizes its significance—the broken arms. The title "Geneviève" draws on a legend: A king has to go off to war. He entrusts his first minister with his young queen. On his return, the minister who has tried in vain to seduce her, tells the king that she has been unfaithful with a page. The page is beheaded, and the queen was also to have been killed. However, the hunter takes pity on the young woman. He takes her deep into the forest. She finds a cave in which to shelter from the wild animals. She lives off berries and roots. A doe gives (?) her some milk. She gives birth to a boy. Having nothing to clothe him in, she wraps him in her long hair. She names him "Schmerzensreich" (Painful). One day, the king goes hunting and gets lost deep in the forest. Suddenly he sees a beautiful young boy. He asks him: "Who are you, what are you doing here?" The boy takes him to his mother. They recognize each other ... great joy. The king takes his wife and child back to the castle on his horse. Now it's the minister's turn to have his head chopped off.

"The legend is like a description of my psychological state: My 'king' had cast me out."

For the last two or three years she has been interested in the writings of C. G. Jung. After his years as a country doctor, in Steinen i. W., her father had realised that loneliness lay at the bottom of many illnesses, the impossibility for many people to find a listening ear. He had attended seminars by Jung in Zurich. (That is why?) his books were easily accessible to M. O.

"This reading helped me a lot. It also helped me make sense of my dreams." From a young age she had noted down the dreams that she thought of some importance.

"But I have never analyzed them, as 'La Femme Surréaliste' (Ed. Obliques) claims."

Going back to the sculpture and the legend of Geneviève, I think that in this case the "king" is an image of the Animus. The Animus is the name that

Jung gives to the masculine (side?) of the female soul, while the Anima represents the feminine side of the male soul. I found out for myself that the "Muse" of a poet, an artist, is also an image of the Anima and that the "Genius" is the image of the Animus in the poet, the female artist. Jung may well have written this somewhere, but I didn't find it in his books.

My "king" had cast me out—it was my "genius" that had sidelined me. In this sort of situation, it's not surprising that one feels "like one's hands are tied." Plus—one doesn't feel oneself. I no longer knew whether I was behaving well or badly. I felt as if I was being pursued. I could no longer be certain of anything. I questioned everything I had done and that I was doing. One evening, in 1946, plunged into dark despond, I decided to get blind drunk (from alcohol?). I got home, hardly able to walk. I picked up two sheets of black paper and covered them with somber splodges—green, ochre and a little white. In the morning I looked at them—they were the first two things I had been pleased with for a long time ("Fleur dans la Forêt" [Flower in the Woods] and "Alentour" [Round About]). I was mildly encouraged. I could tell: "It's still there," although buried deep. Also, some more positive images (things) appeared in my dreams (it was always winter—completely white, devoid of life). In 1949, for example, there was a rabbit running.

I tried to catch it, but it disappeared into a burrow (?). At least it was a living thing!—and a symbol of fertility to boot. Finally, in October 1954, the crisis passed just like that, without external occasion. I know now that this crisis was necessary and formed the basis of/for my ongoing development.

For the first time for a long while, M. O. rents a studio and starts working again with passion and pleasure.

Meret Oppenheim, "Geneviève and the King," around 1971

Emma

A Pioneer

Depth

Thomas Fischer

Jung: in Swiss Psychology

Perhaps the most well-known "class photograph" of the early psychoanalytical movement shows fifty participants of the 3rd International Congress held in Weimar from September 21–22, 1911, grouped around the central luminaries Sigmund Freud and C. G. Jung (see Fig. p. 109). Almost all the important protagonists from the German-speaking region between the two hubs of Vienna and Zurich were present, except for Alfred Adler and Wilhelm Stekel, who by then had already parted ways with Freud's approach. Also in attendance was the neurologist James J. Putnam, who had traveled from Boston in his role as president of the American Psychoanalytic Association (APsaA), which had been founded only four months earlier. It was also the first time that a significant number of women took part in a psychoanalytical congress. Seven of the nine women in the photo were associated with the Zurich group around C. G. Jung who had proudly announced this fact in a letter to Freud ahead of the congress:

"This time the female element from Zurich is going to turn up in force. Sister Moltzer, Dr Hinkle-Eastwick (charming American!), Miss Dr Spielrein (!), as well as a new discovery of mine, Miss Antonia Wolff, a woman of remarkable intelligence with excellent insight into philosophical-religious matters—and last but not least, my wife."

These women were joined in Weimar by doctor Mira Gincburg and Martha Böddinghaus, later Martha Sigg, both members of the Zurich chapter of the Psychoanalytical Association. The renowned Russo-German author Lou Andreas-Salomé, who became a close confidante of Freud's in the years to follow, and Maria von Stach, a leading figure in the German women's movement and former wife of the Jewish writer and philosopher Theodor Lessing, completed the line-up of the group.

Emma Jung was the only "trailing wife" at the Weimar congress. To this day she is mainly known as the spouse of C. G. Jung, who was already famous across the Western world—despite the fact that she had been the first among the participating women to come into contact with the new method of psychoanalysis. She had displayed a keen interest in psychology early on and later became widely known through her own contributions and as a teacher and practitioner of analytical psychology.

Early Insights
at the Burghölzli

Emma Jung-Rauschenbach was born in 1882, the eldest of two daughters of the wealthy Schaffhausen industrialist Johannes (Jean) Rauschenbach. As a young man, her father had taken over the management of the two family-owned companies, the Rauschenbach Maschinenfabrik für Landwirtschaftsgeräte and the International Watch Company (IWC), and had expanded them into successful pan-European corporations. Emma Rauschenbach was by no means predestined to participate in the pioneering work of depth psychology. After completing the secondary school for girls, she wanted to attend an academic high school (gymnasium) and study at a university, but her father would not allow it. Instead, she was sent, aged sixteen, to a distant relative in Paris, to acquire additional language and artistic skills and to prepare herself for running the kind of household that befitted her social rank. But her great intellectual curiosity and keen literary and scientific interests were already evident during her year there. Following the return to her parents' house in Schaffhausen, a prospective physician and son of a country parson called Carl Gustav Jung—who was loosely acquainted with the Rauschenbach family through his mother—began courting the eighteen-year-old Emma. For her, Carl's interest in philosophical-religious questions of life and human psychology—which was evident in his being drawn to the field of psychiatry—held the promise of an interesting perspective on life, despite what seemed his uncertain career prospects at the time. "You see, I'm not marrying a brilliant position or a fortune, I'm marrying a person," she wrote in a letter to him on January 26, 1901, still under her maiden name Emma Rauschenbach. "My soul needs a soul and not external things."

In 1900, Carl took up his first position as an assistant physician at the Burghölzli psychiatric clinic in Zurich. This also marked the beginning of Emma's deep engagement with psychology. She initially supported her fiancé in researching and reading English and French texts for his dissertation *Zur Psychologie und Pathologie sogenannter Okkulter Phänomene* (1902; *On the Psychology and*

Pathology of So-called Occult Phenomena, 2024). At the same time, she eagerly read all the other literature on the subject that Carl recommended to her. The clinic director Eugen Bleuler and his wife Hedwig Bleuler-Waser, herself a doctor of German studies, also encouraged all the physicians' wives to volunteer and actively participate in the everyday operation of the clinic. Thus, following her marriage in February 1903, Emma Jung soon became part of the Burghölzli research community.

Already under Bleuler's predecessor Auguste Forel, the Burghölzli had been seen as one of the leading clinics in German-speaking psychiatry, which was drawn to the psychological-psychotherapeutic approach. Bleuler, who was known for his research on schizophrenia, was the first European clinic director to take an interest in Freud's concept of psychoanalysis and went on to make the Burghölzli a key location for research on this method. As senior physicians, C. G. Jung and his colleague Franz Riklin gained an international reputation for themselves and the clinic with their series of diagnostic association studies conducted between 1903 and 1905. Emma Jung not only figured prominently among the test subjects in the so-called "word association experiments," but also took on the official role of research assistant for the project, together with the young assistant physician Kurt Wehrlin. It was their duty to help record the test material and to process the obtained test results for C. G. Jung and Riklin's publications. When the "Zurich school" around Bleuler began exploring with the psychoanalytical method of dream interpretation in 1900, it wasn't just the doctors but also their wives who took part in reciprocative dream interpretation and observation of complexes. Emma Jung thus became acquainted with Freud's psychoanalytical approach early on and her years at the Burghölzli can rightly be described as self-directed studies in the field of modern psychology.

In 1906, when C. G. Jung first corresponded directly with Freud, his wife was therefore already familiar with Freud's ideas and concepts. In this context, it is evident that she wasn't merely playing the part of a polite, supportive wife when she accompanied her husband on his first visit to Vienna in spring of 1907, and likewise when she participated in the conversations with Freud on his return visit to the Burghölzli clinic in the summer of 1908. This is further corroborated by the fact that Freud sent her a series of specialist books after his trip to Zurich. Later, Carl himself expressed his pride about the lasting impression his wife had made on Freud in a letter he wrote to her on October 10, 1908: "I am always terribly delighted that Freud was so impressed by you."

Correspondence with Freud

Freud was thus already well acquainted with Emma Jung when she had to stand in for her husband at short notice in the spring of 1910 to complete the program for the second *International Psychoanalytical Congress* in Nuremberg. The letters exchanged between Emma Jung and Sigmund Freud in the following two years testify to a conversation between equals. Freud treated her with an esteem that went far beyond the scope of a personal exchange about domestic affairs. In the course of their correspondence after the Weimar congress, Emma Jung candidly admitted to Freud in a letter on November 24, 1911, that she herself at times felt overshadowed by the extent to which all attention was directed at her husband: "From time to time I feel conflicted, wondering how I might be able to assert myself beside Carl; it feels as if I don't have any friends and that everyone who interacts with us actually just wants to engage with Carl, apart from a few boring people who are of no interest to me whatsoever.

The women are all in love with him of course, and the men immediately shut me out anyway, seeing me simply as the wife of their mentor or friend."

Freud's reaction to this is interesting. Appreciating her full competence and independent judgment as a psychoanalyst, he encouraged her on December 1, 1911, in a letter, to start writing her own psychoanalytical works: "I have always admired your keen understanding and your valuable thoughts when you voiced them during one of our rare encounters, and I think I never made a secret of this. So I wouldn't be surprised if

Mrs Emma appears as an author in her own right one day and relates her observations on an aspect of a child's life, on someone's inner life or on a piece of historical writing. I am certain that it will be good, and if the yearbook doesn't want to take it then the new journal, which could perhaps be called 'Imago', will be readily on hand."

The fact that Emma Jung, a mother of four, at times felt burdened by the prominent position of her husband—the man personally selected by Freud as the crown prince within psychoanalytical circles—wasn't only because of Carl's dominant intellect and his exceptional capacity for work. Contributing to her feelings of insecurity wasn't only because of the dominant intellect and exceptional capacity of her husband; it was also due to three of the other women attending the Weimar congress.

The strength of her marriage to Carl had already been called into question years before, following Sabina Spielrein's arrival. Spielrein is seen as C. G. Jung's first real "psychoanalytical patient" at the Burghölzli, where she was treated 1904/1905. During her later medical studies in Zurich a personal relationship developed between Spielrein and Carl that was characterized by strong transference and counter-transference. It was a situation that also loosely involved Freud as the "father" of psychoanalysis, and it wasn't until 1909 that C. G. Jung was able to at least partly break away from his personal entanglement. In 1911, under supervision by Eugen Bleuler, Spielrein was the first woman to receive a doctorate with a dissertation on psychoanalysis: *Über den psychologischen Inhalt eines Falles von Schizophrenie*. She traveled to Weimar as "Miss Dr."

Later, a similar situation developed between C. G. Jung and Toni Wolff, who had come to him for treatment in 1910. The difference here was that Carl conducted this relationship openly from 1913 and Emma Jung had to come to terms with this "second woman" in her marriage. Carl's praise for his protégé's "remarkable intelligence with excellent insight into philosophical-religious matters" in the quoted letter to Freud were the result of Wolff's studies at the University of Zurich, where she attended lectures on theology, philosophy and mythology. "Sister Moltzer," also mentioned in the letter, was Maria Moltzer from Amsterdam, an heiress of the director of Amsterdam's Bols liquor factory. She had come to Zurich in 1905 to work at the Lebendige Kraft sanatorium as a nurse. The sanatorium was run by Max Bircher-Benner, through whom she met C. G. Jung in 1910. She worked as his research assistant in psychoanalysis, before they went their separate ways in 1918. Freud suspected that her relationship with Carl was also more than merely analytical. What is undisputed is that all three women—Emma Jung, Toni Wolff, and Maria Moltzer—were important to C. G. Jung at the time of his separation from Freud and his resulting inner crisis.

Research Work
with C. G. Jung—the Break
with Freud

In 1909 and 1910, Carl and Emma Jung initially tried to take an analytical approach to resolving their marriage problems together. When the endeavor proved unsuccessful, Emma was encouraged by her husband to visit his colleague Leonhard Seif in Munich for a short analysis in autumn of 1911. This gave rise to a phase of intensive psychological self-exploration. Even though other women had a presence in the life of Carl, Emma remained closely connected to her husband and his research.

After Carl had withdrawn from the Burghölzli clinic in 1909, Emma continued to actively support him in his private practice at their newly constructed house in Küsnacht. During 1911 and 1912, she also carried out extensive research and provided editorial assistance for his upcoming key work *Die Wandlungen und Symbole der Libido (Psychology of the Unconscious: a study of the transformations and symbolisms of the libido)*. For his part, C. G. Jung increasingly introduced his wife to his practical work by telling her about interesting cases. As the editor of the *Jahrbuch für psychoanalytische und psychopathologische Forschungen* he also entrusted her with the translation into German of Ernest Jones's article "Some Cases of Obsessional Neurosis," which appeared in 1912 in the same edition as the second part of C. G. Jung's libido paper.

Without a medical degree, neither Emma Jung, nor Toni Wolff or Maria Moltzer could formally join the Zurich chapter of the International Psychoanalytical Association when it was founded in 1910. This was different for Weimar attendee Mira Gincburg, who had studied in Zurich and was one of several Russian and Eastern European women doctors who were introduced to psychoanalysis during their residency as assistant physicians at the Burghölzli. However, the Zurich chapter was open to the inclusion of laypersons and welcomed the three women from early on to participate in their meetings and discussions.

The Weimar congress was in many ways the high point and turning point of the international psychoanalytical movement. Emma Jung was one of the first to notice the increasing friction between Freud and her husband in Weimar. Following the congress, in autumn 1911, she wrote to Freud on her own initiative and without the knowledge of her husband, asking him to expound on his evidently diverging views regarding the recently published first part of *Wandlungen und Symbole der Libido*. She probably did so in part out of worry for the relationship between the two men, but presumably also because of her close involvement in the publication's making. Despite her efforts, the relationship between Vienna and Zurich could not be fixed in the long run.

The break between Freud and her husband led to a split in the psychoanalytical movement after 1912. At that point Emma also broke off contact with Freud and his group in Vienna. The vast majority of the Zurich chapter resigned from the International Psychoanalytical Association in summer 1914 and regrouped as the *Verein für Analytische Psychologie* (Association for Analytical Psychology). Emma Jung, Maria Moltzer, and Toni Wolff had all been intensively involved in the IPA's activities over the previous years and, following a change in statutes passed by the Zurich group of doctors and psychologists in January 1914, they were the first laypersons to be accepted to the new society. To become associate members they had to publish a scientific paper to demonstrate the depth of their knowledge of psychoanalysis. This was Emma's first independent paper on the psychological motifs in the Grimm fairy tales of the Two Brothers. She had completed work on the manuscript in autumn 1913 and—following a break due to the birth of her youngest daughter—presented her paper at two meetings of the Society for Analytical Psychology in autumn 1914.

The "Zurich Women" after the Weimar Congress

Like most of the women who participated in Weimar, the American physician Beatrice Hinkle also remained part of C. G. Jung's circle. Having co-founded one of the first psychotherapeutic clinics in the United States in 1908, she had come to Zurich around 1910 to study psychoanalysis. She soon made a name for herself in the English-speaking world, among other things as the translator of C. G. Jung's *Wandlungen und Symbole der Libido* into English (*Psychology of the Unconscious*, 1916). Martha Böddinghaus, who was originally from Munich and had come to Zurich in 1910 to undergo analysis with C. G. Jung, went on to marry one of his close friends, the Küsnacht businessman and olive oil manufacturer Hermann Sigg. She became an early follower of C. G. Jung's and was part of the group of women around Emma Jung who played a central role in the establishment of analytical psychology in Zurich during the years after Weimar.

Mira Gincburg was the only one among what became known as the "Zurich women" who remained unequivocally allied to Freud's cause, especially after her marriage in 1913 to the psychiatrist Emil Oberholzer whom she had met at the Burghölzli. The couple belonged to just a handful of Freudians in Zurich after 1914. Sabina Spielrein married a Russian Jewish physician and left Zurich in 1912. She lived in Berlin for two years, where she worked as a psychoanalyst and gained recognition with her publications on child and dream analysis. She subsequently returned to Switzerland for a few years—moving first to Lausanne, then to Geneva—without however becoming affiliated with the new Jungian association or the remaining Freudian therapists. She was tragically killed in the Soviet Union during the Second World War.

For Emma Jung, the years after the Weimar congress were among the most intensive of her life. Not only did she and Carl have a family of five children to rear, Emma's own analytical work was now also significantly taking shape. In 1914 she started a long-term analysis with Carl's colleague Hans Schmid-Guisan, which soon developed into a close friendship and resulted in a wealth of personal psychological material in the form of dream chronicles, texts, images, and active imagination. Similar to her husband with his *Red Book*, she laid this material out in a book bound in marbled paper. This is now being exhibited, for the first time after more than 100 years.

Alongside pictorial illustration, Emma Jung discovered poetry as a special form of expression in her own work. In particular the central motifs from the dreams and fantasies she had in connection with her individuation process were consolidated through poetry. During 1915 to 1919, these endeavors led to the creation of what might be called a personal cosmology, in which she created a new base for her development from mother and wife to a person independently connected to the world.

The Grail Legend and Other Contributions to Analytical Psychology

For Emma Jung, the Zurich Psychology Club her husband founded in 1916 soon became the most important forum in which to discuss her further ideas and work. The club served as a place where analysts and their analysands could exchange thoughts and ideas outside their usual analytical setting. The forty founding members, of whom twenty-four were women, appointed Emma Jung as the club's first president, a role she occupied until 1919. Emma was also one of the three initiators of the first women-only evening at the club launched in May 1921. Here specific women's issues and subjects of analytical psychology could be explored from a female perspective.

At a time when the feminist avant-garde overlapped with a nascent conservative counter-movement, the women of the Psychology Club didn't call the conventional societal framework into question as such. The majority of them saw themselves as "medial types," as Toni Wolff put it in the unpublished manuscript of the lecture "Einige Gedanken zum Individuationsprozess der Frau" at the Psychology Club on May 12, 1934. They considered men and women to be equal but essentially assumed a dualistic world view according to which the genders differ in "nature" and consequently also differ in their destiny. Thus the women primarily sought independence through engaging with their inner life and their distinct psychology and less through examining their role in society.

It was from this background that Emma Jung's first publication *Ein Beitrag zum Problem des Animus* (*Animus and Anima: Two Essays*) emerged. C. G. Jung included the paper in his 1934 anthology *Wirklichkeit der Seele*—presumably in recognition of his wife's theoretical contribution to the development of the concepts of anima and animus. Indeed, in a talk at the Psychology Club in 1916, Emma Jung had already spoken about the pandora as an "artificially created image" within men and about the psychological counter-phenomena of the imago within women, presaging the anima and animus before they existed as concepts.

The second subject with which Emma Jung gained a lasting reputation in Jungian analytical psychology was the legend of the Holy Grail, specifically the psychological interpretation of the different forms of medieval grail legends. Her work on this spanned decades, as she developed her expertise by giving talks and lectures at the Psychology Club and the C. G. Jung-Institute Zurich, founded in 1948. Her engagement in the topic also resulted in a lively exchange with intellectuals and academics such as the mythology researcher Karl Kerényi and the physicist Wolfgang Pauli.

Emma Jung's later work, in particular her papers on the animus and anima and the manuscripts on the grail legends published posthumously by Marie-Louise von Franz, were remembered for years after her death in 1955. But her role in the early years of the psychoanalytical movement has largely been forgotten. Her story outlined here serves as a reminder that from the very beginning Emma Jung was an early exponent and pioneer in the history of Swiss depth psychology.

Bibliography:

Emma Jung, *Animus und Anima*, Zurich 1967 (current edition, Leinfelden-Echterdingen 1996).

Emma Jung and Marie-Louise von Franz, *Die Graalslegende in psychologischer Sicht*, Zurich and Stuttgart, 1960 (current edition, Stuttgart 2001).

Susanne Eggenberger-Jung, "Emma Rauschenbach: Portrait of Her Childhood and Youth" in *Dedicated to the Soul: The Writings and Drawings of Emma Jung*, edited by Ann C. Lammers, Thomas Fischer and Medea Hoch, Princeton 2025. pp. 1–21.

Thomas Fischer and Medea Hoch, "Emma Jung and Analytical Psychology" in *Dedicated to the Soul: The Writings and Drawings of Emma Jung*, edited by Ann C. Lammers, Thomas Fischer and Medea Hoch, Princeton 2025, pp. 29–59.

Thomas Fischer and Christfried Toegel, "Der Briefwechsel zwischen Emma Jung und Sigmund Freud" in *Luzifer-Amor* 73, 1/2024, pp. 173–210.

Sigmund Freud and C. G. Jung, *The Freud/Jung Letters, The Correspondence between Sigmund Freud and C. G. Jung*, edited by William McGuire, translation by Ralph Manheim and R. F. C. Hull, Princeton 1974.

Annatina Wieser, *Zur frühen Psychoanalyse in Zürich, 1900–1914*, Inaugural Dissertation University of Zurich, 2001; online at: luzifer-amor.de/downloads.

Andreas Peglau, "Sigmund Freud in Weimar: Ein Foto aus dem Jahr 1911 – eine Momentaufnahme der psychoanalytischen Bewegung" in *Weimar-Jena: Die grosse Stadt* 5, 3/2012, pp. 228–238.

Anton M. Fischer, *Sigmund Freuds erstes Land – Eine Kulturgeschichte der Psychotherapie in der Schweiz*, Giessen 2013.

Anima figures are the nymphs, swan maidens, undines, and fairies, familiar from so many legends and tales. As a rule, they are of enticing beauty but only half human; they have fish tails, like the nixie, or turn into birds, like the swan maidens. Often they appear as more than one, especially as three; the undifferentiated animus also likes to appear as more than one.

With charms or enchanting songs these beings (sirens, the Lorelei, and so on) lure a man into their realm, where he disappears forevermore; or else—a very important point—they try to bind the man in love, that they may live in his world with him. Always they have something uncanny about them, and there is a taboo connected with them that must not be broken. [...]

Pythia, the sibyls and the Muses are feminine beings and may be likened to the northern seeresses; their sayings are of an irrational kind that looks like madness from the standpoint of reason or the logos. Faculties such as these, however, do not belong to woman only; there have always been masculine seers and prophets, too, who are such by virtue of a feminine, receptive attitude which makes them responsive to influences from the other side of consciousness.

Because the anima, as the feminine aspect of man, possesses this receptivity and absence of prejudice toward the irrational, she is designated the mediator between consciousness and the unconscious. In the creative man, especially, this feminine attitude plays an important role; it is not without cause that we speak of the conception *of a work, of carrying out a thought, delivering oneself of it, or brooding over it. [...]*

For the integration of the anima, the feminine element, into a man's conscious personality is part of the individuation process. In this connection, however, a point of special importance must be taken into consideration, for the feminine element which must become an integrated component of the personality is only a portion of the anima, namely, its personal aspect. The anima also represents the archetype of womanhood, which is suprapersonal in nature and therefore cannot be integrated.

Behind the elemental beings of our study stand the divine figures of Cybele and Aphrodite—in the last analysis, the Goddess Nature. This archetypal background explains the irresistible force which can emanate from such an anima figure; for if in it Nature herself is encountered, then it is understandable that a man may be overcome and fall into its power. This happens particularly when no differentiation is made between the archetypal and the personal aspects of the anima. Indeed, confusing the two aspects is what gives the anima superior power, and that is why it is most important to discriminate between what belongs to the "personal" and what to the "suprapersonal".

C. G. Jung tells of a man's dream in which a female figure of more than life size and with a veiled face stands in a church—in the place of the altar. Indeed, like the Platonic ideas, the archetype of the anima is of superhuman nature and dwells in a celestial place. Though distinct from the personal, feminine components of the soul, she is nevertheless the primal image standing behind them and shaping them to her likeness.

As Great Mother and Goddess of Love, as "Mistress," or by whatever other name she may be called, the anima in her archetypal aspect is to be met with reverence. On the other hand, a man must come to terms with his personal anima, the femininity that belongs to him, that accompanies and supplements him but may not be allowed to rule him.

When the anima is recognized and integrated a change of attitude occurs toward the feminine generally. This new evaluation of the feminine principle brings with it a due reverence for nature, too; whereas the intellectual viewpoint dominant in an era of science and technology leads to utilizing and even exploiting nature, rather than honoring her.

Fortunately, signs can be observed today pointing in the latter direction. Most important and significant of these is probably the new dogma of the "Assumptio Mariae" and her proclamation as mistress of creation. In our time, when such threatening forces of cleavage are at work, splitting peoples, individuals, and atoms, it is doubly necessary that those which unite and hold together should become effective; for life is founded on the harmonious interplay of masculine and feminine forces, within the individual human being as well as without. Bringing these opposites into union is one of the most important tasks of present-day psychotherapy.

Emma Jung, "The Anima as an Elemental Being," publ. 1955

"Man the machine" had been the war cry of the radically materialistic Enlightenment, which saw mind and body as inextricably linked. The mind of a person could be inferred from the body, it was argued. Johann Caspar Lavater, who developed the theory of physiognomy, believed character was written into the face. The model that Walter Morgenthaler created for the Swiss National Exhibition of 1914 assembled the various forms of shock therapy then available to psychiatry in a kind of dolls' house. Morgenthaler was also the first psychiatrist in the world to hail the work of one of his patients as art. It was thanks to him that Adolf Wölfli became an icon of "Art brut." Artistic creativity would henceforth become an increasingly popular form of therapy.

The Swiss artist Heidi Bucher's work *The Parlour Office of Doctor Binswanger* reminds us that in the early days of psychoanalysis, the role of patients like Anna O. was as crucial as it was repressed. Dr. Binswanger's hospital in Kreuzlingen, whose patients included the ballet dancer Vaslav Nijinsky, was soon offering not just cold baths but also electroshock and insulin shock therapy. The 1950s saw the pharmaceutical company Ciba Geigy develop a whole gamut of psychotropic drugs such as "Tofranil." The next big breakthrough today is expected to come from psychoactive substances such as LSD, the first clinical trials of which were conducted at the Burghölzli hospital in 1949.

MERET OPPENHEIM
La fin embarassée (End and Confusion), 1971

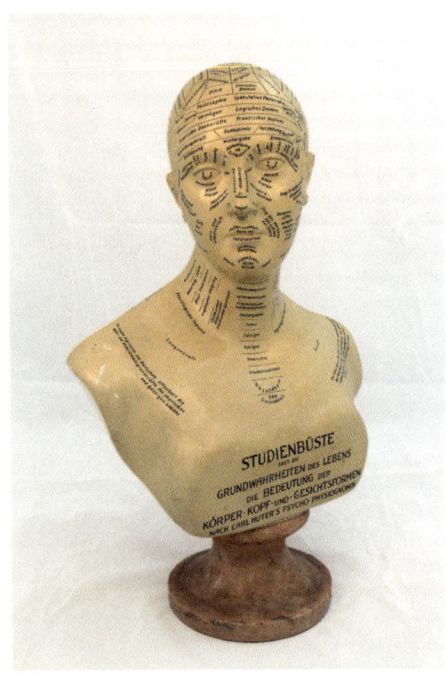

Phrenological study bust after
Carl Huter's psychophysiognomics,
early twentieth century

Physical treatment methods according to
E. Horn (1818), models by Dr Walter Morgenthaler
for the Swiss National Exhibition, 1914

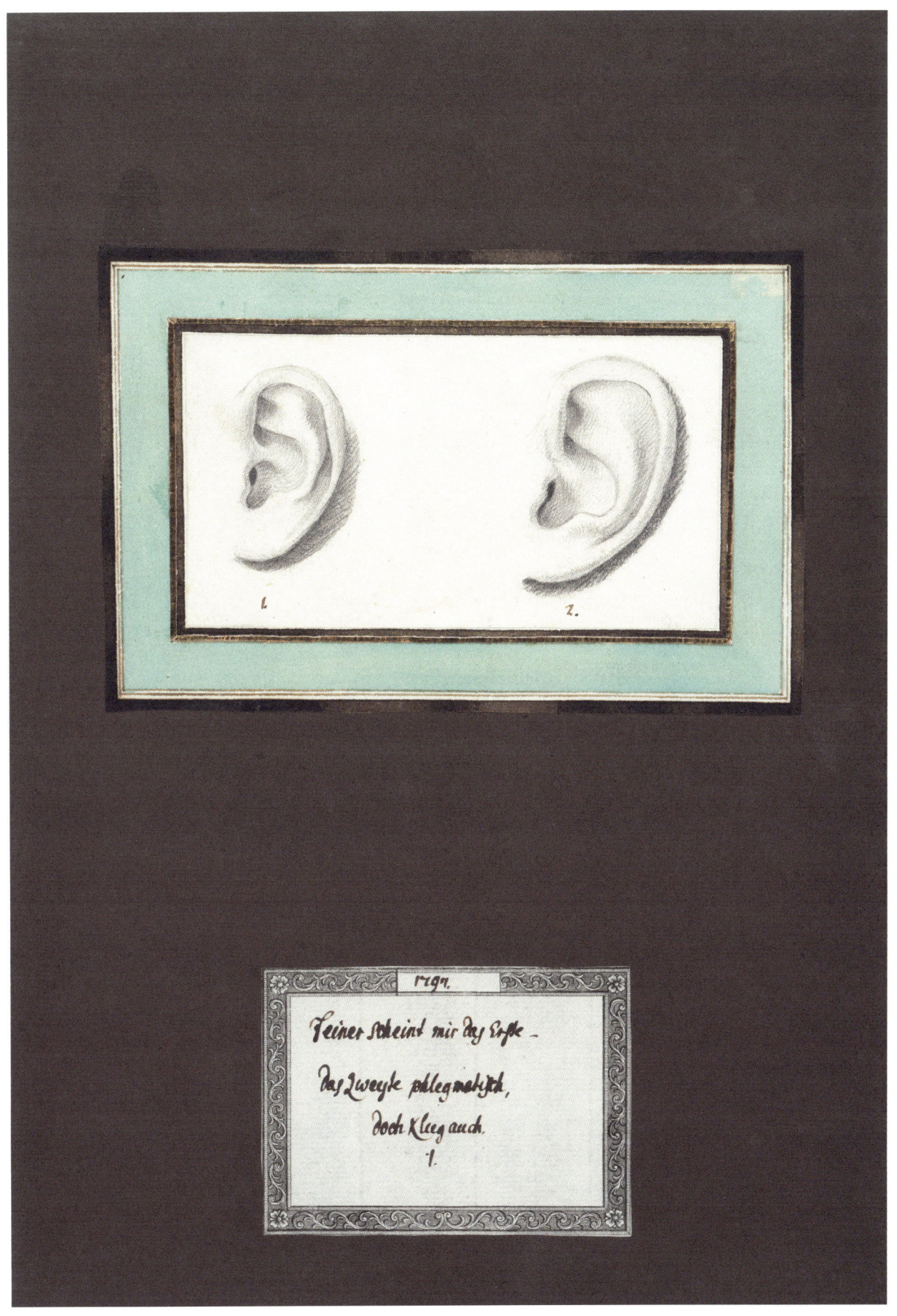

Anonymous (Lavater circle of artists),
Two Ears: One Fine, One Phlegmatic, 1797

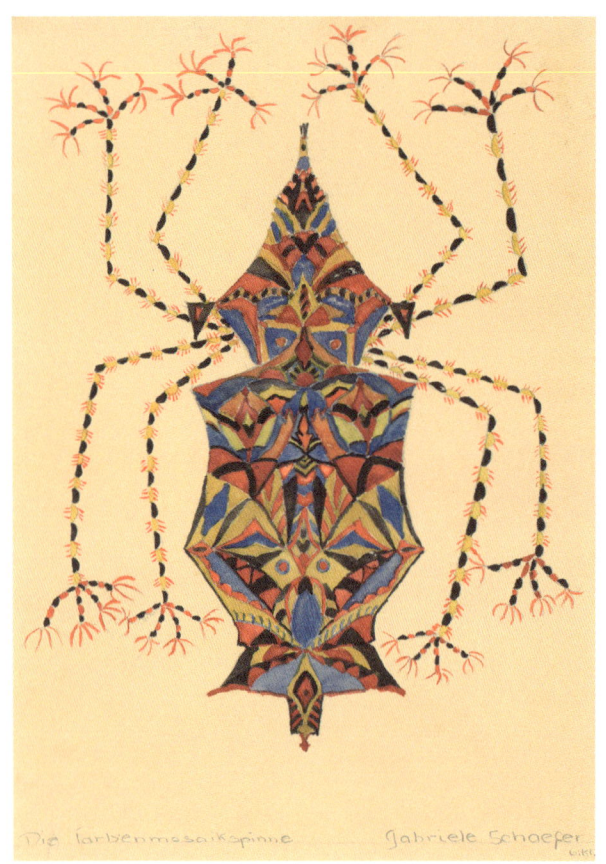
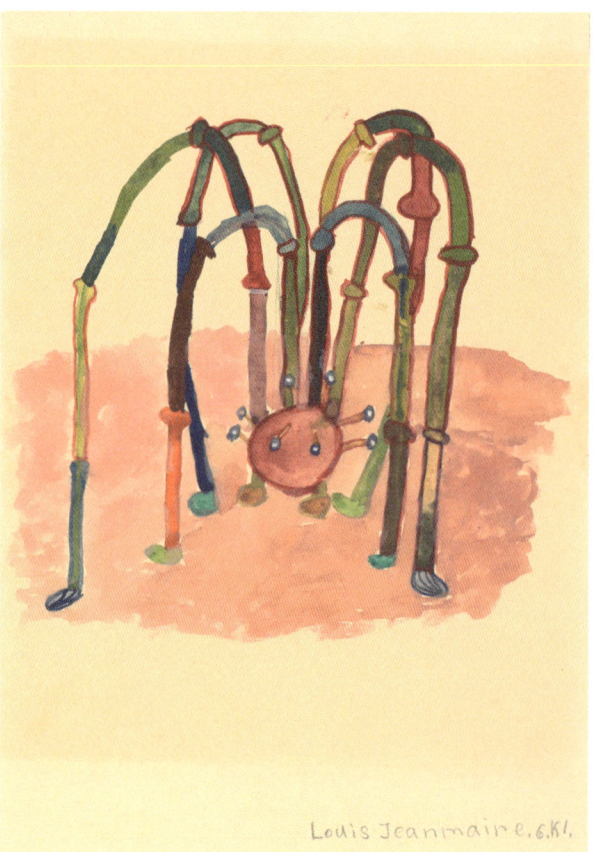

GABRIELE SCHAEFER, age 12,
Die Farbenmosaikspinne, 1934

LOUIS JEANMAIRE, age 12,
Hexenspinne, 1934

Hebephrenia (subtype of schizophrenia),
patient photograph by Hermann Rorschach,
c. 1910–1913

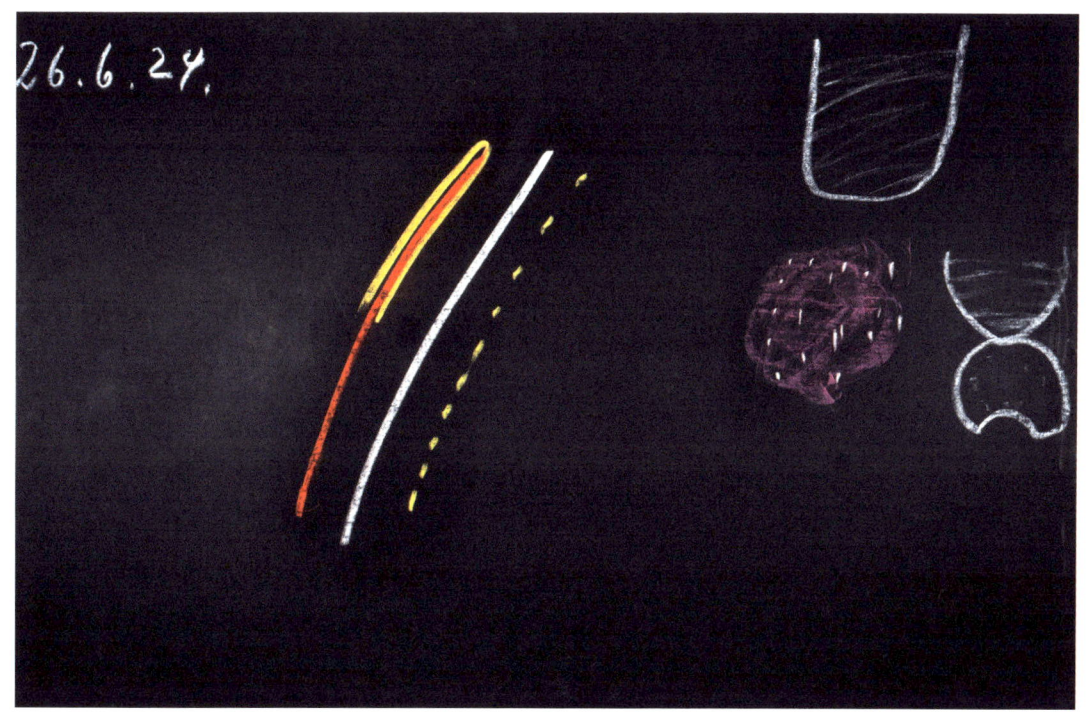

RUDOLF STEINER, blackboard drawing for
Heilpädagogischer Kurs, 26.6.1924

Erika Mann and Annemarie Schwarzenbach,
1933

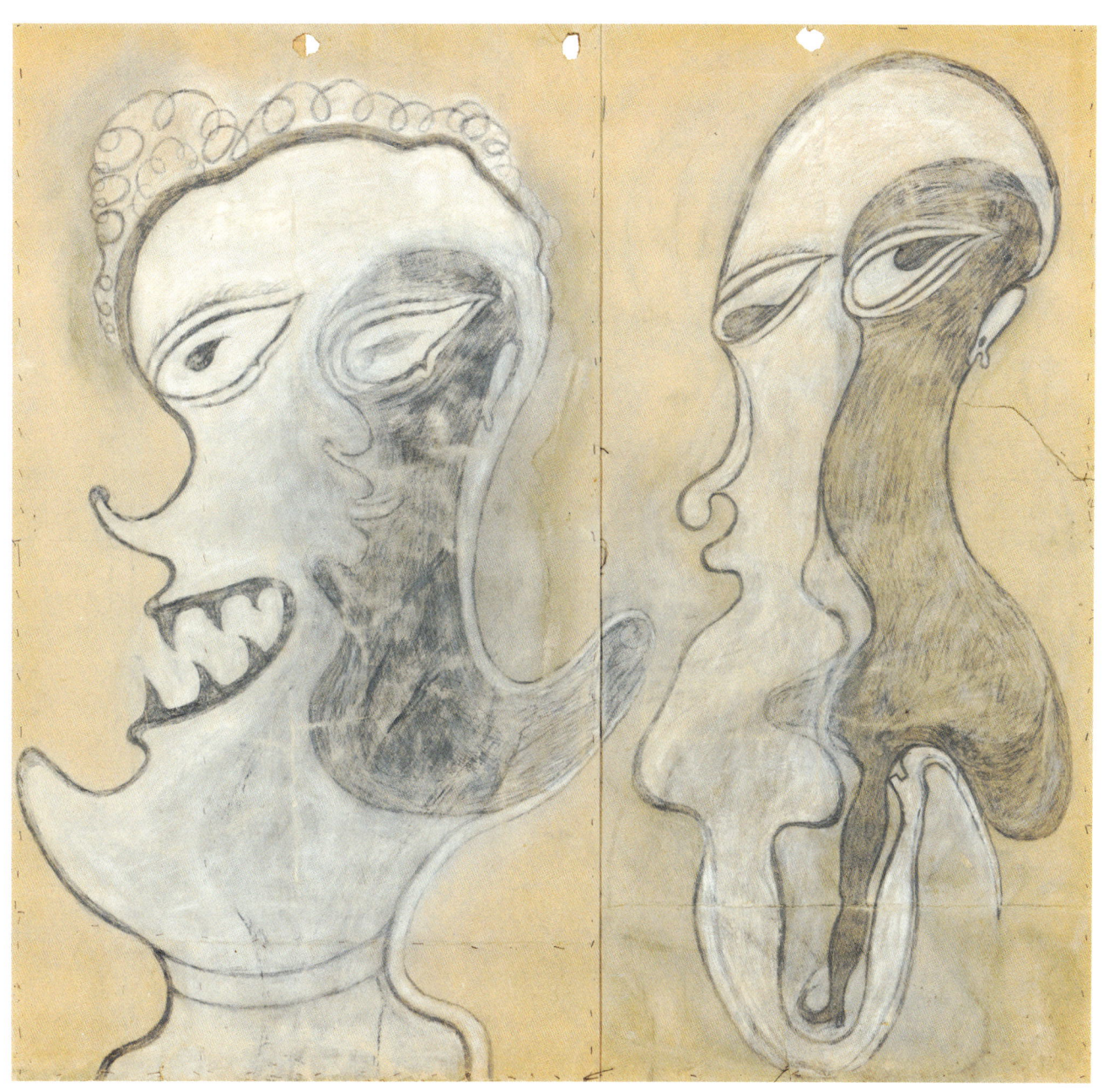

HEINRICH ANTON MÜLLER
Untitled, 1917–1922

ADOLF WÖLFLI
Lunatic = Asylum Band = Hain, 1910

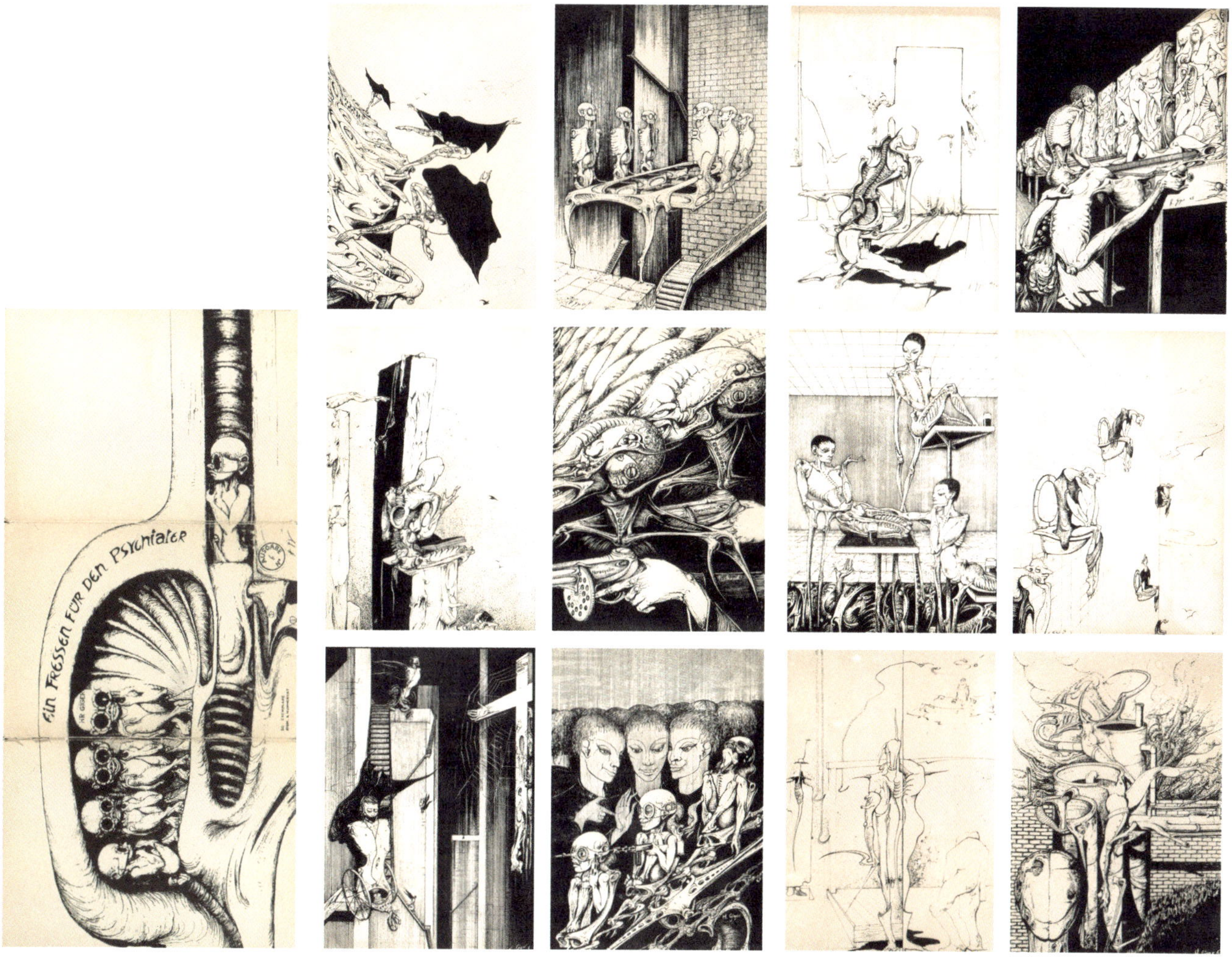

H. R. GIGER
A Feast for the Psychiatrist, 1966

Tin boxes with three different pharmaceutical
test substances, late 1960s

Microgram sheet,
Robert Walser, 1926

ERNA SCHILLIG
Paare mit Bäumen und Tieren, c. 1930

PAUL THEK
Untitled (Mushroom), 1969

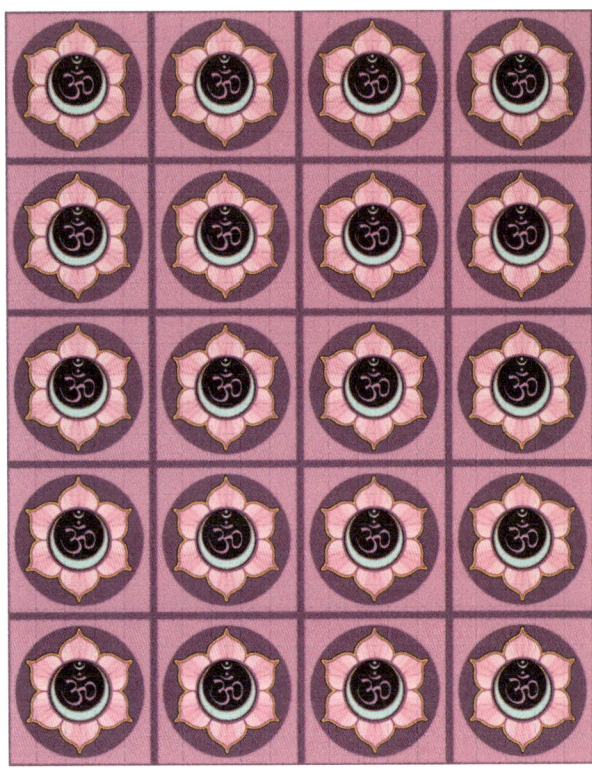

Blotter: absorbent paper used as a common carrier
medium for substances such as LSD

HEIDI BUCHER, *Das Bad, Häutung Bellevue*, photographed by Gaechter and Clahsen, 1988

VASLAV NIJINSKY
The Eye, 1818–1819

Psychi
A Child of an Ambi

On the History of Psychiatry in Nineteenth and Twentieth Century Switzerland

Urs Germann

atry:

valent Modernity

Psychiatric knowledge influences how we define mental distress, how we talk about difficulties in partnerships, the family, and professional life, and how we gauge social abnormalities. Yet many of those who have come into contact with psychiatry associate it with strain and stigmatization. To make better sense of the ambivalent relationship between society and psychiatry, it helps to consider its history.

Although medicine has had to address conditions such as "frenzy," "melancholy," and "hysteria" since ancient times, the history of psychiatry only begins in the modern age, around 1800. The image of the Parisian physician Philippe Pinel liberating "mad people" from their real and imaginary chains during the French Revolution can be regarded as the conceptual founding of the discipline. That emancipatory gesture was coupled with the assurance of modern medicine that, contrary to prevailing ignorance and prejudice, the sufferings of the mind deserved to be treated and cured every bit as those of the body. The people hitherto dismissed as "lunatics" were to become productive citizens with equal rights.

This change in attitude manifested itself in the "lunatic asylums" that, starting in the 1840s, were built to replace the old "madhouses" and hospital wards for the insane, both in Switzerland and elsewhere in Europe. The Asile des Vernets in Geneva built in 1838 is an early example of this. By the First World War, all the large and medium-sized cantons had at least one institution for the treatment and care of the mentally ill. Since the opening of the institution in Mendrisio (1898), this also included Ticino. Some of these facilities, such as the Waldau near Bern (1855), the Königsfelden near Windisch (1872), and the Cery near Lausanne (1873), were rather grand, often barrack-like new buildings. Elsewhere, in St. Urban (1873) and Rheinau (1869), for example, old monasteries were repurposed and dedicated wards in other institutions were set aside for the insane, as happened at the Realta in Graubünden (1855). Basel's Friedmatt (1886), by contrast, was built as an airy, stand-alone pavilion. Nevertheless, those who could afford the cost tended to seek treatment in a private clinic such as the famous Bellevue sanatorium in Kreuzlingen (1857) or Les Rives in Prangins (1930).

Meanwhile, psychiatry was advancing as a scientific discipline. Switzerland's *Irrenärzte* ("lunatic doctors"), as they called themselves, formed their first professional association in 1864. Psychiatry was recognized as an examination subject for students of medicine in 1888 and has had its own specialist journal since 1917. Zurich's clinic, the Burghölzli, soon became an academic hotspot, and until well into the twentieth century, almost all Swiss psychiatrists (very few of whom were women at first) completed at least part of their training at Zurich University Hospital. It was the director of the Burghölzli, Eugen Bleuler, who wrote *Lehrbuch der Psychiatrie*, the textbook first published in 1916 that would shape how Swiss physicians understood psychiatry for nearly a century to come.

The initial optimism did not last long, however. The new institutions were soon overcrowded and the number of long-stay patients rose steadily, necessitating the building of new wings. Psychiatry was increasingly perceived as all about care rather than confinement, especially at long-stay institutions such as those in Bellelay and Perreux. Economic and social structural change and the erosion of family safety nets led to more and more mentally troubled, alcohol-dependent or violent people being dumped in the nearest mental hospital, while industrial society, with its focus on the division of labor, productivity, and performance, became less and less tolerant of what were perceived as disruptions of all kinds, both social and mental.

Yet the first half of the twentieth century also saw the development of "small psychiatry" alongside these large institutions. The term refers to both those neurologists and psychiatrists who treated the neuroses of well-heeled clients in their private practices—the Bernese psychotherapy pioneer Paul Dubois is an early example of such a practitioner, as is C. G. Jung, who opened a practice in Küsnacht in 1909—as well as all the newly equipped small outpatient clinics, most of them affiliated with existing institutions that served a broader swath of the population. While this development helped lower the threshold for obtaining psychiatric help, it also gave rise to a tendency towards psychologization and pathologization. More and more people sought psychiatric advice for psychological difficulties and everyday problems. In the interwar period, child and adolescent psychiatry was established at the interface between hospitals, schools, child and youth welfare services. André Repond, a pioneer of the mental hygiene movement, which aimed to promote mental health, for example, opened a medical-educational service in the Valais that he ran from the clinic in Malévoz.

Coercion in the Name of Order

Contrary to its heroic founding narrative, psychiatry still must operate within the constantly changing parameters defined by patient well-being at one extreme and the public's legitimate interest in order and safety at the other. State institutions, in particular, had long been part of the disciplinary apparatus with which the liberal-democratic state sought to "correct" the "misfits" on the fringes of society, either by forcibly integrating them or rendering them "harmless." Stigmatization arose from this endeavor, since to the middle classes of the fin de siècle, a stay in a psychiatric clinic was tantamount to "social death." Indeed, until the second half of the twentieth century, most patients were institutionalized against their will, whether by their own families, the physicians treating them, or the authorities. Their treatment, moreover, might entail a range of coercive practices, from the straitjacket and lidded bath of the nineteenth century to isolation and compulsory medicalization and fixation, which are still delicate issues for today's psychiatry.

There were times when Swiss psychiatry actually prided itself on being a guardian of public order and hygiene, especially around the turn of the twentieth century, when the battle against alcoholism, hereditary diseases, criminality, and social neglect was spurred on by degeneration theory. An understanding of disease that regarded societal factors uncritically as "reality" added greatly to the pressure to conform and fall into line.

It was in this climate that psychiatrists established themselves as indispensable expert witnesses for authorities and courts seeking to ascertain a person's fitness for society. Besides judging the mental capacity or neediness of struggling individuals, they also tended to read atypical lifestyles as a sign of abnormality. While Swiss psychiatry of the 1930s did indeed set itself apart from the "racial hygiene" being propagated by the Nazi regime, there were some in the field who nevertheless espoused the forced sterilization of ostensibly "inferior" people, marriage prohibitions, and restrictive naturalization standards. Thus, they became willing accessories to the sterilization of women who might otherwise be denied an abortion or whose children might become a burden on welfare services. They also recommended the castration of sex offenders and even of homosexual men—at least until homosexuality was depathologized in the 1970s. To those on the receiving end, such interventions often came to be associated with powerlessness and violence.

Even if the last third of the twentieth century saw those earlier forms of coercive care set aside in favor of more subtle forms of support and control, psychiatric clinics have remained the final catchment basin for those vulnerable people who fall through all the other social safety nets. Among them, at least until the 1970s, were those young people who could no longer bear the repressive regimes of the care homes in which they had been forced to grow up. In the course of time, they would be joined by drug addicts, homeless people, and traumatized migrants.

Therapies and Experiments

In addition to such coercive treatments, another difference between psychiatry and somatic medicine was the notorious imprecision of psychiatric diagnoses and the therapeutic impotence of those making them. Indeed, psychiatry's therapeutic arsenal had long consisted of little more than confinement in an asylum or psychiatric hospital, where patients could be shielded from their home environment, closely supervised, and made to do collaborative work in an effort to bring about "social healing." Inevitably, therefore, any new approaches to treatment raised great expectations that quickly escalated into passionate demands for normalization. The high degree of autonomy enjoyed by the directors of Switzerland's clinics made them especially willing to experiment, which in turn led them to develop a highly eclectic therapeutic style.

In the late nineteenth century, surgical procedures on the brain were just as much an accepted approach to setting the mind to rights as were hypnosis sessions. Eugen Bleuler then opened the discipline to Freudian psychoanalysis, after which the completion of a course of training analysis was considered de rigueur among Swiss psychiatrists, at least until the 1970s. Psychoanalysis in its turn spawned two important new departures after the Second World War: first the application of psychotherapy to treat schizophrenics and second ethno-psychoanalysis.

The more active forms of treatment applied during the interwar years, including more intensive forms of occupational therapy and somatic "cures," also raised new hopes, especially since the latter, being invasive, were imagined to be more effective. The psychiatric hospital in Münsingen near Bern, for example, became a veritable "Mecca" for insulin shock and electroconvulsive therapy during the 1930s, attracting not only doctors but also patients and their families from all over Europe. There was also a brief surge in psychosurgical interventions after the war, with the aim of pacifying the more disruptive patients if only to relieve the institutions housing them.

What all these therapies had in common was their uncertain effectiveness, even when measured by the standards of the day. Again and again, the initial euphoria flipped over into disillusionment. The "pharmacological turn," as the advent of the first psychotropic drugs in the 1950s is often called, followed the same pattern, though its consequences were much more far-reaching. Not only did the new substances promote a biological understanding of mental illness, but they also changed the everyday work of psychiatric hospitals and their nursing staff with lasting effect, as well as introducing the pharmaceutical industry as a new and powerful player in the world of psychiatry. The choice of drugs available grew exponentially as the neuroleptics, tranquilizers, and antidepressants were joined by both Ritalin, which before long was being prescribed for a whole host of hyperactive children, and LSD, which also found its way into 1960s counterculture (and in the 1970s was outlawed).

In spite of all these advances, the dividing line between experiment and therapy remained as wafer-thin as ever. Psychiatrists at a number of Swiss hospitals, including the pioneer of antidepressants Roland Kuhn of Thurgau, are now known to have tested unlicensed preparations without either the knowledge or the consent of their patients and free from all government oversight. Nor was it only the big university hospitals in places like Basel and Zurich that were involved in this practice; many smaller institutions such as those in Marsens and Wil were as well. Yet it quickly became clear that while the new drugs might alleviate symptoms, they could not *cure* the mentally ill; and they had distressing side-effects, too.

The boom in psychopharmacology reached its zenith in the 1990s, when "happiness pills" such as Prozac were marketed as panaceas for even the most trivial everyday worries. But with no major new breakthroughs in the offing and only unsatisfactory returns, the pharmaceutical industry decided to scale back its research in this area. A few years ago, however, a number of Swiss university hospitals began experimenting with psychedelics again, and as in the past, the hopes and expectations are high.

Critiquing the System and Fostering Openness

The societal changes that Switzerland underwent in the 1960s did not leave psychiatry unscathed. At least initially, the country's underfunded hospitals profited from the expansion of social services made possible by the boom years. Dilapidated buildings could at last be repaired and refurbished, dedicated new complexes built, working conditions improved, and, where the seriously depleted labor market allowed, additional staff hired. Perimeter walls were torn down, new departments opened, and the rigid separation of the sexes relaxed. The mainstreaming of psychotropic drugs shortened hospital stays and at the same, the number of short hospital stays for the purpose of crisis intervention increased, which led to the emergence of what has come to be called "revolving-door psychiatry."

The waves made by the student revolt of 1968 then came crashing down on psychiatry, too. No longer could hospital hierarchies, forced hospitalization, and the "immobilizing" of disruptive patients be uncritically accepted. On the contrary, the younger generation of psychiatrists came to see psychiatry as the very epitome of a repressive system in urgent need of humanizing. Grassroots groups that sympathized with the anti-psychiatry movements in other countries sprang up in many places and there were public protests, including one sparked by the death of a young man who had been hospitalized in Geneva in 1980. Meanwhile, both patients and former patients began organizing at the local level. The year 1978 saw the founding of the Pro Mente Sana organization, for example, which champions the rights of people with impaired mental health.

Yet the closure of psychiatric hospitals, which the group around psychiatrist Franco Basaglia had pioneered in Italy, for example, was never really on the agenda in Switzerland, not even in progressive cantons like the Italian-speaking Ticino. The focus was rather on institutional reforms and the further expansion of "small psychiatry," meaning the provision of local structures, outpatient clinics, walk-in services for addicts, and both day and night clinics, which together would reduce the number of inpatient admissions while still helping those in need. Elderly patients and individuals with intellectual disabilities who had hitherto been institutionalized were transferred to care homes and sheltered housing and special workshops funded by disability insurance made it easier for people to enter or re-enter the world of work and replace the work in clinics, which is often associated with constraints. As early as the 1960s, Canton Vaud placed its faith in the French model of *sectorization*—basically a variant of care close to home—while in German-speaking Switzerland it was Canton Basel-Landschaft that pioneered the decentralization of mental health services. One good example of the revolution in social psychiatry that took place in the last quarter of the twentieth century is the Soteria house in Bern, which opened in 1982 and still exists to this day. Here, according to the Soteria concept, schizophrenia patients are treated in normal apartments in the city and were given both minimal medication and psychosocial support, provided by fostering close relationships between the sick and their carers.

The turn of the millennium then saw the advent of neuropsychiatry, to hopes for the effectiveness of standardized diagnostic manuals and checklists, brain scans, and biomarkers, though none of these has led to any fundamental change in psychiatric practice. Around the same time, attention to mental health began to creep into everyday life on an unprecedented scale as one epidemiological survey after another revealed a precipitous rise in the incidence of depression, anxiety, and attention deficit disorders. Going to a therapist became perfectly normal. The stigma once attached to having mental health issues and the consumption of psychotropic drugs began to wane and would decline even more sharply when social media made baring one's soul to the world the norm. Swiss psychiatry still relies heavily on inpatient services and psychiatric clinics, most of them now privatized, and has been investing in a third generation of complexes over the past few years. The expansion of outpatient services such as treatment in the home or therapy involving psychiatric survivors (working with patients on a peer-to-peer basis), by contrast, has been thwarted by the fee structures governing it.

Bibliography:
A monographic history of Swiss psychiatry has yet to be written. The past few years have nevertheless seen the publication of several in-depth studies of historical developments in specific regions or fields. What follows is a small selection of these:

Cristina Ferreira, Ludovic Maugé, Sandrine Maulini, *L'Homme-bus: Une histoire des controverses psychiatriques (1960–1980)*, Chêne-Bourg 2020.

Silas Gusset, Loretta Seglias, Martin Lengwiler, *Versorgen, behandeln, pflegen. Geschichte der Psychiatrie in Graubünden*, Basel 2021.

Mirjam Janett, Urs Germann, Urs Hafner (eds.), *Das Problem Kind. Zur Geschichte der Kinder- und Jugendpsychiatrie in der Schweiz im 20. Jahrhundert*, Basel 2023.

Marietta Meier, Mario König, Magaly Tornay, *Testfall Münsterlingen. Klinische Versuche in der Psychiatrie 1940–1980*, Zurich 2019.

In 1900 I completed my medical studies. I left Paris in August to go to the Waldensee Sanatorium, near Berne in Switzerland. [. . .] I had, accordingly, specialized in the study of the so-called "diseases" of the will and, to be more exact, nervous troubles, obvious tics, habits common to every living human, caused by the phenomena of that congenital state of hallucination which is, in my opinion, the continuous and irradiating activity of consciousness.

Hysteria, the Great Hysteria, was then much in fashion in medical circles. Following the preliminary work of the schools of Montpellier and la Salpêtrière, which had, so to speak, done no more than define and situate the object of their studies, a number of foreign men of science, particularly the Austrian, Freud, had taken up the problem, had gone into it more amply, more profoundly, had lifted it, extracted it from its purely experimental and clinical domain to make of it a kind of pataphysics of social, religious and artistic pathology. [. . .] A kind of key to dreams for use by psychiatrists, as codified by Freud in his works on psychoanalysis, which Dr Stein was, as it happened, just putting into practice for the first time in his highly fashionable sanatorium in Waldensee. [. . .]

All those who have written on the subject are filled with prejudice. Before searching out and examining the mechanism of causes of disease, they treat of 'disease as such', condemn it as an exceptional and harmful condition, and start out by detailing the thousand and one ways of combating it, disturbing it, destroying it; they define health, for this purpose, as a 'normal' condition that is absolute and immutable.

Diseases are. We do not make or unmake them at will. [. . .] Diseases are a transitory, intermediary, future state of health. It may be that they are health itself. [. . .]

The doctors of today are not physicians: Prophylaxis! Prophylaxis! . . . they cry; and to save face they ruin the future of the species.

In the name of what law, of what morality, of what society are they allowed to rage on? They intern, sequester, isolate the most striking individuals. They mutilate our physiological geniuses, the bearers and forerunners of the health of tomorrow. Proudly they term themselves princes of science, and, suffering from persecution mania, assume the easy posture of the victim. Obscure and obscurantist, they dress their language in tatters of Greek and, rigged out thus grotesquely, insinuate themselves everywhere in the name of a rational shopkeeper's liberalism. As for their theories—hippomammary droppings. They have made themselves tools of a vulgar bourgeois virtue that was formerly the monopoly of bigots; they have put their science at the service of state police forces and organized the destruction of all that is most deeply idealistic (i.e. independent).

They castrate for crimes of passion and even take their knives to the lobes of the brain. Senile, impotent eugenists, they imagine they can extirpate all evil. Their vanity is equalled only by their rascality, and hypocrisy is the only check on their levelling rage, their hypocrisy, their concupiscence.

Just look at the alienists. They have made themselves lackeys of the rich man's crime. On the model of Sodom and Gomorrah they have set up their topsy-turvy heavens; they have built bordello-like retreats where only banknotes cause the doors to open, whose sesame is gold. There, all is arranged to maintain and encourage the rarest of vices.

There, the most refined of sciences panders to disordered and maniac minds whose sybaritism is of a complexity so frighteningly modern that the crotchets of a Ludwig II of Bavaria or a Marquis de Sade seem like pretty games. There, crime is the rule. Nothing is monstrous or contrary to nature. All that is human is alien to it. The prothesis functions in rubbery silence. Rectums of silver are inserted, and vulvae of chromed leather. The last of the egalitarian communards, the Drs Guillotin, make cynical incisions in aristocratic lower backs and loins. They have appointed themselves spiritual directors of the spinal fluid, and practise coldly the laparatomy of consciences. They make forcible use of ether, opium, morphine and cocaine, and force is there, regardless of whether it is used to restrict or push up the dosage.

All is based on a ready-reckoner established according to unshakeable statistics. They work out combinations of douches and poisons; they calculate nervous prostration against heightened sensitivity. History has never known such a secret society of spoilers and ravagers; what is told of the Inquisition and the Jesuits does not approach their virtuosity in the art of exploiting the blemishes of escutcheoned families. And these are the hands to which today's society has been confided! And these are the hands that shape our society of tomorrow!

And this is the point to which I have been coming: I wanted to draw up a terrible accusation against these psychiatrists, expose their psychology, circumscribe and define their misshapen professional conscience, destroy their power and deliver them up to public obloquy.

For my purposes I could have found no better place than the celebrated house of Waldensee.

Blaise Cendrars, "Pataphysics of Pathology," 1926

Not Simply

On the History of Child Psychiatry

Ursina Klauser

a Diminutive Adult

For a long time, psychiatry barely concerned itself with children at all. The psychiatric institutions founded all over Europe throughout the nineteenth century were geared toward adult patients and only in exceptional cases were children admitted and treated there. When in 1887, German psychiatrist Hermann Emminghaus published one of the first systematic treatises on mental illness in childhood, he described the psychiatrist as a specialist in the mental health of adults, opining that children would be unlikely to enter his "sphere of observation."

Outpatient Psychiatry and Observation Wards

It was only at the beginning of the early twentieth century that child psychiatry began to take shape and establish itself as a separate medical discipline. The presence of a sufficient number of children under a psychiatrist's charge was a necessary precondition for this, yet there were so few children in any one institution that they were barely noticeable as a distinct cohort. Besides, until the end of the nineteenth century, classical psychiatry remained firmly focused on "diseases of the mind," that is, on the most serious mental and psychological disorders.

This did not change until after the new century when various new approaches to psychiatry were proposed, the character of many psychiatric institutions changed, and new clinical pictures were defined. Psychoanalysis, which in Switzerland was enthusiastically embraced, played an important role here, with psychiatrists now addressing even relatively minor disorders and abnormalities. They diagnosed neuroses, for example, and treated nocturnal enuresis (bedwetting) by using autosuggestion to elicit the inner conflicts underlying the problem. As of 1900, for example, the Münsterlingen Psychiatric Hospital, located in the far north-eastern corner of Canton Thurgau, numbered many such cases.

Children, too, were increasingly accepted as belonging within psychiatry's ambit. The creation of more and more outpatient facilities alongside the closed institutions was a crucial factor. These lowered the barrier to access and brought both new groups of prospective patients along with a very different range of conditions to treat. Here, right from the start, it was clear that children could no longer be treated as marginal figures. When having to assess a child's criminal responsibility, foster care options, or readiness for school, for example, the authorities frequently deferred to the nearest outpatient clinic to make the decision for them. Parents, too, turned to them for advice, if their child was struggling at school, had been caught thieving, lying, or playing truant, was wetting the bed or was otherwise behaving abnormally.

Münsterlingen's outpatient records for 1920, for example, mention a worried father who in his consultation with the director explained that his thirteen-year-old son had been restless, unable to sleep, and somehow "different" since being beaten by his teacher. There is also an account of a mother whose son, despite all her admonitions, had become a notorious thief and liar; another mother sought advice for her nine-year-old daughter, who seemed disturbed and had developed mysterious tics. In another instance, it was the welfare services asking for guidance in a case involving a girl of school age whom they describe as "sadly not quite normal." The 1920s also saw psychiatrists being asked to establish whether boys facing charges of theft were of sufficiently sound mind to be held criminally responsible for their actions.

Against this backdrop of a growing intake of minors, the perception of children as a distinct category of patient became increasingly widespread among psychiatrists. Having embraced this new cohort, however, they were immediately confronted with new questions and problems. Whereas initially they had dealt only with isolated cases, the number of child referrals now rose sharply, especially those to outpatient services. Despite the lack of any exact figures for the patients seen in Münsterlingen in the early twentieth century, it is clear that children accounted for around a third of all its outpatients. By 1950, the hospital was examining about 100 children per year, a figure that in the next twenty years later was to increase by a factor of ten. The Burghölzli in Zurich began offering outpatient consultations in 1910, and within just a few years had a caseload that included 100 children.

Meanwhile, separate institutions for the long-term care of children were established. The accommodation of children and adolescents in psychiatric hospitals alongside mentally ill adults had long been regarded as a last resort, and by the early twentieth century came ever louder demands for specialized facilities. The model preferred throughout Switzerland was the so-called "observation ward," in which children might be accommodated, monitored, and in some cases treated for weeks or months at a time. The first such ward was the Stephansburg in Zurich, which opened in 1921. Although located on the same site as the psychiatric institution Burghölzli, the Stephansburg was housed in a separate building "to spare its little patients any contact whatsoever with sick adults," as its first annual report emphasized. Some thirty children were admitted in the first year alone, and soon similar wards were being created elsewhere, specifically in Schaffhausen (1925), Bern (1936), and Lausanne (1939). By the mid-twentieth century, there were more than a dozen such wards for children in Switzerland.

The Concept of Development and Child Psychiatry as a Field in its Own Right

Drawing a clear line between children and adults was crucial to the founding of child psychiatry as a discipline. A child was "not simply a diminutive adult," wrote Swiss psychiatrist Moritz Tramer in the early 1930s, echoing his German colleague August Homburger, who just a few years earlier had stressed that a child was not merely a "smaller scale adult." The mind of a child, argued Homburger, was utterly different.

Both men were following an insight first popularized in the eighteenth century. It was then that Jean-Jacques Rousseau laid the foundation for a new understanding of childhood and child-rearing in his novel *Emile; or On Education* published in 1762. The impact of Rousseau's view of children as fundamentally different from adults was at first felt most forcefully in education, though as the nineteenth century progressed, it began to have a bearing on other questions as well. Human development now became a field of intense interest as both biologists and psychologists began to treat children and adults as distinct entities, each of which merited closer scrutiny. The view of children as fundamentally different rested on the realization that a child is still developing and not yet fully formed.

Development, moreover, entails more than just physical growth. Inspired by the theory of evolution, more and more researchers began to redefine it as a process of structural change. They also believed that by studying the process of individuation, they might learn more about the evolution of humanity as a whole; hence their enthusiasm for childhood as a field of study worthy of interest. This newfound fascination with the development of the mind, and of intelligence, language, emotions, and morals, was at first fed by the researchers' observations of their own offspring, followed by that of much larger groups. The scientist Charles Darwin began making notes about his own children soon after the birth of his first son in 1839, and would draw on those observations in two of his publications from the 1870s. Having drawn inspiration from the works of others, Darwin himself inspired numerous other studies. One of these was William T. Preyer's work, *Die Seele des Kindes* of 1882 (published in English as *The Mind of the Child* in 1888), which was also based on the author's close study of his own son's early development. Preyer's observations led him to conclude that while there were certainly differences in how individual children developed, the sequence of developmental stages invariably remained the same. *Die Seele des Kindes* met with great interest and soon became a classic for the nascent field of child psychology. Among the other important specialists in this field to directly or indirectly draw on Preyer's findings were William L. Stern, Karl and Charlotte Bühler, and, somewhat later, Jean Piaget. Thus, child psychology became established as a discipline in its own right.

Homburger and Tramer were among the psychiatrists of the early twentieth century to build on these changes. Basing their work on the findings of child psychology and their own experience as practicing psychiatrists, they explicitly considered children as human beings who were still developing and stressed that any psychiatric engagement with them must bear this in mind. Development, as a criterion, was crucial not just to their treatment but also to the recognition of any psychological abnormalities and disorders that they may present. Broad studies and psychometric tests, including intelligence tests, provided a basis for comparisons and averages, thanks to which childhood development could be understood as a clear timeline of phases, according to which children might be judged "normal" or "abnormal." To be able to identify a psychological abnormality in a child, it always had to be considered against the background of its development.

Tramer was the first to cite this as a reason for elevating child psychiatry to the status of independent discipline. While others before him had concerned themselves with the psychopathologies of childhood, they had always understood these as a subdiscipline of psychiatry as a whole, or even pediatrics. Tramer, by contrast, took the view that child psychiatry should be a separate discipline with its own institutions, training programs, and professional associations. It was in part to underscore this claim that in 1934 he launched the *Zeitschrift für Kinderpsychiatrie*, the first scientific journal dedicated to child psychiatry. Published in Switzerland, it soon enjoyed recognition in other countries, too, even if not all the responses to Tramer's work were positive. In fact, the idea of child psychiatry as a distinct entity remained controversial right up to the mid-twentieth century, as many psychiatrists continued to insist that there was no need for a special "children's table."

It was not until after the Second World War that child psychiatry was at last able to establish itself on firm footing. Switzerland introduced the title Doctor of Child Psychiatry in 1953 and the first professional association was founded four years later. The International Association for Child Psychiatry came into being only after the war's end, in 1948, though the principles on which it rested had been established years earlier. The first International Child Psychiatry Congress, held in Paris in the summer of 1937, had attracted medical practitioners from more than twenty different nations, including Tramer from Switzerland. Such cross-border networks were crucial to the new field's professional standing. The same twenty-year period also saw the publication of the first dedicated textbooks. Tramer's *Lehrbuch für allgemeine Kinderpsychiatrie* of 1942, for example, was held in high esteem far beyond Switzerland and translated into both French and Spanish. Leo Kanner, a physician who had left Berlin and emigrated to the USA in 1924, published his own English language textbook *Child Psychiatry* in 1935. Both books became standard works in the field and have been reprinted multiple times.

From a rather different perspective, psychoanalysis also made a decisive contribution to the new view of the child and of childhood that took hold in the early twentieth century, not least because of the importance it attached to preverbal experience. It also provided child psychiatry with specific diagnostic and therapeutic tools that did not rely on comparisons with averages but instead sought to understand children in their own world and on their own terms.

Many of the first child psychiatrists were influenced by psychoanalysis and made use of depth psychology in their work. They had children paint and draw, tell stories, and interpret pictures, and gave them figures to play with as well as asking them about their dreams. This fact alone attests to the serious effort now being made to approach children as categorically different from adults. Some of the most important groundwork here was laid by women. Even in the early days of the twentieth century, while Sigmund Freud and C. G. Jung devoted themselves primarily to adult patients, psychoanalysts such as Anna Freud, Melanie Klein, Sabina Spielrein, and Hermine Hug-Hellmuth had understood that children, and, by extension, child psychoanalysis, had needs of its own, and had given lectures, published papers, and developed specific methods—most of them based on play—to that end. They were thus instrumental in enabling child psychiatry to get a foothold in diagnostic and therapeutic practice as a discipline of its own.

Bibliography:
Urs Hafner, *Kinder beobachten. Das Neuhaus in Bern und die Anfänge der Kinderpsychiatrie*, 1937–1985, Zurich, 2022.
Mirjam Janett, Urs Germann, and Urs Hafner (eds.), *Das Problem Kind. Zur Geschichte der Kinder- und Jugendpsychiatrie in der Schweiz im 20. Jahrhundert*, Basel 2023.
Ursina Klauser, *"Schwierige" Kinder. Ambulante kinderpsychiatrische Praxis in Münsterlingen,* 1910–1980, Dissertation University of Zurich, 2024 (in publication).

Let us now turn to the first words "papa" and "mama". It is very important to pay attention to how the baby pronounces these words. He does not at first say "mama" and "papa" but "mö-mö-mö", "pö-pö-pö": the vowel sound is thus roughly an ö and the number of syllables to begin with is unrestricted. If we carefully watch the baby's mouth as it says "mö-mö-mö" and then try to imitate its movements ourselves, we see how closely these movements are related to those of suckling. The act of suckling is present in the "mö-mö-mö" sounds. [...] It is therefore not a daring conclusion to assume that when the baby first utters "mö-mö-mö, sounds which are linked to certain movements in suckling, it also experiences the pleasurable sensations of suckling.

We do not need to imagine that there are clear images in the baby's mind: they need not be either the image of the mother or of suckling itself, they could be quite vague sensations of warmth, of softness (in contact with the mother's body), of liquid, of fullness, etc. The baby will naturally always want to repeat these sensations; so it will instinctively bring its mouth into a position which produces the sounds we have been discussing. The connection between the "mö-mö" sounds and the corresponding sensations becomes increasingly close, it becomes constant; the baby will seek to produce these sounds in order to invoke in itself a certain group of sensations which are both desired and familiar. Because certain sounds are now linked to quite specific psychic contents, to sensations, perhaps even ideas, we can already talk about words which indicate these contents, or indeed represent them.

These first words are still autistic, that is they exist only for their own sake. This first autistic stage is distinguished from the later "magical" stage to the extent that magic assumes an external world which can be influenced, whereas in this first autistic stage we do not yet need to assume an external world separate from the child. The emergence of the word "mö-mö" already in the autistic stage however throws light on the origin of magic, namely the belief in the omnipotence of words and especially of a name.

Just as we may not approach a sacred animal or a king, and just as we ourselves must avoid objects, especially food, which are used by that person, because otherwise we would die on the spot, so we may not speak his name. [...]

When in time and with further psychic development the idea of an object, the mother, becomes differentiated from the ill-defined cluster of sensations, the original connection between action = word and the now differentiated object "Ma-ma" (later mother), persists. By speaking the name it would be possible actually to evoke a certain group of sensations which will later be represented by a person. If this name is altered or damaged in any way, the psychic content connected with it (in this case = the person) is also damaged. Thus it happens that in magic the name of a person represents the person himself and whatever happens to the person's name will happen to the person himself. The separating of the word (name) from the event is a secondary process; originally it was one and the same. [...]

The word "mö-mö" reproduces suckling in its truest sense. "Pö-pö", "bö-bö" etc correspond more with the time when the satisfied infant is playing with the breast, now letting go of it, now latching on to it again. If the baby is not too hungry and is thus in a good mood, it enjoys repeating the movements that produce "pö-pö", "bö-bö" and similar sounds. But when the feeling of hunger becomes more imperious the sucking movements become more energetic and the mouth takes on the specific shape for suckling, for grasping the nipple firmly. This shape produces the "mö" sound. If the hunger becomes altogether too severe then every sensible sound stops and gives way to a reflex process, crying. Among certain mammals the noises arising from labial sounds remain their only language for their whole life. With others it is not the case. Why should that be so? [...]

The word "Mama" (in baby pronunciation "mö-mö-mö") reproduces the act of suckling. The word Papa (="pö-pö") stems from the phase when the satisfied infant is playing with the breast. Both words owe their origins to suckling. Like no other, the act of suckling is fundamental to the most important experiences of the child's life: here it gets to know the bliss of having its hunger stilled, but it learns too that this bliss has an end and has to be won all over again. The infant experiences fort the first time the fact that there is a world outside itself, its contact with the mother's body plays a part in this by offering some resistance to the movements of the infant's mouth. And finally the infant learns that there is a refuge in this external world which is desirable not only because there its hunger is satisfied, but because it is warm and soft and protected from all dangers. If we have once in our lives felt "Let this moment last for ever, it is so beautiful" it was surely at this time. Here the child learns for the first time to love, in the widest sense of the word, that is to experience contact with another person, independently of feeding, as the highest bliss.

Sabina Spielrein, "The Origin of the Child's Words Papa and Mama," 1922

and Their Shadows

Christine Lötscher
& Gesa Schneider

Heroic Epics

*C. G. Jung
in Pop Culture*

As a figure in pop culture, C. G. Jung is most likely to appear alongside his paternal friend and later antagonist Sigmund Freud. Such male pairings—Schiller and Goethe, Friedrich Dürrenmatt and Max Frisch spring to mind—inevitably beg the question of which of the two was the greater or more successful. At first glance, some might observe that Freud's theories are much more firmly established in everyday life than are Jung's. The terms "Freudian Slip," "repression," and "Oedipus Complex," for example, are very much part of everyday parlance. But anyone who engages seriously with the rivalry between Freud and Jung is bound to conclude that it is Jungian thinking that has had the more profound impact on popular culture. The way in which popular narratives, from Grimm's fairy tales to blockbusters like *Harry Potter* and the superhero multiverses of Marvel and DC, are read and interpreted is deeply influenced by Jung, as is the way we relate them to our own life stories. To put it simply, we are all heroes in a myth that has us forever growing and becoming, maturing and metamorphosing, and that myth is fueled by a collective unconscious and its timeless symbols.

Storytelling is steeped in three specific elements of Jungian depth psychology above all others: the theory of archetypes, individuation theory, and the concept of the shadow. Expressed in popular science terms, archetypes in the Jungian sense are patterns of thought and action that influence consciousness. An archetype cannot be grasped but must be experienced through the medium of symbolic images, such as those of dreams and myths. In his individuation theory, Jung illustrates how a person becomes an "ego," a "self." The concept of the shadow is an important aspect of the individual personality as well as being a factor in the collective unconscious. The shadow of a person contains whatever stands in the way of his or her own positive self-image.

The Hero's Journey from Fairy Tales to Hollywood

The tale of the hero who sets out to seek his fortune is noteworthy for its combination of all three elements. After suffering setbacks, overcoming obstacles, and recruiting helpers en route, the hero eventually returns home triumphant. That this form of narrative has become deeply embedded in globalized popular culture is in part owing to the work of Jung's assistant Marie-Louise von Franz, whose books analyzing the symbolism of fairy tales were very popular in the second half of the twentieth century.

A work that had an even greater impact on the popularization of Jung was Joseph Campbell's *The Hero with a Thousand Faces* (1949), which is a study in comparative mythology. Campbell was an US-American literary scholar who dedicated his life to the study and sharing of myths and who in pursuit of this was influenced profoundly by Jung. Campbell identified the hero's quest as an archetypal model that he called the "monomyth." Almost all narratives follow the same basic pattern, he argues, in that they basically tell the story of the hero's individuation with special prominence given to the process of becoming an adult. According to this reading, the journey undertaken by both ancient heroes such as Homer's Odysseus and modern heroes such as Frodo in J. R. Tolkein's *Lord of the Rings* or Harry in Joanne K. Rowling's *Harry Potter* series should be understood as an inner development. The figures whom the hero encounters en route are archetypes and as such symbolize the experiences through which humans mature. The mentor, for example, is a source of wisdom and support, the adversary the figure behind whom the Jungian shadow lurks, the anima the feminine facet of the self, and the self itself the protagonist, whose individuation entails combining conscious and unconscious elements to forge the mature, holistic-thinking, sentient, and sensitive individual that he or she is destined to become.

The ultimate popularization of Jung's theories of individuation and archetypes was the translation of Campbell's hero's journey into the screenplay of director George Lucas's *Star Wars*. After that Hollywood blockbuster par excellence,

Campbell's model would provide the basis for scriptwriting assignments. That pop genres such as fantasy, space opera, or romance—generally entailing the chance encounter of two complementary elements—are all inspired by Jung is only logical, given that he continued developing his romantic theory of the unconscious in his analytical psychology.

Jung expert Micha Brumlik has elaborated how Jung's concept relates to the Romantic philosophy of the self as a subject that undergoes development and self-discovery. That a lot of subtlety and complexity fell by the wayside between Friedrich Wilhelm Joseph Schelling and today's superhero films is especially apparent in the theory of archetypes, which has forfeited its original dynamism in favor of a rigid symbolism that turns archetypes into stereotypes.

Stereotypes and the "Manosphere"

The radicalism with which social media's "manosphere" continues to insist on the complementary nature of the sexes is having dramatic consequences, and in young people especially is widening the gap between the world of men and the world of women. The men who are drawn to the "manosphere" imagine themselves to be living in a society dominated by feminist values. They regard themselves as victims of a misandrist culture that they have to fight simply to defend their very existence. Ironically, the appropriation of archetypes can have the effect of not just invoking the behavioral patterns typically referred to as "toxic masculinity" but actually cementing them. The question of what masculinity is or can be in the twenty-first century still rests heavily on the life models developed by Jung, which in turn took their cues from the heroic male figures of myth. It is hardly surprising, therefore, that the Canadian psychologist Jordan Peterson has had such extraordinary success at propagating a worldview in which men are disadvantaged and have to reclaim "their" world. This worldview, which can only come at the cost of equality, has tremendous pulling power for young men seeking a direction in life.

Peterson, often billed as the "father" of the "manosphere," claims Jung as one of his principal sources of inspiration. In his lectures he celebrates Jung as a unique visionary, as a genius, and hence uses Jungian concepts for his advice to people on how to realize their full potential. He tells his mainly male audiences that men use the idea of (stereotypically) female perfection as a source of motivation and drive. He laments that many women simply do not understand this. They do not understand that men see them as the "manifestation of a judgmental ideal," and that to be able to enter into a relationship with a real woman, a man first has to sacrifice his relationship with the ideal woman. Peterson spices his explanations with comparisons from fairy tales and myth, including characters like Harry Potter and superheroes. What he is basically saying is that men go out into the world either as fairy tale princes or mythic heroes and that to realize their potential must be ready to face their fears over and over again, especially their fear of rejection by women.

Against this backdrop, Jung's ongoing popularity as a source of inspiration among feminist psychologists may seem paradoxical. One such psychologist in Switzerland is Verena Kast, whose books about finding the self, the nature of loving, and grief have attracted large audiences over the decades. As an icon of feminine interpretations of Jung, Kast approaches his work with both the seriousness of the scholar and the autonomy of a feminist. Kast has done Jung a great service by popularizing his depth psychology through readily comprehensible explanations of his theories of individuation, archetypes, and the shadow and by embedding these in specific, everyday situations.

Pop Music and Type Tests

That Jungian depth psychology can be made to speak to an audience of emancipated women on the one hand but also co-opted for an audience of conservative men on the other points to how the ubiquity of therapy narratives influences the contemporary pop culture spread by social media as does almost nothing else. These include for example breakup songs from the US pop singer Taylor

Swift's that give courage to millions of broken hearts: "I can do it with a broken heart!" as well as the K-Pop (Pop music from South Korea) boy band BTS, who celebrate Jung as the guru of self-discovery and whose albums both have titles that explicitly reference Jung: *Map of the Soul—Persona* (2019) and *Map of the Soul—7* (2020).

The enthusiasm for therapy in the world of pop music is closely interwoven with the pop psychology available on social media. TikTok, for example, has become an amalgam of entertainment and therapy, offering everything from counseling to dating advice and book tips. This supposedly feminist counseling did not come out of nowhere. It perpetuates the counseling culture that arose within the second-wave feminism in the 1960s and since then has gone mainstream, as Taylor Swift's success proves. For Gen Z (people born between 1995 and 2010), therefore, the search for a holistic concept of the self is not at all "cringe," but rather a matter of course, almost a sacred duty—at least for a certain, female-coded bubble.

While it would be absurdly simplistic to blame Jung (in true Freudian style) for this polarization of the sexes, there is in fact a direct line connecting the two running from archetypes and individuation theory to a peculiar interpretation of natural "masculinity," the evidence cited for which is to a high degree culturally specific, namely the narratives of myths and fairy tales. That the relationship between symbols, the human psyche, and sociocultural reality described by Jung is a good deal more complex is all too often disregarded with the result that esoteric thinking, in the guise of rationality, has become not just admissible but socially acceptable.

A further reduction of archetypes to stereotypes is apparent in what, even today, is still the most frequently applied test in the world of business: the Myers-Briggs Test, also known as the MBTI (Myers Briggs Type Indicator). Based on the typology of Jung's *Psychological Types* (1921), it was developed by Katharine Cook Briggs and her daughter Isabel Myers and first published in 1944.

The test (an abridged version of which can be found on the internet) sets out to ascertain the personality type of the person taking the test. The model assesses type according to four functions (thinking/feeling, sensing/intuition), each of which is refined by the attributes "introverted" or "extraverted." The test is still widespread in large corporations, which use it in pursuit of their goal of making the business as profitable as possible. Whether the typologies and categories it defines hold true has never been proven. In spite of this—or perhaps because of it—the test still plays a huge role in translating what are usually male self-assessments and self-perceptions into action. What makes the test effective, in other words, is that people believe in it.

The beauty of the Myers-Briggs test is that every type can become a self-fulfilling prophecy. As chance would have it, the two authors of this text are both ENFP according to the test (meaning extraverted, intuitive, feeling, and prospecting). Individuals with these attributes are "free spirits with an unquenchable appetite for new experiences and perspectives," blessed with a "lively imagination that enables them to see possibilities that others perhaps do not recognize," and, best of all, they are "driven by a deep-rooted desire to make the world a better place." If, therefore, this test, contrary to our better judgment, really were effective, we could indeed hope to overcome the sex binary. One could re-appropriate Jung, *and* rewrite the heroic epics entirely in the spirit of the quote: "personal growth means: greater awareness, more behavioral options, a stronger self, more permeability," which the Internet attributes to him and which now enjoys a life of its own.

Bibliography:
Micha Brumlik, *C. G. Jung zur Einführung*, Hamburg 2004.
Joseph Campbell, *The Hero With a Thousand Faces*, New York 1949.
Debbie Ging, "Bros v. Hos: 'Postfeminism, Anti-feminism and the Toxic Turn in Digital Gender Politics,'" in *Gender Hate Online: Understanding the New Anti-Feminism*, Cham 2019.
C. G. Jung, *Memories, Dreams, Reflections*, recorded and edited by Aniela Jaffé, translation by Richard and Clara Winston, New York 1989.
Verena Kast, *Die Tiefenpsychologie von C. G. Jung. Eine praktische Orientierungshilfe*, Ostfildern 2020.
Jordan Peterson, *What Women Don't Understand About Men*: https://www.youtube.com/watch?v=1aY49YU8uBQ (accessed September 10, 2024).
Jordan Peterson, *Your Potential Future Self: How To Apply Jungian Psychology To Your Life*: https://www.youtube.com/watch?v=TnT8FoX4H3I (accessed September 10, 2024).
Marie-Louise von Franz, *Psychologische Märcheninterpretation. Eine Einführung*, Küsnacht 2012.
Emma Jung, *Animus und Anima*, Zurich 1967 (current edition, Leinfelden-Echterdingen 1996).

There was once a man, Harry, called the Steppenwolf. He went on two legs, wore clothes and was a human being, but nevertheless he was in reality a wolf of the Steppes. He had learnt a good deal of all that people of a good intelligence can, and was a fairly clever fellow. What he had not learnt, however, was this: to find contentment in himself and his own life. The cause of this apparently was that at the bottom of his heart he knew all the time (or thought he knew) that he was in reality not a man, but a wolf of the Steppes. Clever men might argue the point whether he truly was a wolf, whether, that is, he had been changed, before birth perhaps, from a wolf into a human being, or had been given the soul of a wolf, though born as a human being; or whether, on the other hand, this belief that he was a wolf was no more than a fancy or a disease of his. It might, for example, be possible that in his childhood he was a little wild and disobedient and disorderly, and that those who brought him up had declared a war of extinction against the beast in him; and precisely this had given him the idea and the belief that he was in fact actually a beast with only a thin covering of the human. On this point one could speak at length and entertainingly, and indeed write a book about it. The Steppenwolf, however, would be none the better for it, since for him it was all one whether the wolf had been bewitched or beaten into him, or whether it was merely an idea of his own. What others chose to think about it or what he chose to think himself was no good to him at all. It left the wolf inside him just the same.

And so the Steppenwolf had two natures, a human and a wolfish one. This was his fate, and it may well be that it was not a very exceptional one. There must have been many men who have had a good deal of the dog or the fox, of the fish or the serpent in them without experiencing any extraordinary difficulties on that account. In such cases, the man and the fish lived on together and neither did the other any harm. The one even helped the other. Many a man indeed has carried this condition to such enviable lengths that he has owed his happiness more to the fox or the ape in him than to the man. So much for common knowledge. In the case of Harry, however, it was just the opposite. In him the man and the wolf did not go the same way together, but were in continual and deadly enmity. The one existed simply and solely to harm the other, and when there are two in one blood and in one soul who are at deadly enmity, then life fares ill. Well, to each his lot, and none is light. [. . .]

For the close of our study there is left one last fiction, a fundamental delusion to make clear. All interpretation, all psychology, all attempts to make things comprehensible, require the medium of theories, mythologies and lies; [. . .]

The division into wolf and man, flesh and spirit, by means of which Harry tries to make his destiny more comprehensible to himself is a very great simplification. It is a forcing of the truth to suit a plausible, but erroneous, explanation of that contradiction which this man discovers in himself and which appears to himself to be the source of his by no means negligible sufferings. Harry finds in himself a "human being," that is to say, a world of thoughts and feelings, of culture and tamed or sublimated nature, and besides this he finds within himself also a "wolf," that is to say, a dark world of instinct, of savagery and cruelty, of unsublimated or raw nature. In spite of this apparently clear division of his being between two spheres, hostile to one another, he has known happy moments now and then when the man and the wolf for a short while were reconciled with one another. Suppose that Harry tried to ascertain in any single moment of his life, any single act, what part the man had in it and what part the wolf, he would find himself at once in a dilemma, and his whole beautiful wolf-theory would go to pieces. For there is not a single human being [. . .] who is so conveniently simple that his being can be explained as the sum of two or three principal elements; and to explain so complex a man as Harry by the artless division into wolf and man is a hopelessly childish attempt. Harry consists of a hundred or a thousand selves, not of two. His life oscillates, as everyone's does, not merely between two poles, such as the body and the spirit, the saint and the sinner, but between thousand and thousands.

Hermann Hesse, "For Madmen Only," 1927

Art and Insanity

A Crack

*Otto Gross and
the Resistance to Psychiatry
and Psychoanalysis*

Stefan Zweifel

in the Wall

The Randlingen Asylum suddenly appeared to the constable as a giant spider that had spun a great web over the entire region, leaving the ensnared families to flail around helplessly in a futile attempt to free themselves.

Friedrich Glauser, Matto regiert, 1936

The consistent and uncompromising application of psychological methods to reconquer the life of the unconscious mind entails battling against adjustment itself, and with it the principle of authority, whether in the immediate family, in our interpersonal relations, or in our relations with the state, capital, and institutions.

Otto Gross, "Zur neuerlichen Vorarbeit: vom Unterricht," 1920

"At about 4 o'clock this afternoon, Otto Gross escaped over the wall of the A-2 garden," C. G. Jung wrote in a note dated June 17, 1908. Gross's leap over the wall of Zurich's Burghölzli psychiatric hospital was a watershed in the history of both the imagination and anti-psychiatry, in that it became emblematic of the escape of the conformist ego—the ego that only ever nods along and, like a donkey, answers everything with one loud Y-E-S, "Yes, I am paranoid. Yes, I am schizophrenic"—from the clutches of psychiatric and psychological terminology.

This leap over the wall of normality also came to symbolize the avant-garde, which at the time was spearheading the advance into the realm of unreason—even anti-reason. Simplistically psychologized, Gross embodied the omnipotence fantasy of the rebellious adolescent, who, spurred on by his boundless admiration for the "delinquent ego" of *poètes maudits* such as Arthur Rimbaud (incidentally an admiration that in this somewhat polemical text I share), rises up against the figure of the "father." Indeed, Gross himself, as a cokehead who wrote extensively about the "pan-sexualization" of society, became the very incarnation of Rimbaud's declaration: "The poet must make himself a visionary." This, according to Rimbaud, should be done by radically "deranging all the senses" and using "every conceivable form of poison" for the sake of "love, suffering, and insanity."

When Gross's father had him interned in 1913, the magazine *REVOLUTION!* ran an open letter of protest penned by Blaise Cendrars and signed by Guillaume Apollinaire and various other avant-gardists: "I was horrified to hear of Dr. Gross's clandestine detention and precipitous referral to a madhouse [...] organized by his father," Cendrars wrote. "From the bottom of my heart, I support your protest and denounce these unworthy machinations of a bigoted father (our fathers are all bigoted!), who without a moment's hesitation has wrecked the work of a mind that in France is highly prized."

In fact, Gross's discovery of psychoanalysis was itself a form of protest against his father, Hans Gross, who as the author of a *Handbuch für Untersuchungsrichter, Polizeibeamte und Gendarmen* (1893; *Handbook for investigating magistrates, police officers and gendarmes*) had called for "degenerates" to be sent to Africa. He had also put high hopes in the brain research taking place at the time, thanks to which, "it will eventually be possible, when working at the dissecting table, to objectively conclude: '*That was a homosexual.*'"

Sigmund Freud, meanwhile, regarded Gross as the only person who, if only he were "healthy enough," might make a contribution of his own to "his" psychoanalysis. As C. G. Jung's "twin brother minus *Dementia praecox*" (as Jung put it in a letter to Freud), Gross himself, however, eluded such norms of what constituted good health, for as Cendrars opined, disease may even be "health itself."

Gross thus became a figure of Dark Romanticism's "para-nomadism," that is to say, a paranoid psychotic, a psychogeographical vagabond, and as such impossible to pin down. Later, Gross refused to be either institutionally or even socially straitjacketed, and, being of an anarchic and anarchistic disposition, gladly associated himself with the Dadaists in Zurich and Friedrich Glauser in Ascona. He once shared a train compartment with Franz Kafka, to whom he chatted away about art and psychoanalysis in a way that even Kafka found "barely intelligible."

His flight was always a "conceptual flight," even if the Burghölzli under Eugen Bleuler diagnosed it as symptomatic of *Dementia praecox*, or schizophrenia, to borrow today's term. Gross, for his part, saw its potential quite differently: "The stream of ideas must have flowed in the same direction as that of normal people but was freer and lighter, so that what we had before us was not a mentally ill person, but a genius."

Sadly, Gross, unlike Cendrars, was never given the chance to write such texts himself. The fictional Gross in Cendrars's novel *Moravagine* (1926) flees to Russia under the Nihilists, a group driven by its unshakeable conviction that everything had to be blown apart—God, the emperor, the tsar, capital, monotheism, and monogamy—and was even building its own bombs to finish off the tsar. Similarly, the real Gross, shortly before his death, had planned to blow up a transformer at the Prater (amusement park) and with it most of Vienna: the madman as explosive device, an ego-bomb whose detonation will shatter everything, its splinters forming a pattern that defies categorization; whose fragmented face resembles nothing so much as a yearning for a different order, a "Waving not Drowning."

To us "normies" it remains as alien as the antics of the Dadaists did to many members of Jung's Psychological Club, who when they visited the Cabaret Voltaire were utterly bewildered by what they saw. The Dadaists performing there had at first used classical cabaret to protest against the war. And when that protest dissipated in the lukewarm applause of their Zurich spectators, they took to lambasting all of Western culture, including the enlightened thinking of Kant—and Voltaire, for that matter—whose rationality had not only not prevented a world war but, once hijacked by technophilia, had actually enabled it. Reason, moreover, might place itself at the service of all nations and ideologies; hence the large numbers of soldiers who took the writings of Goethe and Voltaire with them to the trenches.

So it was the language on which our culture rests that had to be dissolved, the Dadaists eventually realized. After all, is there not a hierarchy in every sentence we speak? On the battlefield of grammar, is it not the subject that is the commander-in-chief, dispatching verbs to order around its soldier-like objects? "Anlogo bung!" as Hugo Ball would say.

When performing his first phonetic poems at the Cabaret Voltaire in 1916, Ball became so nauseous and dizzy that he broke into a sweat and had to be carried off the stage. Fleeing the nihilistic and destructive forces of Dada, he decided to return to sense—and to God, on Monte Verità.

Monte Verità:
The Other Truth about Reason

During his stay on Ascona's "Mountain of Truth," Ball became a follower not just of God but also of psychoanalysis. Sadly, his *Exorzismus und Psychoanalyse* project would remain forever a fragment, though he did begin practicing as an analyst. His first patients were the wife and daughter of Bernhard Lang, who in 1916 became Hermann Hesse's analyst, despite Hesse's decision to discharge himself from the Sonnmatt sanatorium after a stay of just twelve hours. Hesse also had himself analyzed by Johannes Nohl at the foot of Monte Verità, and during further analysis sessions with Lang kept a very long and detailed dream diary. He embarked on yet another course of analysis, this time with Jung himself, in 1921, though by 1925–26 he was back with Lang, ardently averring that "no one understands the dark and wild side of the soul as you do!"

While psychoanalysis might liberate an artist from a creative block, it could not turn any random person into an artist, as Hesse wrote in his article "Künstler und Psychoanalyse" as early as 1918: "He who had not been a poet before, who had not felt the inner structure and pulse of psychic life, could not be turned into an interpreter of souls by any amount of analysis." Writing to Jung sixteen years later, however, Hesse seemed more anxious to underscore the dangers of psychoanalysis for artists, since "those who take it seriously might easily have to refrain from all artistic activity for the rest of their lives. That is fine if the person is just a dilettante, but in the case of a Handel or a Bach, I feel we could do without psychoanalysis if we got a Bach in return."

This ambivalence was similarly apparent to another visitor to Monte Verità, Friedrich Glauser, whose "word salads" at the Cabaret Voltaire prompted Emmy Hennings to hail him as a "young Rimbaud." Glauser was once again on the run from the police and psychiatry when he visited Hennings and Ball in Ticino, and in the course of his life would see the inside of seventeen psychiatric hospitals all told. At least his few weeks of analysis with Max Müller in Münsingen had opened his eyes to the infantile roots of his cocaine and morphine addiction: "The analysis had only just begun when an assertion sprang to mind that I just had to say out loud, even while laughing at its stupidity: 'I am the mother.' The whole of my analysis thereafter turned on that one sentence. My mother died when I was four years old. I lived alone with my father and played the role of the absent mother... Taking narcotics was a welcome method of creating ever new conflicts in which I played the part of the suffering female. Society later took on the role of the father, at least in my inner life."

As in the case of Gross, drug addiction is interpreted as a provocation on the part of the father and a repressive society. Ultimately, addiction would triumph, both for Glauser and for Gross. The former soon stopped allowing analysts to peer into soul, and with his wry sense of humor resolved that "Any analysts wishing to venture into the depths of my psyche in their search for gold must expect to have to put on diving suits with heavy lead soles, and then, duly protected and armored, to have to dive down to fifty meters below the level of consciousness. Instead of gold, though, which probably *is* there," he continued, "they will have to content themselves with squid, and squid, of course, spit like a true castration complex, since they prefer to remain in the dark."

At the Waldau:
Art Brut and Anti-Art

Glauser found "the atmosphere in Waldau significantly more amenable than that in Münsingen." At the Waldau, they promoted the healing power of creativity, and in 1915, Walter Morgenthaler had even declared the works of one of the inpatients there to be art. The works in question were those of Adolf Wölfli, and included both his autobiographical writings describing his own inner universe—which stacked up formed a pile over two meters high even then—and his innumerable drawings, which before long had spilled over onto his closet, and from there onto the walls and even the ceiling of his cell, with the result that Wölfli eventually lived literally inside his own art.

Wölfli was a great mental traveler who described what he saw and experienced on his imaginary journeys all over the world in cascades of wordplay inspired by just a few back numbers of the magazine *Ueber Land und Meer* and his own psychogeographic visions: "And now: And now: Weer about to stage our jurney forever in hot pursioot with an inkwiring mind, a 3-fold team of 4 drawing us from west to east across the southerly half of the sky, thru most respectable and most elegant villidges, markets, hamlets large and small, and yes, thru great and mighty cities, elegant and majestic cultures, flora-a and vegetaytion, but also across vast moors, steppes, swamps, marshes, prairies and jungles [. . .] all the way to the God-Father-Sky-Star-Giant Glacier."

Another future pioneer of psychoanalysis to be infected by the power of this creativity was Lou Andreas-Salomé who through her friendship—actually her love affair—with Nietzsche had already developed a Dionysian ear for madness. On September 22, 1922, after reading Morgenthaler's study, she sent it forthwith, along with a picture of Wölfli, to her lover, the poet Rainer Maria Rilke. Her accompanying letter would lay the groundwork for her friendship with Freud and her career as a pioneer of Freudian psychoanalysis: "I read and read and am still reading the book by Wölfli in the Waldau. You see: to interact with such people, to learn how to view and understand them—how I long for this! Psychoanalysis, you know, must treat only those it regards as curable and thus as neurotics, and the only asylums it considers appropriate are Waldau and Zurich's Burghölzli (from which psychoanalysis once learned many things, back when Bleuler was still involved in it) [. . .] What must have seized you most forcefully, I imagine, is the fact that the core compulsions of the creative artist clearly reappear in the schizophrenic—that in both of them, active and passive, seeing and shaping are incomprehensibly the same . . . This is the incredibly moving, gripping thing about the psychotic: that, though incurable himself, he does impart something to us that goes even beyond us (if only we make the attempt, which has been under way for about a decade now, to understand him in his dialect.)"

Morgenthaler had undoubtedly taken a first step towards understanding this "dialect." And even if today, the worldwide triumph of "Art brut" that then ensued might also be viewed critically as "appropriation," how else can delusion be understood, if not by first bringing it back into the fold of reason?

The Spider of Reason

It was during a stay in the psychiatric hospital in Münsingen that the French philosopher Michel Foucault translated the existentialist essays of Ludwig Binswanger and Roland Kuhn. He also took part in Fasnacht and the hospital's "Fools' Festival" of 1954, whose parade of "lunatics" featured "wicked Mrs. Geigy" and "Dame Largactil," among others. The the paradox of letting "fools" out of the asylum so that they could play the part of "fools" was certainly not lost on him.

Throughout this life, Foucault would study the sanity in insanity as the repressed truth of pure reason, a realm that either banishes "lunatics" altogether—as cities did once with the Ship of Fools—or overpowers them and keeps them locked up, as did the lunatic asylums that came later, many of which were built as panopticons to permit constant monitoring by the eye of reason.

Foucault was in the vanguard of the antipsychiatry movement that in the 1970s campaigned to have patients liberated from the institutions housing them. His aim was to prove that psychiatric hospitals could neither critique nor conceptualize the delusions of the mentally ill without at the same time destroying their very essence, which might also be said of great works of art. Great "madmen" of the stature of Freud's most famous cases—the Rat Man or President Schreber, for example—wove such a dense web of associations that not even Freud himself could ever wholly untangle them. Similarly, the works of great authors can never be adequately deciphered as mere "symptoms."

After all, the "spinners" of such yarns are engaged in a battle against the web of reason. Their works can never be wholly explained and are more like the webs that spiders are known to spin after consuming psychoactive substances: bizarre webs full of holes and irregularities. What matters is that they elude the great spider of the hospital, which according to Glauser had the whole country, the whole of bourgeois, common-sensical Switzerland, in its grip. The only treatment they should receive was that demanded by Annemarie von Matt, who is quoted in the foreword as one of those women whose rebellion against their fathers seems rather less adamant. The patients, she said, should simply be set free and left to roam the Swiss countryside—and burrow holes in it.

In Praise of Idiocy

The revolt and raging of the insane, their shaking of the bars of reason whose grids compartmentalize the world, was an attempt to get cognition and emotion flowing again in order to flush out the foundations of all those walls that prevent us immersing ourselves in what is real, our sensory impressions of which can be overwhelming. Describing the courage of poets in 1800, the German poet Friedrich Hölderlin wrote that they went through life completely bare, by which he meant naked, unprotected, helplessly exposed to impressions of all kinds, and responded to these in their own, idiosyncratic idiom. (The Greek word for "own" is *idios*, which is why, in a certain sense, the great poets might indeed be called idiots.)

Take the paranoid Rousseau on his Ile St. Pierre or Hölderlin in his tower in Tübingen, who in the end could do no more than stammer "*oui, oui*"—yes, yes—while bending over the flowers in his garden. Far from being the sound of a donkey braying in unison with healthy common sense, however, his affirmation was actually more like a "*oui-ja*," a word that fled German to join the language of "the other," which is what the French stands for here. The flower is wholly there in this babbling. Yes, yes, is a pure affirmation of the present. It is as open as the mouth when it forms the French word *oui*, as open to the impression made by the flower as Novalis was to his own little blue flower, and with it the Romantic view of the world, a world absorbed entirely by the *ich* so that the *ich* becomes one with the world, eluding the constraints of reason to become pure perception.

It was from just such figures, figures as steeped in Dark Romanticism as is this essay, that Félix Guattari and Gilles Deleuze took their cues for their *Capitalism and Schizophrenia*. Published in the 1970s at a time when the asylums really were opening their doors, the work sets out to wrest itself free from the Oedipal triangle of father-mother-child and the dead weight of Freudian terminology. It seeks rather to dance its way to freedom, much as had Vaslav Nijinsky—until he, too, after a short visit to the Burghölzli in 1919, was so overpowered by psychiatry, so weighed down by the gravity of reason, that he grew fat and hence too heavy to o'erleap the wall of the Bellevue Sanatorium and Ludwig Binswanger's consulting room, which Heidi Bucher kindly transformed into a kind of padded cell.

And so they all dreamed—the Nietzschean philosophers and the artists and authors whose works are scattered among our museums—dreamed of cracking open the walls of the museum, too, and of new people who might drift freely, roam freely, unbound by anything, and ready to reinvent themselves in an instant, like a wheel turning on its own axis that with each new revolution surpasses itself once again. The dynamic of excess and ecstasy that no pharmaceuticals can tame—this "schizoid" art—exposes the limits of psychiatry and psychology and with them the fault line in our perception, indeed a fault line in the whole world, engendering in us the desire to get out into the open, into the Great Other.

Bibliography:
Blaise Cendrars, *Moravagine*, translation by Alan Brown, New York 2004.
Friedrich Glauser, *"Jeder sucht sein Paradies…" —Briefe, Berichte Gespräche*, edited by Christa Baumberger, Zurich 2022.
Emanuel Hurwitz, *Otto Gross—Paradies-Sucher zwischen Freud und Jung*, Zurich: Suhrkamp, 1979.
Walter Morgenthaler, *Madness and Art. The Life and Works of Adolf Wölfli*, translation and introduction by Aaron H. Esman, Lincoln 1992.
J.J. Rousseau, *Reveries of the Solitary Walker*, a new translation by Russell Goulbourne, Oxford 2011.

Nietzsche lost his head because he thought. I do not think and therefore will not lose my head.

I know everyone will say that Nijinsky has gone mad, but I don't care, for I have already behaved as if I were a madman at home. Everyone will think this, but I will not be put in a lunatic asylum, because I dance very well and give money to anyone who asks me. People like eccentrics, and they will therefore leave me alone, saying that I am a mad clown. I like lunatics because I know how to talk to them. [. . .]

I did not like reading the New Testament, because I could not understand it. The book was lovely and the print beautiful. I did not feel the New Testament. I read Dostoevsky. Dostoevsky was easier for me to understand, and therefore I swallowed him whole as I read him. I swallowed him in great chunks because when I read "The Idiot," I felt that the Idiot was not an "idiot" but a good man. I could not understand "The Idiot," because I was still too young. I did not know life. I now understand Dostoevsky's "Idiot" because people take me for an idiot. I like feeling and therefore pretended to be an idiot. I was not an idiot, because I am not nervous. I know that nervous people are subject to madness, and therefore I was afraid of madness. I am not mad, and Dostoevsky's Idiot is not an idiot. [. . .]

St. Moritz, Suvretta House:
I was nervous because God wanted to arouse the audience. The audience came to be amused. They thought that I was dancing to amuse them. I danced frightening things.

They were frightened of me and therefore thought that I wanted to kill them. I did not want to kill anyone. I loved everyone, but no one loved me, and therefore I became nervous.

I was nervous and therefore transmitted this feeling to the audience. The audience did not like me, because they wanted to leave. Then I began to play cheerful things. The audience cheered up. They thought that I was a boring artist, but I showed that I could play cheerful things.

The audience started laughing. I started laughing. I laughed in my dance. The audience too laughed in the dance. The audience understood my dances, for they wanted to dance too.

I danced badly because I kept falling on the floor when did not have to. The audience did not care, because I danced beautifully. They understood my tricks and enjoyed themselves. I wanted to dance more, but God said to me,

"Enough." I stopped. The audience dispersed. The aristocrats and the rich people begged me to dance again. I said I was tired. They did not understand me, because they insisted. I said that the movements of one aristocratic lady were excited. She thought I meant to offend her. I then told her that she had a feeling for movement. She thanked me for the compliment. I gave her my hand, and she felt that I was right. I like her, but I feel that she came in order to be introduced to me. She likes young men. I do not like this life, and therefore I asked her to leave me, and made her feel it. She felt it and therefore did not give me the opportunity to continue the conversation. I wanted to speak to her, but she felt the opposite. I showed her the blood on my foot. She does not like blood. I gave her to understand that blood was war and that I did not like war. I asked her a question about life by showing her a prostitute's dance. She felt it, but did not leave, because she knew I was playacting. The others thought I would lie down on the floor and make love. I did not want to complicate the evening and therefore got up whenever it was necessary. I felt God throughout the evening. He loved me. I loved Him. Our marriage was solemnized. [...]

My wife wants me to go to Zurich to see a specialist for nerves, in order to have my nervous system examined. I promised her 100,000 francs if she is right about my nerves being in a bad way. I will give it to her if the doctor says that I have bad nerves. If she loses I will not pay her. I have not got this money now, but I have promised it to her. I will play on the Exchange, but for that reason I will have to stay several weeks in Zurich. I will go there within the next few days. I have no money and hope my wife will give me some. I will go with her. She will take me with her own money. I have a little in the bank, about 200 frs. I will play with them. I want to lose my last money that they may give me some more. God will help me to win and I am not afraid. He wants me to break the Stock Exchange.

Vaslav Nijinsky, "The Clown of God," 1919

Appendix

SHORT BIOGRAPHIES

ALAIN DE BOTTON is an Anglo-Swiss writer, philosopher, and broadcaster. He has written numerous novels and essays on philosophy, aesthetics, and architecture. His most recent publication is *A Therapeutic Journey*. He founded a new school in London called the School of Life in 2008.

THOMAS FISCHER holds a doctorate in history and works as an editor for the Zurich-based Foundation of the Works of C. G. Jung. He was project manager and co-editor of *The Art of C. G. Jung* (2019) and *Emma Jung—Dedicated to the Soul* (2025). He is a great-grandson of Emma and Carl Jung.

URS GERMANN is a historian and research associate at the Institut für Medizingeschichte at the University of Bern. He has been studying the history of psychiatry for many years and has written several books and articles on the subject.

ITA GROSZ-GANZONI of Winterthur, Switzerland, is a psychoanalyst and has been an active member of the *Psychoanalytical Seminar Zurich* (PSZ) since 1971. Besides being a practicing psychotherapist, she was on the board of further education of the PSZ for many years and is also active as a supervisor and lecturer.

MICHAEL JAKOB is Professor of Comparative Literature at the University of Grenoble. He also teaches Theory and History of Landscape at the Accademia di Architettura di Mendrisio and at Harvard Graduate School of Design. He is a curator of international exhibitions and the director of documentary films.

VERENA KAST is a psychologist and psychotherapist trained in Jungian psychoanalysis. She was a professor in the field of anthropological psychology at the University of Zurich and a training analyst and supervisor at the C. G. Jung-Institute Zürich, Küsnacht. Kast is also a prolific author with a particular interest in the handling of emotions, the imagination, and dreams in therapeutic processes.

URSINA KLAUSER is a historian. From 2016 to 2019 she was a member of the research group that investigated the drug trials conducted at Münsterlingen Psychiatric Hospital, and in 2023 she was awarded a doctorate by the University of Zurich for her dissertation on the history of outpatient child psychiatry. She has been working as a research archivist at the Thurgau State Archives since autumn 2022 and at the same time is involved in various educational and research projects.

ELIZABETH LEUENBERGER-KAJS a Swiss-American who has lived in Zurich since 2000, has her own practice as a depth psychologist and Jungian psychoanalyst in Erlenbach, Canton Zurich. As a trained photographer, she has always been interested in images. Her interest in images and the production of images by the unconscious is also proving to be of great service to her as curator of the image archive of the C. G. Jung-Institut Zürich, Küsnacht, a position she has held since 2023.

CHRISTINE LÖTSCHER is Professor of Popular Literatures and Media at the University of Zurich and a literary critic. Her field of research includes popular genres such as fantasy, science fiction, crime, and horror, as well as coming-of-age narratives in the Anthropocene. She is also interested in treatments of sex and gender in romantic novels and on social media.

LOTHAR MÜLLER is a journalist, literary and cultural critic who lives in Berlin. He wrote for the arts and culture pages of the *Süddeutschen Zeitung* until 2020 and is an honorary professor of the Humboldt-Universität zu Berlin. His most recent works are *Freuds Dinge. Der Diwan, die Apollokerzen und die Seele im technischen Zeitalter* (2019), *Spinnen. Ein Porträt* (2024), and *Die Feuerschrift. Giacomo Casanova und das Ende des alten Europa* (2025).

PETER SCHNEIDER is a Zurich-based psychoanalyst, author, columnist, and lecturer in clinical psychology. He is also a co-editor, alongside Dana Mahr and Alexandra Papadopoulos, of the EPF Essays series. He was previously Professor of Developmental Psychology in Bremen and visiting Professor of History and Epistemology of Psychoanalysis in Berlin.

GESA SCHNEIDER has been director of the Museum zu Allerheiligen in Schaffhausen since July 2024. Holding a doctorate in Literary Studies, she ran the Literaturhaus Zürich from 2013 to 2023 and was co-director of the Museum Strauhof from 2015 to 2018. She is active in various organizations and foundations and as a moderator of literary events both in Switzerland and abroad.

MURRAY STEIN holds a doctorate in religion and psychological studies from the University of Chicago and a diploma in Analytical Psychology from the C. G. Jung-Institut Zürich. Since 2004, he has been on the Faculty of the International School of Analytical Psychology Zurich (ISAP-ZURICH). The author of Jung's *Map of the Soul* (1998) and many other books and articles, he is currently working on assembling his collected writings. From 2001 to 2004 he was President of the International Association for Analytical Psychology (IAAP).

STEFAN ZWEIFEL is a freelance author, translator, and curator. He holds a doctorate in philosophy from the University of Zurich and has translated the works of Marquis de Sade, Jean-Jacques Rousseau, Marcel Proust, and many other authors into German. He is head of the Eventi letterati Monte Verità. Together with Juri Steiner he has curated three exhibitions at the Swiss National Museum: *Dada Universal* (2016), *Imagine 68* (2018), and *The Exhausted Man* (2020). He lives in Zurich with his two children.

ITEMS ON LOAN FROM

Aargauer Kunsthaus Aarau
Marco Witzig, Adliswil
Dätwyler Stiftung, Altdorf
Staatsarchiv Uri, Altdorf
Fondazione Eranos, Ascona
Fondation Beyeler, Riehen/Basel
Historisches Museum Basel
Novartis Archives Basel
Pharmaziemuseum der Universität Basel
Archiv Hermann Rorschach, Archiv für Medizingeschichte der Universität Bern
Nachlass Eberhard W. Kornfeld, Bern
Adolf Wölfli Stiftung, Kunstmuseum Bern, Bern
Pharmazeutisches Kontrolllabor, Bern
Robert Walser-Stiftung Bern
Schweizerische Nationalbibliothek: Schweizerisches Literaturarchiv, Bern
Psychiatrie-Museum Bern
Anna Koellreuter, Biel
Bündner Kunstmuseum Chur
Collection Daniel & Natalia Hug, Cologne Germany
Kirchner Museum Davos
Rudolf Steiner Archiv, Dornach
Freies Deutsches Hochstift/Frankfurter Goethe-Museum
Staatsarchiv des Kantons Thurgau (StATG), Frauenfeld
Centre Jean Piaget, Université de Genève
Bibliothèque de Genève
John Neumeier Stiftung, Hamburg
Ursula Hauser Collection, Switzerland
Familienarchiv Jung, Küsnacht
C.G. Jung-Institut, Zürich/Küsnacht, Bildarchiv
Collection de l'Art Brut, Lausanne
Kunstmuseum Luzern
PZM Psychiatriezentrum Münsingen AG
Bibliothèque publique et universitaire de Neuchâtel
Kanton Schaffhausen, Staatsarchiv Schaffhausen
Stiftung Nietzsche Haus in Sils Maria
Kantonsbibliothek Nidwalden, Nachlass Annemarie von Matt
Nidwaldner Museum, Stans
Albertina, Wien
Österreichische Nationalbibliothek, Wien
Studio und Archiv Paul Parin und Goldy Parin-Matthèy, Wien
Emma Kunz Stiftung, Würenlos
Abteilung Entwicklungspädiatrie, Universitäts-Kinderspital Zürich
C.G. Jung-Arbeitsarchiv, ETH-Bibliothek, Zürich
Fischli Weiss Archive, Zürich
Freud-Institut Zürich
Graphische Sammlung ETH Zürich
Kunsthaus Zürich
Sammlung Maja Hoffmann/ LUMA Foundation, Zürich
Universität Zürich, Institut für Evolutionäre Medizin (IEM)
Basler Psi-Verein
Stiftung der Werke von C.G. Jung, Zürich
Stiftung Pestalozzianum, Zürich
Susanne Seiler, Zürich
The Estate of Heidi Bucher, Zürich
Zentralbibliothek Zürich
Museum für Gestaltung Zürich/ Grafiksammlung und Kunstgewerbesammlung/Zürcher Hochschule der Künste

IMAGE CREDITS

IN PICTURES I

15 Henry Fuseli, *The Nightmare*, 1790–1791, oil on canvas, 76.5 × 63.6 cm. Freies Deutsches Hochstift / Frankfurt Goethe Museum, IV–1953–033, Photo: David Hall

16 Adolf Wölfli, *Zungsang = Skt. Adolf = Roosali*, 1917, From: *Hefte mit Liedern und Tänzen*, booklet 15, p. 383, pencil and collage on newsprint, 99 × 69/70 cm, A 9294 – 54(XV/p. 383). © Adolf-Wölfli-Stiftung, Kunstmuseum Bern

17 Annemarie von Matt, *Helvetisches Verkehrs-NETZ in Rosarot*, 1956, pencil and coloured pencil on paper, collaged, bound into a booklet, 17.5 × 10.5 cm. Reproduction of the works and reproduction of the texts by Annemarie von Matt with the kind permission of the Bildhauer Hans von Matt-Stiftung, Stans

18 Caspar Wolf, *Thunderstorm and Lightning over the Lower Grindelwald Glacier*, 1774–1775, oil on canvas, 54 × 82 cm. Aargauer Kunsthaus Aarau, 242, Photo: Brigitt Lattmann

20 Henry Fuseli, *The Silence*, c. 1795–1799, oil on canvas, 63.5 × 51.5 cm. Kunsthaus Zürich, 1976

20 Friedrich Nietzsche, *Composition*, 1889, 21 × 16,5 cm. Stiftung Nietzsche Haus, Sammlung Rosenthal

21 J.J. Rousseau, *Les Confessions, Premier Manuscrit*, 1769–1771, 25 × 20 cm. Bibliothèque publique et universitaire de Neuchâtel, Ms. R 17

22 Thomas Hirschhorn, *Nietzsche-Map*, 2003, cardboard, paper, plastic film, print, marker, biros, 412 × 240 cm. LUMA Stiftung, Photo: Stefan Altenburger Photography © 2024, ProLitteris, Zurich

24 Guy Debord, *The Naked City. Guide psychogéographique de Paris*, May 1957, plan printed in Copenhagen, 33 × 48 cm. Bündner Kunstmuseum Chur, acquisition 2016, inv. no. 12582.000.2016 © Guy Debord Estate

25 Alphonse G., *New electro-mechanical, rotating machine for steering a submarine*, 1886/1887, ink on paper, 23 × 26 cm. Psychiatrie-Museum Bern

25 Henry Fuseli, *Satirical self-caricature of Fuseli entering Switzerland after his stay in Italy*, 1778, pen and brown ink on paper, 24.1 × 19.3 cm. Kunsthaus Zürich, Grafische Sammlung, gift from Paul Ganz, 1938

26 C. G. Jung, *Female Half-Figure*, c. 1920, wood, carved, painted, 12.8 × 7.5 × 5.5 cm. © 2007 Stiftung der Werke von C. G. Jung, Zurich, Photo: Alex Wydler

27 C. G. Jung, *Spherical Vision III*, 1919, gouache on paper, 21.5 × 28 cm. © 2007 Stiftung der Werke von C. G. Jung, Zurich, Photo: Alex Wydler

29 Heidi Bucher, *The Parlour Office of Doctor Binswanger, Bellevue Sanatorium*, Kreuzlingen, 1988, gauze, fish glue and latex, 360 × 525 × 525 cm. The Estate of Heidi Bucher, cortesy the Estate of Heidi Bucher and Lehmann Maupin, New York, Hong Kong, Seoul and London

IN PICTURES II

60 Masturbation bandage, nineteenth century. Medizinische Sammlung Universität Zürich – Institut für Evolutionäre Medizin (IEM), MHSZ 14230

60 Louise Bourgeois, *Fillette (Sweeter Version)*, 1968, cast, latex over plaster, 59.6 × 26.6 × 19.5 cm. Ursula Hauser Collection, Switzerland © The Easton Foundation / 2024, ProLitteris, Zurich

61 Marlene Dumas, *Nuclear Family*, 2013, oil on canvas, 200 × 180 cm. Fondation Beyeler, Riehen / Basel, Photo: Robert Bayer

62 Cornelis Huijberts, *Sezierter und mehrfach quergeschnittener menschlicher Penis*, before 1744, copper engraving, vellum, 27.3 × 21.4 cm. Graphische Sammlung ETH Zürich

63 Kerim Seiler, *Holotypes (LA)*, 2007, Clip frames, ink, paper, 214.6 × 316.2 cm. Collection Daniel & Natalia Hug, Cologne Germany © 2025, ProLitteris, Zurich

63 Goldy Parin-Matthèy among the Dogon photographed by Paul Parin, third trip, Mali, 1959–1960. Studio und Archiv Paul Parin & Goldy Parin-Matthèy

64 + 65 Evaluation of the Rorschach Test by Goldy Parin-Matthèy of Elisa Ajé from the Dogon, Mali, 1966. Studio und Archiv Paul Parin & Goldy Parin-Matthèy

66 Evaluation by Hermann Rorschach of Eugen Bleuler's Rorschach Test, c. 1920. Archiv des Instituts für Medizingeschichte der Uni Bern, Archiv Hermann Rorschach, Rorsch HR 3:3:5:6_05

67 Preliminary drawing of the second Rorschach plate, Hermann Rorschach, 1917–1918. Archiv des Instituts für Medizingeschichte der Uni Bern, Archiv Hermann Rorschach, Rorsch HR 3:3:1:2, [3] IIr

68 C. G. Jung sitting in his study photographed by Yousuf Karsh, 1958. Courtesy of the Stiftung C. G. Jung, Küsnacht, Photo: Yousuf Karsh, Ottawa

68 Max Pollak, *Portrait of Sigmund Freud at his desk*, 1914, soft-ground etching and dry point, 86 × 73 × 1.5 cm. © Freud Museum London

68 Sigmund Freud's model of the soul, in: *Neue Folge der Vorlesungen zur Einführung in die Psychoanalyse*, Sigmund Freud, Vienna, 1933. Internet Archive 2025

69 Letter from C. G. Jung to Sigmund Freud, January 6, 1913. ETH Bibliothek Zürich, Hs 1056:31092

70 Robert Fludd, *Tomus secundus, in tractatus tres distributa*, 1619–1621. Wellcome Collection, London

71 Fischli / Weiss, *Jacques Lacan at the Age of Two Recognizes His Image in the Mirror for the First Time*, from the series *Suddenly This Overview*, 1981–2012. Courtesy Fischli Weiss Estate © 2025, ProLitteris, Zurich

71 Sophie Taeuber-Arp, *Dr. Komplex (Le Dr. Oedipus Complex, savant contemporain, qui dira le prologue C. G. Jung)*, 1918, puppet, wood, turned, painted, 38 × 19 × 19 cm. Museum für Gestaltung Zürich, Kunstgewerbesammlung, ZHdK, Photo: Umberto Romito & Ivan Šuta

71 Sophie Taeuber-Arp, *Freudanalytikus, Freudanalise, mage Freudanalise*, 1918, Marionette, Holz, gedrechselt, 61 × 17 × 17 cm. Museum für Gestaltung Zürich, Kunstgewerbesammlung, ZHdK, Photo: Umberto Romito & Ivan Šuta

72 Letter from C. G. Jung to Sabina Spielrein with diagram, 20.12.1917, p. 4. ETH Bibliothek Zürich, Hs 1056:30679

73 *Destruction as the Cause of Becoming*, Sabina Spielrein, 1911, offprint. © 2007 Stiftung der Werke von C. G. Jung, Zurich, Photo: Susanne Eggenberger-Jung

73 Sabina Spielrein at the Jean-Jacques Rousseau Institute, Geneva, 1921. Archives Institut J. J. Rousseau, Université de Genève

IN PICTURES III

96–99 C. G. Jung, *The Red Book – Liber Novus*, 1913–1930, paper, ink, gold, leather. © 2007 Stiftung der Werke von C. G. Jung, Zurich, Photo: Fabian Feigenblatt

100 Patient image 016.APAJ from the C. G. Jung Collection, 1929, Bildarchiv, C. G. Jung-Institut Zürich © C. G. Jung Institut Zürich, Küsnacht

100 Patient image 039.BMAX from the C. G. Jung Collection, 1928, Bildarchiv, C. G. Jung Institut Zürich. © C. G. Jung Institut Zürich, Küsnacht.

101 Olga Fröbe-Kapteyn, *Untitled (Visions – Final Series – #5)*, 1937, chalk pastel, pencil on paper, 42 × 29.5 cm. Eranos Foundation, Ascona (Switzerland). All rights reserved

102 Patient image 002.ABHG from the C. G. Jung Collection, Bildarchiv, C. G. Jung-Institut Zürich © C. G. Jung Institut Zürich, Küsnacht

102 Patient image 002.ABAB from the C. G. Jung Collection, Bildarchiv, C. G. Jung-Institut Zürich © C. G. Jung Institut Zürich, Küsnacht

103 Patient image 009.AIBH from the C. G. Jung Collection, 1929, Bildarchiv, C. G. Jung-Institut Zürich © C. G. Jung Institut Zürich, Küsnacht

103 Patient image 021.AUAC from the C. G. Jung Collection, Bildarchiv, C. G. Jung-Institut Zürich © C. G. Jung Institut Zürich, Küsnacht

103 Patient image 006.AFAI from the C. G. Jung Collection, Bildarchiv, C. G. Jung-Institut Zürich © C. G. Jung Institut Zürich, Küsnacht

104 Hélène Smith, drawing of a transmission, c. 1908, 18.6 × 11.3 cm. Bibliothèque de Genève, Ms. fr. 7843/3

105 Patient image 009.AIAK from the C. G. Jung Collection, 22.5.1917, Bildarchiv, C. G. Jung-Institut Zürich © C. G. Jung Institut Zürich, Küsnacht

105 Patient image 009.AIAL from the C. G. Jung Collection, 22.5.1917, Bildarchiv, C. G. Jung-Institut Zürich © C. G. Jung Institut Zürich, Küsnacht

105 Patient image 009.AIAR from the C. G. Jung Collection, 22.5.1917, Bildarchiv, C. G. Jung-Institut Zürich © C. G. Jung Institut Zürich, Küsnacht

105 Patient image 009.AIAS from the C. G. Jung Collection, 22.5.1917, Bildarchiv, C. G. Jung-Institut Zürich © C. G. Jung Institut Zürich, Küsnacht

106 Soul model by C. G. Jung from: *Analytical Psychology: Notes of the Seminar Given in* 1925, p. 129. Design realisation by Martina Brassel

107 C. G. Jung photographed by Henri Cartier-Bresson, c. 1959. Courtesy of the Stiftung C. G. Jung, Küsnacht © Fondation Henri Cartier-Bresson

107 Emma Jung photographed by Camille Ruf, Zurich, 1905. © Familienarchiv Jung Küsnacht, Photo: C. Ruf Zurich

107 Manuscript *Red Book* with original ribbon, C. G. Jung, c. 1930. © 2007 Stiftung der Werke von C. G. Jung, Zurich, Photo: Fabian Feigenblatt

108 Letter from Emma Jung to Sigmund Freud, Küsnacht, 1912, first page. © 2007 Stiftung der Werke von C. G. Jung, Zurich

108 Synthesis of Emma Jung's cosmology in a picture painted by her, c. 1919. © 2007 Stiftung der Werke von C. G. Jung, Zurich

109 Third International Psychoanalytical Congress photographed by Franz Vältl, Weimar, 1911. Courtesy of the Familienarchiv Jung Küsnacht, Photo: Franz Vältl, Grand Duke of Saxony's court photographer

110 Manuscript *Symbols of Transformation*, Part 2, C. G. Jung, c. 1912, p. 15. ETH Bibliothek Zürich, Hs 1055:15

IN PICTURES IV

153 Meret Oppenheim, *La fin embarassée (End and Confusion)*, 1971, oil on canvas, 110 × 84 cm. Bündner Kunstmuseum Chur, Deposit Susanne and Peter Gartmann Collection, 2024 © ProLitteris, Zurich, Inv. No. 13462.000.2024

154 Phrenological study bust after Carl Huter's psychophysiognomics, early twentieth century. Medizinische Sammlung Universität Zürich – Institut für Evolutionäre Medizin (IEM), MHSZ 13021

154 Physical treatment methods according to E. Horn (1818), models by Dr Walter Morgenthaler for the Swiss National Exhibition, Bern, 1914. Psychiatrie-Museum Bern

155 Anonymous (Lavater circle of artists), *Two Ears: One Fine, One Phlegmatic*, 1797, pencil drawing, 29.6 × 20.5 cm. Österreichische Nationalbibliothek, LAV 314, 3999

156 Gabriele Schaefer, age 12, *Die Farbenmosaikspinne*, 1934, 29.7 × 21 cm. Stiftung Pestalozzianum, Zurich

156 Louis Jeanmaire, age 12, *Hexenspinne*, 1934, 29.7 × 21.1 cm. Stiftung Pestalozzianum, Zurich

157 *Hebephrenia* (subtype of schizophrenia), patient photograph by Hermann Rorschach, c. 1910–1913. Archiv des Instituts für Medizingeschichte der Uni Bern, Archiv Hermann Rorschach, Rorsch HR 4_2_1_16–13

157 Rudolf Steiner, blackboard drawing for *Heilpädagogischer Kurs*, Dornach, 26.6.1924, chalk on paper, 105 × 154 cm, GA 317.02. Rudolf Steiner Archiv, Dornach

158 Erika Mann and Annemarie Schwarzenbach, Lavandou, 1933. Schweizerisches Literaturarchiv, A-5-08

159 Heinrich Anton Müller, *Untitled*, 1917–1922, chalk on tinted paper, 78 × 82 cm. Collection de l'Art Brut, Lausanne (Suisse), Photo: Danielle Caputo, Atelier de numérisation, Ville de Lausanne

160 Adolf Wölfli, *Irren = Anstalt Band = Hain*, 1910, From: *Von der Wiege bis zum Graab*, booklet 4, p. 203, pencil and coloured pencil on newsprint, 99.7 × 72.1 cm, A 9243 – 20(IV/p. 203). © Adolf-Wölfli-Stiftung, Kunstmuseum Bern

161 H. R. Giger, *A Feast for the Psychiatrist*, 1966, c. 180 × 120 cm. Private Collection of Marco Witzig

161 Tin boxes with three different pharmaceutical test substances, late 1960s. © Staatsarchiv des Kantons Thurgau

162 Microgram sheet, part of the *Tagebuchfragment*, Robert Walser, 1926. © Keystone SDA / Robert Walser-Stiftung Bern, 295r

163 Erna Schillig, *Paare mit Bäumen und Tieren*, c. 1930, pastel chalk, 61.5 × 46 cm. Staatsarchiv Uri

164 Paul Thek, *Untitled (Mushroom)*, 1969, latex, colour, 9 × 12 × 15.5 cm. Kunstmuseum Luzern, 94.84w

164 Blotter: absorbent paper used as a common carrier medium for substances such as LSD. Pharmazeutisches Kontrolllabor, Berne

165 Heidi Bucher, *Das Bad, Häutung Bellevue*, photographed by Gaechter and Clahsen, 1988, 59.5 × 42 cm. The Estate of Heidi Bucher, courtesy the Estate of Heidi Bucher and Lehmann Maupin, New York, Hong Kong, Seoul and London, © Gaechter + Clahsen Fotografen Zurich

167 Vaslav Nijinsky, *The Eye*, 1818–1819, paper, ink. 20.5 × 25 cm. Stiftung John Neumeier, Hamburg, 8287

BIBLIOGRAPHY CREDITS QUOTES

38 C.G. Jung, "The Swiss Line in the European Spectrum," in *The Collected Works of C. G. Jung*. Volume 10, edited and translated by Gerhard Adler and R. F. C. Hull. Princeton: Princeton University Press: Bollingen Series, 1978. © 1970 Princeton University Press

48 Sigmund Freud, *The Interpretation of Dreams*. Translated by Abraham Arden Brill, London: G. Allen & Unwin, Limited, 1915

56 J.J. Rousseau, "Reveries of the Solitary Walker," in *The Confessions of J. J. Rousseau*. Third edition, volume II, anonymous translation. London: printed for G. G. and J. Robinson, 1796.

80 Paul Parin, in conversation with Stefan Zweifel, Zurich, 2008. Translated by Astrid Freuler. © Stefan Zweifel

90 Anna Koellreuter (ed.), *What is this Professor Freud like? – A Diary of an Analysis with Historical Comments*. Translated by Ernst Falzeder and Kristina Pia Hofer, London: Karnac Books Ltd, 2016. © 2016 Karnac Books Ltd, London. Reproduced with permission of the Licensor through CCC

118 C.G. Jung, *The Red Book*. Edited by Sonu Shamdasani, New York: W. W. Norton & Co., 2009. © 2009 W. W. Norton & Co., New York. © 2007 Foundation of the Works of C. G. Jung, Zurich

126 Sigmund Freud and C.G. Jung, *The Freud/Jung Letters: The Correspondence between Sigmund Freud and C. G. Jung*. Edited by William McGuire, translated by Ralph Manheim and R. F. C. Hull, Princeton: Princeton University Press: Bollingen Series, 1994. © 1974 Princeton University Press, Princeton, New Jersey

138 Lisa Wenger and Martina Corgnati (eds.), *Meret Oppenheim—My Album: The autobiographical Album "From Childhood until 1943" and her handwritten biography*. Zurich: Scheidegger & Spiess, 2022. © 2022 Lisa Wenger, Martina Corgnati and Scheidegger & Spiess

148 Emma Jung, *Animus and Anima: Two Essays*. Translated by Cary F. Baynes and Hildegard Nagel. First published 1957 by Analytical Psychology Club of New York. © 2007 Foundation of the Works of C. G. Jung, Zurich

174 Blaise Cendrars, *Moravagine – A novel*. Translation by Alan Brown, 12 Kendrick Mews Kendrick Place London SW7. © 1968 Peter Owen. Reproduced with permission of the Licensor through PLSclear

182 "The Origin of the Child's Words Papa and Mama," in Colne Covington and Barbara Wharton (eds.), *Sabina Spielrein: Forgotten Pioneer of Psychoanalysis*. Hove: Brunner-Routledge, 2003. © 2003 Coline Covington and Barbara Wharton. Reproduced with permission of the Licensor through PLSclear

190 Hermann Hesse, *The Steppenwolf*. Translated by Basil Creighton. New York: Henry Holt and Company, 1929, p. 53–54; 76–77.

200 Vaslav Nijinsky, *The Diary of Vaslav Nijinsky*. Edited by Romola Nijinsky, New York: Simon and Schuster 1936

**IMPRINT
PUBLICATION**

This publication is supported by
Nancy Swift Furlotti, Recollections, LLC
Otto Gamma-Stiftung
Pro Anima Stiftung
Stiftung zur Förderung der Psychologie
 von C. G. Jung (SFPJ)
Stiftung der Werke von C. G. Jung
Susan Bach Foundation
UBS Culture Foundation

Editor
Swiss National Museum

Concept and editing
Stefan Zweifel, Pascale Meyer

Essays
Thomas Fischer, Urs Germann, Ita Grosz-Ganzoni, Michael Jakob, Verena Kast, Ursina Klauser, Elizabeth Leuenberger, Christine Lötscher, Lothar Müller, Gesa Schneider, Peter Schneider, Murray Stein, Stefan Zweifel, interview with Alain de Botton

Project coordinator, Scheidegger & Spiess
Anthonie de Groot

Translation
Bronwen Saunders, Astrid Freuler

Copyediting
Camilla R. Nielsen, George Johnson,
Sarah Quigley (Interview Alain de Botton)

Proofreading
George MacBeth

Design and typesetting
Martina Brassel

Lithography, print, and cover
TBS la Buona Stampa, Pregassona

© 2025 Swiss National Museum and
Verlag Scheidegger & Spiess AG, Zurich

© for the texts: the authors
© for the images: see image credits
© 2024/2025 ProLitteris, Zurich, for all works by Louise Bourgeois, Fischli/Weiss, Thomas Hirschhorn, Meret Oppenheim and Kerim Seiler

Verlag Scheidegger & Spiess AG
Niederdorfstrasse 54
8001 Zurich
Switzerland
www.scheidegger-spiess.ch
T +41 44 262 16 62
E info@scheidegger-spiess.ch

Product safety
Responsible person pursuant to EU
Regulation 2023/988 (GPSR):
GVA Gemeinsame Verlagsauslieferung
Göttingen GmbH & Co. KG
Post Box 2021
37010 Göttingen
Germany
T +49 551 384 200 0
E info@gva-verlage.de

Scheidegger & Spiess is being supported by the Federal Office of Culture with a general subsidy for the years 2021–2025.

All rights reserved; no part of this publication may be reproduced, stored in a retrieval system or transmitted in any form or by any means, electronic, mechanical, photocopying, recording, or otherwise, without the prior written consent of the publisher.

The publisher has made diligent efforts to contact all copyright holders and secure the necessary permissions. If any copyright holder has been inadvertently overlooked, we would appreciate it if they would contact the publisher at their earliest convenience.

Museum's edition
ISBN 978-3-905875-83-6 German
ISBN 978-3-905875-84-3 English

Publisher's edition
ISBN 978-3-03942-277-7 German
ISBN 978-3-03942-278-4 English

**IMPRINT
EXHIBITION**

This publication is published on the occasion of the exhibition *Landscapes of the Soul— C. G. Jung and the Exploration of the Human Psyche in Switzerland* at the Landesmuseum—Swiss National Museum Zurich, 17th of October 2025 to 15th of February 2026

Overall management
Denise Tonella

Curator
Stefan Zweifel

Project direction and organization
Pascale Meyer, Sophie Dänzer,
Valérie Lüthi

Scenography
Alex Harb

Exhibition graphic
Martina Brassel

Advisory committee
Günhan Akarçay, Heidi Amrein,
Beat Högger, Roman Aebersold,
Sabrina Médioni, Denise Tonella

Project controlling
Sabrina Médioni

Cultural services and museum education
Lisa Engi, Vera Humbel, Tanja Bitonti

Technical management
Mike Zaugg, Ladina Fait

Conservation management
Natalie Ellwanger, Ulrike Rothenhäusler

This exhibition is made possible
with the support of the
UBS Culture Foundation

Cover image
Detail from: Henry Fuseli, *The Nightmare*, 1790–1791, oil on canvas, 76.5 × 63.6 cm. Freies Deutsches Hochstift / Frankfurt Goethe Museum, IV–1953–033,
Photo: David Hall